COMPANION INTO GLOUCESTERSHIRE
AND THE COTSWOLDS

COMPANION INTO

GLOUCESTERSHIRE

AND

THE COTSWOLDS

By R. P. BECKINSALE, M.A.

*WITH FIFTEEN PLATES
AND ENDPAPER MAP*

SPURBOOKS LIMITED

First published by Methuen Ltd.

This edition with new photographs and map by
SPURBOOKS LIMITED
1 Station Road, Bourne End, Buckinghamshire
1973

SBN 0 902875 23 X

Printed offset litho by
Biddles Ltd., Guildford, Surrey

To
MONICA

PREFACE

'Gloucestershire is the finest home
That the Lord God ever made.'
—F.W.H.

THIS BOOK was conceived during my early days at
Burford and matured when fate sent me to spend five
happy years at the school at Chipping Campden. In it I
have attempted to portray the portions of Gloucestershire
which have, after numerous visits, continued to prove
pleasing to me. The following pages therefore represent
the parts of our county that I would gladly show to any
visitor, as at each spot I could say with pride: 'This is
Gloucestershire!' Bristol and Gloucester, omitted in earlier
editions, have now been included, but it seemed folly to
describe Tewkesbury Abbey when every visitor would
spend sixpence on the informative booklet sold in the
building. In place of this shortcoming I hope the reader will
find many compensations, if only in the cosmopolitan
nature of the volume, in the few additions of my own re-
searches, in the references to the modern Gloucestershire
poets and to the wild life of the country-side.

I have made little direct mention of Gloucestershire folk,
but they will know why. It is difficult, unless one is a poet,
to write impartially of one's friends and relatives. To-day
there seems to be a tendency afloat to look on them as a
peculiar race while they in their turn have begun to doubt
if they alone lack the power 'to see ourselves as others
see us'.

For information and frequent hospitality I am indebted,
and hope, in spite of this book, I shall continue to be in-

debted to friends in most parts of the country. Special mention should be made of willing assistance from the Rev. Somerset Bateman, Mr. H. V. Hindle of the Bristol Development Board, Dr. Kenneth Dent, Ph.D., B.Sc., and Mr. W. Burrow, M.A. I would like to seize the opportunity of thanking the Librarian and Staff of Gloucester Public Library for courteous help during many years. The photographs will doubtless disappoint many Gloucestershire lovers. Such noted views as the cloisters of Gloucester Cathedral and the chapter-house at St. Augustine's, Bristol, should, of course, have been included, but these appear so frequently in print that I have preferred more unusual scenes. My friend Mr. W. J. Butt of Bourton-on-the-Water added to his many kindnesses in the past by allowing me to select at will from his large collection of pictures of the North Cotswolds. Mr. G. F. Harris of Barnwood kindly supplied me with the views I wanted of the Central Cotswolds and Forest of Dean, while most of the other photographs were taken by Dr. Kenneth Dent in my presence.

It is a pleasure to thank the following authors and publishers for their permission to reprint extracts from the following works: Mr. Hilaire Belloc and Gerald Duckworth & Co. Ltd. from "Dedicatory Ode" on page 18; Mr. John Masefield and Wm. Heinemann Ltd., from "Tewkesbury Road" (p. 193), "The Daffodil Fields," "The Setting of the Windcock" (p. 238) in *Collected Poems of John Masefield*; Mr. F. W. Harvey and Messrs. Sidgwick & Jackson from 'On Birdlip' (p. 179), 'Elvers' (p. 230), 'Gloucestershire Men' (p. 154), and 'A Ballade of Gloucestershire Towns' (p. 235), in *Farewell*; and from 'Song of Minsterworth Perry' (p .229) in *A Gloucestershire Lad*; and 'Ducks' (p. 38) from *Ducks and Other Verses*; the representatives of Mr. Ivor Gurney and Messrs. Sidgwick & Jackson from 'Near Midsummer' (p. 221) and 'That Country' (p. 78) in *War's Embers*.

Finally, like all other married writers, I cannot express

adequately my debt to my wife. It was only with the assistance of almost every secluded corner in the North Cotswolds that she was finally persuaded to leave her native Campden. Portions of a thesis of hers on the Windrush Valley have been incorporated into this volume and somehow I feel that this preface should be hers acknowledging my humble assistance.

R.P.B.

CONTENTS

ILLUSTRATIONS

CHAPTER I: *The Country around Chipping Campden*

CHIPPING CAMPDEN

THOSE WHO believe in love at first sight should go out of their way, if indeed the road from Stow is not their way, to view Chipping Campden from Westington Hill. The considerable cluster of unobtrusive houses, interspersed with trees whose snowy blossoms in spring tell of cherry and pear, lies in a sweeping fold of the Cotswold Hills just where they are narrowest and where the stone walls begin to give way to green hedgerows. The grey arc of the old-world town nestles in the lee of the 'Ten-o'clock Hoo', a rounded hillock capped by a decaying elm, beyond which rise the bolder lines of the furrows and elm-rows of Dover's Hill. The houses are an integral part of the landscape, as indispensable to it as the trees and stone walls and bold, sweeping outlines of the hills. So natural is the blend of colours that the occasional puff of smoke from a train and the glint of the sun on an unseen greenhouse attract the eye and seem startling and unpardonable intruders. Chipping Campden really consists of three parts; the irregular cluster of rustic houses, some thatched, others with tall box hedges and all gay with flowers in season, which is called Westington; the broad, curving High Street with its stately perspectives and 'islands' of buildings on each side of the Market Square; the humble cottages and dignified buildings next the church at the northern end of the town. The first has a rural stamp, the second a look of pride and wealth, the third an air of nobility and patronage. Not that the town is anything but a unity with its harmony of colour and uniformity of architectural style. It is hard to imagine an insignificant Campden, yet in early Norman times it was a small hamlet with fifty villeins and two mills planted on the slight eminence between the Cattle Brook and its mother-stream, the Knee Brook. The Cattle Brook flowed down the middle of the street called Leasebourne until it was diverted underground, and an iron pump, still standing, was erected where was formerly an open drinking pool. Since then the name has been corrupted into Scuttlebrook, and although its bubbling source at the big stone trough bespeaks of persistency rather than volume, the inhabitants have seized on the opportunity to tell how their grand-fathers raced in tubs down the shallow stream. The tiny hamlet had become a great wool mart by the fourteenth century, and the home of many rich merchants who began to enlarge and beautify the little town.

If you would see the great Perpendicular church, go to the straw-thatched smithy in Cidermill Lane, or stand on the steps of the alms-houses and then turn away contented. Perhaps you *must* go into a church which owes so much to the merchant princes. William Grevel, who on his death in 1401 merited the title of *flos mercatorum lanae totius Angliae,* wished to be buried in the church which was then a-building, and left one hundred marks to further the 'new work'. Tradition says that he built the north aisle, but most of the building dates back to about half a century after his death. The Grevel brass and two others, equally well preserved, are now in the chancel. The tombs of the Hickes family, even greater benefactors to Campden, are to be seen in the south chapel. Alabaster effigies show Sir Baptist Hickes and his wife Elizabeth resplendent in ruffs and coronets; near by, in marble, Sir Edward Noel, Viscount Campden, and his wife Juliana, daughter of Sir Baptist Hickes, are represented at the Resurrection Day in shrouds and coronets and my lord hands his lady gracefully from the opened tomb. The same Sir Baptist Hickes gave to the church its fine, brass falcon-lectern and the carved Jacobean pulpit. Worth a glance too are some fragments of old glass in the tracery of the great east window and the decorated font, but more unique are the remains of a fifteenth-century altar frontal, exquisitely embroidered with representations of the Madonna on a design of flowers, which was copied at the express wish of Queen Mary to form the altar cloth of Westminster Abbey for the coronation of King George V. A richly-worked cope of crimson velvet also hangs framed near by. 'Restoration' in recent centuries has scraped the interior walls and pillars miserably clean, and the old carved oak benches form cupboards and settles for many a house in Campden. The lichen-mottled exterior, however, is almost perfect. The dark grey colour, the harmony of design and the lofty tower, with its ribs and pinnacles, give a more satisfying sense of grace and beauty than any other church in North Gloucestershire.

The church of St. James would have been sufficient delight for the day if you, and every visitor before you, had not glanced across the road at those twisted spiral chimneys. These are part of the ruins of Campden House, begun in 1612 by Sir Baptist Hickes soon after he had bought the manor. Campden owes as much to the Hickes as Fairford owes to the Tames. Sir Baptist Hickes, the younger son of a Gloucestershire merchant who had set up as a mercer in Cheapside, was the brains of the business and achieved such success that he was able to lend large sums of money to King James and to Scottish nobles at the Court. He became fabulously rich, and what was a mere £30,000 for a country house when he could leave £100,000 each to his two daughters and could own another mansion in that part of London still named after his Gloucestershire manor? We wonder what the Campden masons thought as they shaped the stone for those spiral shafts and reared the magnificent house with a wide terrace and flanking pavilions in the Italian style. The edifice was crowned with a transparent dome in which a light burnt after dark to guide benighted travellers on the wolds, a truly 'town' notion for folk who relied upon the tolling of the curfew bell. The great benefactor, now Viscount Campden, died in 1629 and was spared the tragic ending to his grandiose scheme. In May 1645 the mansion was garrisoned for the King by Sir Henry Bard in the absence of the owner who was fighting for His Majesty elsewhere. When the troops were withdrawn to swell the forces at Naseby, the house was wantonly burnt lest it should fall into the hands of the enemy who happened to come no nearer than Warwick. The ruins are quite extensive; the parts that remain of the south front and two airy pavilions or banqueting houses at each end of the terrace are sufficient to show the grandeur of the scheme, which comprised eight acres in all. The main entrance, near the church, has two peculiar gazebos or lodges, which are now used as dwellings, and whose very ingenious chimneys actually come out above the gateway, and it is a strange sight to see smoke curling out from beneath the ornamental pinnacles that seem so detached from any fire-place. Inside the gate is the well in the main courtyard. The small, square building with the tall, spiral shafts was, of course, the almonry, and its stone staircase, common enough in the old house, will testify to the skill of the craftsmen. Still standing, too, are parts of the curtilage walls and two lovely archways where Lady Juliana's carriage drive from Broad Campden bridged the stream and entered the quadrangle.

The alms-house folk will, if you are patient and do not start 'telling' them that so and so is surpassed in such and such a place, draw your attention to the huge barn and to the big washing-tank through which, they say, cattle and carts entering the town were driven so that the streets might not be fouled. In any case you will envy the old people their home, the most exquisite house in Campden. The building takes the form of a capital I in honour of King James I, the royal friend of Sir Baptist Hickes who gave and endowed it for twelve people. Here is the very quintessence of Campdonians; here the Boer War is but yesterday and modern notions are none too welcome. Old Polly Wain, who could dance a jig at ninety, unwillingly consented to broadcast, and did so without knowing it was merely a rehearsal. When asked to speak again next day, Polly became suspicious and would not budge from her lovely home and said what she really thought but not to the British nation. It is at all times a pleasure to gaze at the smooth, gabled face of perfectly fitting stone, at the marvellous symmetry of the windows and steeply sloping roofs, and at the artistic simplicity of the chimneys and corner pinnacles. For pure craftsmanship in stone masonry and for beauty of conception these alms-houses are almost unexcelled. The view from the top of the steps is unforgettable—the smooth, solid face of the grey alms-houses, with their tinge of flowers and communal water-tap in the wall, the church rising serenely up beyond and by it the great gateway and loggia with twisted chimney shafts.

It is a pleasant walk down Calf's Lane past the Court House, the massive building which leans so perceptibly and which is still owned by the Gainsborough family, descendants of the Hickes. Here, too, you may see a very fine columbarium which served the great mansion. Footpaths lead off the lane to two old mills, both with huge over-shot wheels containing fine ironwork, and to the Coneygree, the green field nearest to the churchyard, where you may sit and bless the National Trust as well as Sir Baptist Hickes. Inevitably, however, you will return to the broad High Street which is lined with houses mainly of the late sixteenth and seventeenth centuries and here all that is typical of the Cotswold style of architecture may be found—the square-headed mullioned windows, the steeply-pitched grey-stone roofs, the dormered gables and the projecting lintels resting on cunningly carved brackets.   Grevel's House, built about 1380 by the great William, the flower of English wool merchants, boasts of a two-storied panelled oriel which, with the fine arched doorway and skilfully cut gargoyles, must have been the envy of his contemporaries. Across the street, near the flourishing Maidenhair Tree (*Gingko biloba*) is the austere front of the Woolstaplers' Hall which retains a fine open-timbered room used as a wool exchange in the fourteenth century. Beyond it is the Old Grammar School, founded in 1487 by John Fereby and his wife and rebuilt about 1628.   During these years the stone-masons of Campden must have been very busy for in 1627 the Market Hall was built by Sir Baptist Hickes, probably on the site of an old cross. The upper stories of the dignified houses around it are well worth a study if only for the sun–dials which face the morning sun. The painted one opposite the Grammar School was used to regulate the Town Hall clock until 1854 when I suppose the jog-trot mile to the newly-built railway needed more exact computation. The Market Square is still the scene of markets where the farmers talk of 'shup' and 'baists' and sample the home-brew at the 'Noel Arms' and pass the day with the folk who come to stand and stare. You may not like the Town Hall until you know that the weather-beaten buttresses date back to about 1180 when the then Lord of Campden, Hugh de Gondeville, built a beautiful chapel to Catherine of Alexandria, probably as an act of reparation for having been drawn unwittingly into Henry II's quarrel with Thomas à Becket. The King came here during de Gondeville's lifetime and granted the town its first charter. The newer building blends so successfully with the older houses, and it is so much a part of the social life of the town, that no one dislikes it for being a mixture of 'foreign' architectural styles. A few paces beyond the Market Square is a quaint porch, with a tiny gargoyle representing a dolphin's head, which leads to Poppett's Alley where you may 'thread the eye of a needle' in the Biblical sense. The High Street has other treasures and as a whole it is beautiful; the noonday sun will deepen the shadows under the archways and eaves, winter rain will make the grey mullions glisten and darken, the moonlight adds a mysterious softness which soothes the strength and simplicity of the willing, light-loving stone.

You may well wonder what preserved Campden from decay when the wool trade dwindled and the fortunes of the Hickes family were impaired in the Civil War. The market still went on and the games on Dover's Hill were an annual source of profit. Then, in the eighteenth century, a silk industry came here to take advantage of the mills and clean water. Raw silk was twisted into threads suitable for the weavers of Coventry, but this trade was ruined about 1857 when French silks were allowed into England free of duty. The new railway, which very respectfully (and very sensibly) approached no nearer than a mile to the town did not restore prosperity, and by 1883 the inhabitants numbered less than two thousand. In this year the corporation, founded in 1605, was abolished, and the bailiff's robes and beautiful silver maces of the serjeants are still preserved in the Town Hall. The unspoilt nature of the town proved its salvation, for in 1902 the Guild of Handicraft migrated from the East End of London to the old silk-mill in Sheep Street, bringing a group of intelligent and skilled craftsmen into the slumbering town. These men learnt to love the town of their adoption and were among the first to preserve its old-world charm from commercialism and decay. Things have changed a little since Evans wrote so enthusiastically of the social life of the Guild, but the Dramatic Society flourishes like the green bay tree and the artistic productions in silver, iron, wood, stone and stained glass have acquired a national reputation. The yearly exhibition shows these hand-made objects amidst a setting of paintings and etchings of the neighbourhood in which artists find both health and inspiration.

Once a year, too, the great barns near the church are now filled to overflowing with ten thousand fleeces, and merchants come to Campden from all parts of England. The buyers dressed in sober tweeds prod the bales and pull apart the wool with knowing hands and, in the sample barn, the nods and grunts denote a rise of a farthing a pound. We think of the July of 1481 when the Celys wrote that 'wool in Cotswold is at great price, 13s. 4d. a tod (28 lb.) and great riding for wool in Cotswold as was any this 7 year', but the buyer drives off in his car with watch, not hawk, on his wrist, and to-day the guinea per tod will not buy white wines or rich presents for ladies.

Chipping Campden has retained its saneness in spite of the visitors which throng there, nor does it thrust at you cigarettes and cheap teas. It has more friends than any other town of its size in the world, and the munificence of these has even rescued the Norman Chapel at Broad Campden near by. The Morris Dances are still performed in the street and the old charities remain. Where Leasebourne begins and ends is a mystery which can only be solved by waiting to see if you receive St. Thomas's loaf. A knock at the door, a huge loaf thrust into your hands—and you *are* in Leasebourne. On rare occasions such as the loss of a dog or shortage of water, the town crier will turn out with his bell to give notice to the inhabitants, who at the first 'Oyez' are all at their doors as tense and excited as if it were news of national importance. And how the inhabitants hate change! There is a row of houses off Sheep Street which they knew as Workhouse Bank, and for years this has been altered officially to Gainsborough Terrace; a huge name-plate denotes the change, but the inhabitants read it 'Wurkhus Bank' and so it will always be.

These homely Campden folk used to amuse themselves before the coming of wireless and, with a rare sense of fun and mischief, they have stored up jokes against their grandfathers and even nearer neighbours. Many of these local yarns have found their way into print, and the 'regulars' at the public-houses have a fund of others which, at the price of a pint of bitter, they will embellish and interweave until the listener is duly impressed. There is, however, one tale which cannot be exaggerated and that is the Campden Wonder. It is one of the strangest stories in history; the facts, as related by Sir Thomas Overbury, a contemporary, are briefly as follows: The aged Lady Juliana, Dowager Viscountess Campden, who lived at the Court House, had as her steward a certain William Harrison who had been fifty years in her service. On the 16th of August, 1660, Harrison set out to collect rents from the neighbouring hamlet of Charringworth, and as he did not return by evening his wife sent her servant, John Perry, to look for him. Neither returned that night, and on the next morning Harrison's son met Perry returning alone. Together they learned that the old steward had rested for a while in a house at Ebrington, and they discovered nothing more until a woman showed them a comb and a blood-stained band picked up in a furze brake near by. Although these belonged to the missing man no trace of him could be found. Naturally, Perry was suspected of foul play, and on his arrest told such a rambling and confused story that he was detained in custody. A week later he said he was willing to tell the real facts and revealed to the bench how his mother Joan and brother Richard had persuaded him, much against his will, to join with them in stealing his master's money. After strangling and robbing Harrison in the Coneygree they threw his body into the 'great sink' at Wallington's mill and placed the comb and band in the gorse brake to divert suspicion.

Joan and Richard strongly protested their innocence, yet John persisted in his accusations. As all three were returning from the magistrate's house, out of Richard's pocket dropped a ball of string which he said was his wife's hair-lace; it had a slip-knot at the end and John swore that this string was used to strangle Harrison. The body of the victim could not be found so the judge at Gloucester dismissed the case. At the next assizes a less scrupulous judge presided, or perhaps the discovery that the Perrys had broken into Harrison's house and robbed him of £140 in the previous year may have hardened his lordship's heart. Too late, John declared his confession was false and that he knew nothing of his master's death. All three were hanged on Broadway Hill; the mother, being a reputed witch, suffered first, and John, solemnly declaring that they might hereafter possibly hear of his master's death, died last. John's bones were still swinging on the gallows when, two years later, William Harrison came home alive and well. The old man told a preposterous story of being kidnapped by two horse-men and taken to sea, where he was captured by Turkish pirates and sold as a slave to 'a grave physician, of 87 years of age, who lived near to Smyrna'. Somehow he managed to escape as a stowaway to Lisbon where an Englishman took pity on him and saw that he reached Dover safely. No one seems to have bothered to get to the truth of the story and Harrison carried on with his normal duties as if nothing had happened. The affair, however, sat less easily on Mrs. Harrison's mind, for Wood, in his diary, says that she hung herself soon after her husband's return. John Perry's false accusations may be explained as a peculiar form of lunacy brought about by mental strain, but no one has explained why it was expedient for Harrison to disappear for a while. A romantic explanation believed in by Campdonians is that John, the elder brother, was a wastrel and drunkard, jealous of the steady and industrious Richard who supported his aged mother and was happy in marriage. Spite drove him to connive with Harrison to remain away for two years and to accuse his mother and brother of murder, hoping that by turning King's evidence his own neck would escape the hangman's noose. Probably the only man who knew the whole truth was Harrison and his secret died with him. It still remains a mystery as to what he was doing in the two years, for it is highly improbable that he ever left England.

DOVER'S HILL AND WESTON-SUBEDGE

From close by the Catholic church at Chipping Campden, a footpath leads straight up the green meadows of the Leasow and across the fields near Kingcomb Lane to the summit of Dover's Hill. The view from here never fails to surprise, for the country before us is rarely in the same mood. Sometimes after rain little purple scarves of mist float leisurely in the vale, and occasionally the landscape lies smiling in sunshine and beautifully dappled with shadows of passing clouds. At our feet lies the vale of Evesham, rich with fruit trees and small brown fields which stretch away to a wooded horizon on which the spires of Coventry can be seen when the air is clear enough.

The lower slopes of the hill are clothed in woods and plantations to which tiny springs trickle down through stone drinking troughs or occasionally a pond. Dover's Hill was the site of the famous 'Olympick Cotswold games'; the grassy plateau, now partly divided by a hedge and arable fields, was sufficiently extensive, and the abrupt slopes towards the woods were useful in many ways. Below the steep upper slope a small circular plateau projecting from the Hill, now almost surrounded by Lynches Wood, is said to be the natural arena, where the wrestling took place. Looking down from the hill it is difficult to imagine a more perfect setting for any sports.

During 250 years these elaborately organized games grew so popular as to become a national byword for sport Camdon folk had probably always enjoyed dancing and wrestling at Whitsun just as in 1938 they had a May Queen and a twirling Jack o' the Green, and of course the foot races of Scuttlebrook Wake. These old rustic pastimes were changed into a vast meeting by the energy of a certain Robert Dover, an attorney, born about 1575 at Barton-on-the-Heath near Moreton-in-the-Marsh. Finding himself secure financially,

'Dover, his Knowledge not Imploys
T' increase his Neighbours' Quarrels, but their Joys.'

Through the agency of his friend Endymion Porter, he was given leave by James I to select a place on the Cotswolds where the old English sports and pastimes, which had been so much attacked by the Puritans, might be encouraged. The games were founded soon after 1604, and Dover devoted his time and energy entirely to them for nearly another forty Whitsuns. Endymion Porter, Groom of the Bedchamber to the King, gave Dover an old suit of His Majesty, a wide hat decked with a feather, and a ruff 'purposely to grace him and consequently the solemnity'. Thus arrayed, and on a prancing white horse, Dover superintended the games which began with a salvo of cannons fired in his honour from a tall movable wooden tower. The prizes were valuable and 300 gentlemen are said, in one year, to have worn 'Dover's Yellow favours'. The meeting, which was attended by the nobility and gentry for sixty miles around, is frequently mentioned in contemporary literature. In 1636 poems by Ben Jonson, Drayton and others, mostly of indifferent quality, were collected and published under the title of *Annalia Dubrensia: upon the yearly Celebration of Mr. Robert Dover's Olympick Games upon Cotswold Hills.* Ben Jonson writes that the sports did much to

'Advance true love and neighbourhood,
And do both church and commonwealth the good.'

Captain Robert Dover died in 1641 and was buried at Stanway without monument or inscription, as if to give the lie to Drayton's lines:

'We'll have thy statue in some rock cut out,
With brave inscriptions garnished about;
And under written—"Lo! this is the man
Dover, that first these noble sports began."
Lads of the hills and lasses of the vale,
In many a song and many a merry tale,
Shall mention thee, and having leave to play,
Unto thy name shall make a holiday.'

The Civil War stopped the games for a while, but they were revived under Charles II and continued with brief intervals up to 1851. It seems that much of their former rustic nature went with the death of Dover, and then the games began to attract crowds so great as to be almost uncontrollable. In the early years of the nineteenth century many a tree and barn sported the following notice:

Dover's Ancient Meeting
(date)
On Thursday in Whit-week
on
Dover's Hill
near
Chipping Campden, Glos.
The Sports will commence
With a good match of Backswords
for a purse of guineas.
To be played by 9 or 7 men on a side. Each side
must appear in the ring by 3 o'clock in the afternoon
or 15s. each pair will be given
for as many as will play.
Wrestling
for belts and other prizes
also
Jumping in bags and Dancing
And a Jingling Match for 10/6
As well as Divers Others of celebrated
Cotswold and Olympick Games.

The 'Divers Others' included cudgel-playing, the quintain, leaping, pitching the bar, playing at balloon, walking on hands, a dance of virgins, hunting a hare which was not to be killed, and horse-racing.

As time went on the horse-racing became an increasingly important feature of the games, and towards 1850 some 30,000 people, including the worst characters from the industrialized areas in the Midlands, attended the meetings. No doubt the disorderly element was increased by the 'navvies' employed in digging the railway tunnel which pierces the hill just to the west. The morals of the whole neighbourhood were being corrupted when, in 1851, the last meeting was held and shortly afterwards the ground was enclosed.

The National Trust has recently acquired a large portion of the hill which, with its short turf and rough slopes, its health-giving breezes and distant views, would still form an excellent site for the revival of the old-world games. Now, however, the woods are solitary and quiet save for the wood-pigeons and the green wood-peckers that laugh so derisively at the ghosts of the vanished multitudes.

The lane bordering Dover's Hill on the west winds down the slope through the trees and orchards of the scarp to Weston-Subedge. The straggling village, hidden in fruit-trees, has taken no notice whatsoever of the ancient Buckle Street near to which is scarcely a building of the parish. Some of the old houses have an upper story of half-timber work, but many more are skilfully built of nicely shaped blocks of freestone which seem to have been used alike for gabled cottage and large sized residence. The village hall has been fashioned out of an old barn, and near by is a house with a 'priest's hiding-hole' as the villagers say. Several early seventeenth-century houses may be found here, including one with a sculptured doorway and another with a sun-dial (1624) supported on either side by a cherub's head. The tiny post office is more picturesque even than that at Stanton, and it contrasts markedly with the neigh-bouring farm-house, a lovely creeper-clad symmetrical building shaded by a flourishing cedar and backed with a square dovecot. The vast rectory, formerly a residence of the Bishops of Worcester, contains some portions dating back to the time of William Latimer, who built it 'as big as a college'. Latimer was rector of Weston and Saintbury where he was buried in 1545. In his younger days he travelled in Italy and studied Greek at the University of Padua. He shares with his friends Grocyn and Linacre the honour of planting the study of Greek at Oxford, where he was a Fellow of All Souls. Erasmus praises his upright life and great learning, but Latimer seems to have been so busy at Weston-Subedge that he could find no time to help Erasmus with a second edition of his Greek testament nor did he leave behind him any notable written work, Just outside the wall surrounding the rectory grounds is a long, low cottage bearing the date 1634, which has the air of a former alms-house. The church of St. Laurence will not greatly interest antiquarians save, perhaps for the medieval tower and the large altar stone of pre-Reformation age. The carving of a queer, crouching animal near the font may have come from the old manor-house which stood in the adjacent field where traces of a moat can be seen. A brass on the chancel wall shows William Hodges in the dress of Elizabeth's time.

At the north end of the village you will find a large patch of garden allotments rented at relatively low cost to each parishioner as a compensation for the loss of their common lands. Weston-Subedge retained much of the field-system of agriculture up to 1852, and the old Field Account Book was printed in 1904 by Mr. C. R. Ashbee, the benefactor who brought the Guild of Handicraft to Chipping Campden. It tells, for instance, how at the Vestry Meeting of October 25th, 1849, the Weston-Subedge parishioners decided to plant 'Gravels' with vetches, the Aston field with beans, the 'long field' with wheat and not allow the sheep to feed upon the young wheat after Christmas next. Each year a solemn declaration was made to weed properly, hoe, manure, and cultivate the lands.

Typical entries between the Michaelmasses of 1850 and 1851 show the cares of the holders and incidentally the cost of labour.

7 weeks keeping crows off wheat .	£2	9	0
260 perches of trenching in the pasture. ½d.		10	10
15 days keeping birds off beans and wheat		5	0
Received for raising stone, Bold Gap Quarry ·	3	10	0
14½ days putting up wall on Farr Hill; furzing same, cleaning pool at Narrows, stopping up holes after races, etc.		16	11

Bold Gap is the quarry now clothed with beeches on Dover's Hill, and the Narrows are grassy meadows lying between Weston Park Woods and Campden Woods above Campden House. So the whole of Dover's Hill and the lands stretching to the Narrows belonged to the parishioners of Weston, and as the latter entry says, was used every Whitsun as a race-course. The beans and wheat-fields are now under orchards and strawberries, but men are still employed to keep off the birds and an ear-splitting bang and terrific rattle of tin cans often startle the innocent visitor more than the impudent thrushes and blackbirds.

'A lovely river all alone,
  She lingers in the hills and holds
A hundred little towns of stone,
  Forgotten in the western wolds.
                        —HILAIRE BELLOC

NEAR ADLESTROP the bank of the slow-flowing Even-lode affords a cool shade where the muddy pool-loving stream hides its trout that are less fat and speckled than their brothers in the Windrush and Coln. Behind us, in Oxfordshire, lies Daylesford, the home of Warren Hastings, who loved this winding stream; before us, the ancient trackway from Rollright to Stow, the *Via Regia*, leads on as a modern highway to the distant hill that is crowned with a tall church tower. Gradually as we climb up out of the lowland its humid heat gives way to cooling breezes, and we come refreshed into the little town of Stow. Stow-on-the-Wold, or Stow St. Edward as it was known till the sixteenth century, is not to be taken by surprise, for in whatever direction you approach it the climb is steep, except perhaps on the Broadway side.

The height, however, brings its own reward, and the beech-lined precipice towards the south is a mass of copper and gold in autumn, and the clean boles are a delight all the year round. The hill on which Stow stands is nearly 800 feet high, and in its almost isolated majesty overlooks on the east the wide green valley of the Evenlode. To the west, across the huge furrow of the Dikler stream, the rolling limestone downs recede, curve upon curve, until the greyish fields and clear-cut plantations merge into the

18

distant horizon. What curious fancy induced our ancestors to settle on this bleak, windy outpost where there is scarcely enough level ground for the local cricket club? Summer is certainly pleasant here with its invigorating airs 'as cool as the oldest and driest iced-champagne', but in winter Stow-on-the-Wold, where the wind blows cold, is less comforting.

Overcoats are pierced by the pitiless elements, and house doors become possessed of the strength of ten thousand devils. Neither could abundant water have tempted the first dwellers here because drinking-water was scarce at Stow until Mr. Joseph Chamberlain gave £2,000 to provide a constant water supply. Obviously, then, it must have been the view which gave rise to this hill-top town, the highest in Gloucestershire, not so much on account of its scenic as its strategic value. The great Fosse Way came from Moreton-in-Marsh direct to Stow, where it climbs the hill and plunges straight down on the other side, not out of contempt of natural obstacles, but because of a military instinct which appreciated the importance of this look-out post.

The natural clearing on the hill-top was probably the site of a fortress in Celtic times, and hither the great Roman artery drew the minor trackways until all roads hereabouts led to Stow, and solely because the Romans elected to climb the hill, you and I have no choice in the matter. The sites of two Roman villas have been found east of the 'Unicorn', but it has been shown that the few existing earthworks are the remains of a medieval castle which have determined the curious triangular plan of the town.

Stow St. Edward grew up around its wide market-place, and has even encroached upon this scene of its famous fair. The triangular clean-looking town has an honest non-consequential aspect, and its diversified grey-stone houses are not individually of great interest. The chief glory of

NAUNTON

Stow is the church of St. Edward, an ancient structure much rebuilt and enlarged since its original foundation about the year 870. It was dedicated in the fourteenth century in honour of St. Edward the Confessor, and one hundred years later the wealthy woolstaplers reared the tall, massive tower and made the great windows which heighten the vista of pointed arches and illumine the realistic faces of the stone corbels supporting their new roof. In their alterations the merchants spared the greater part of the older building, and the two Decorated windows on either side of the porch are fine examples of thirteenth-century work. It is interesting to notice that the earliest walls consist of thin slates and much mortar whereas the newer portions were constructed of skilfully-shaped, large blocks of oolite. Captain Hasting Keyte, one of the Keytes of Ebrington, lies in the chancel: he was slain, as the inscription records, *ex parte regis* at the battle of Stow, the last encounter of the Civil War in the open field. On March 21st, 1646, upon some unenclosed land near Donnington, a mile north of the town, three thousand royalists under old Sir Jacob Astley put up a brave but hopeless resistance to the Cromwellians. Astley and many other officers were captured and hundreds of prisoners were confined for some days in the church which, for a long time afterwards, remained in a sorry plight.

The fine, large painting of the Crucifixion over the altar is the work of Gaspard de Crayer (1610), a noted Flemish artist and pupil of Rubens. It was presented a century ago by Joseph Chamberlain, who was lord of the manor and has been Stow's greatest benefactor. The many memorials here to the Chamberlains date back at least to 1667: the family probably came to England at the Conquest, and after returning to France some time later, came over again during the Huguenot persecutions. In Rudder's day the Rev. John Chamberlain was lord of Maugersbury Manor and owned estates also in other parts of Gloucestershire. The fourteenth-century cross in the market square has been given a new headpiece in honour of Joseph Chamberlain.

The little triangular town has several pretty alleyways leading off from the wide market-place, where the stocks still remain under a great elm. The Town Hall, now partly a museum, is guarded by a figure of St. Edward. Here you may view the Royce collection of relics of British and Roman times, including numerous flints, coins and fragments of pottery. These ancient finds take on a remoter antiquity when seen after the notable Christie Crawford collection of Civil War relics. We can gain a vivid picture of Commonwealth England from the armour and books and letters housed here, but even more interesting are the paintings, mainly contemporary portraits of such well-known people as Charles Stuart, Henrietta Maria, Nell Gwynn, Elizabeth Bourchier the wife of Cromwell, and the Duchess of York, the very same picture which was seen by Pepys in Peter Lelys' studio.

Almost facing the Town Hall stands St. Edward's House, which has a handsome fluted front, and incidentally, two big stone boots at the base of the steps leading up to its niched doorway. The Elizabethan school-house with rounded windows is also worth noticing as it occupies the site of a fifteenth-century chantry school which was reconstructed, according to the Latin inscription, at the expense of Richard Shepman, a merchant of London.

Stow retains its unassuming air even on fair days, when the streets hum with business and all the neighbourhood swarms up the hill. The fairs began in 1477 when Edward IV authorized two to be held each year on the feasts of St. Edward the Confessor and St. Philip and James, October 24th and May 12th by our modern calendar. The fair acquired a great reputation, especially for sheep, of which in Defoe's day 20,000 were sold at one fair, as well as for cows, cheese and horses. Within living memory all the neighbouring people bought their garden tools and implements at the fair, which is now devoted mainly to ironmongery, hops and general merchandise.

The horse trade has revived a little of late years and the spring sale lasts for two days. Here you may see nearly 300 horses, and the whole gamut of horse terms would not account for them all. There are hunters and hacks, cobs and ponies, cart-horses and colts, not to mention geldings. A fine bay gelding will fetch seventy guineas while a cob would be cheap at twenty; a steady pony will cost a dozen guineas, and although you could get four wild ones for the same money, take my advice and buy the former as it will not show a burning desire to bolt to its Welsh mountains or Dartmoor tors. The Fosse is crowded with horses and each in its turn paces the Roman road, the graceful hunter with a nimble tread, the cart-horse with his powerful plodding thump and the cob with its carefree I-want-to-go-home trot. There are prizes for the best groomed horses, and all, except the wild-eyed ponies, have their coats brushed to a glossy nicety and their manes and tails neatly clipped and plaited with brightly-coloured ribbons. How grateful must they be for this social holiday away from the dusty furrow and everlasting sheep of the hills. The great event is a red letter day in the calendar of all the neighbouring villagers whose humdrum lives are quickened a while when the flares of the pleasure-fair sparkle away on the hill. We can well understand the feelings of the Cotswold farmhand who, having migrated to Australia, told the officials that he was 'Thirty last Stow Fair', and found to his utter amazement they had not heard of that great event.

MORETON-IN-THE-MARSH AND BOURTON-ON-THE-HILL

Country people like to be precise in rural matters and the towns-man's 'sheep' becomes in the Cotswolds a 'tup', a 'wether' or a 'ewe'. Bourton-on-the-Hill was distinguished from Bourton-on-the-Water, Stow St. Edward became Stow-on-the-Wold and Moreton Henmersche was corrupted into Moreton-in-Marsh. Henmersche twisted the tongue and meant little to travellers or inhabitants; it was misspelt and jostled about, appearing as Enmarsh or Hindmarsh until every one knew that the name should be in-Marsh, for was not the town in the damp lowlands. For who was to know that the Fosse Way came to this point on the tiny Evenlode simply because a large patch of dry gravel afforded a firm crossing of the river. Or who was to guess that 'mersche' was related to 'marc', signifying a march or boundary, for Moreton-in-March as it should have become is near the borders of several counties, and two miles to the east stands the Four Shires Stone where Gloucestershire meets Oxfordshire and Warwickshire and used to meet parts of Worcestershire.

In British times a tribal boundary ran near the site of the town which was then safeguarded by a camp, part of which is still to be seen in the recreation ground consisting of a tall earthwork capped by a hawthorn hedge. Moreton, too, is on a more natural boundary, for it lies in the broad trench of the Evenlode that divides the typical Cotswold country on the west from a less determinate hilly scenery to the east.

The Romans have much to answer for in Moreton. The Fosse Way has become lined with buildings making a main street as straight as a ruler, and you would see through Moreton at one glance if the Town Hall did not mercifully break the geometrical exactness. It is a wide and pleasant tree-lined street, but it lacks the curving beauty of Campden, or the honest-to-goodness air of Stow.

The position of Moreton close to both Vale and Wold brought markets and trade so that shop-windows are many, but, fortunately, the houses were usually well built of stone. The old 'White Hart Inn' is said to have lodged Charles I on the night of July 2nd, 1644, and the Cottage Hospital possessed until recently the chair and footstool actually used by the King at his trial.

During the Stuart epoch, Moreton fell on hard times and its wool and weaving trade disappeared. Before the end of the eighteenth century the population had dwindled to 600 souls in spite of the introduction, in 1742, of a large linen-cloth business by a certain Mr. Busby, who bought the 'Manor House' which still stands in the High Street. The house dates from 1680 and Mr. Busby acquired it very cheaply, solely because it was supposed to be haunted by the ghost of Dame Creswyke, the wife of a previous lease-holder. Perhaps the indecipherable inscriptions on the walls lost their meaning for the spirit of Dame Creswyke after Mr. Busby had re-decorated the house with loot from old Moreton Church; the unhappy dame never reappeared to see the fragments of carved stones, among them an old font, a piscina and two fine gargoyles that still decorate her garden.

Flax was grown throughout the eighteenth century upon the clay lands of this district, and as many as forty linen-weavers found employment at Moreton, not to mention the work done on cottage looms in the neighbouring hamlets. By 1807 the flax-cultivation had almost ceased, but the spinning still occupied the women during winter evenings and the weaving persisted to well within living memory. At the opening of the railway here in 1845 a beautiful linen cloth, of local manufacture, was presented to each of the directors.

The site of a Norman church has been found in the Congregational cemetery, and the new church, which consists mainly of nineteenth-century work, has little of interest except perhaps the efforts of a local rhymester. Among the many epitaphs we read of an uncommon domestic accident:

> 'Here lies the bones of Richard Lawton
> Whose death alas, was strangely brought on;
> Trying one day his corns to mow off
> The razor slipped and cut his toe off.'

In the High Street an ancient curfew tower may be seen, but its bell is not now rung. The market house, a noble building on round pillars, was restored by Lord Redesdale, and the hotel near by repeats the name for, as at Stow, the town had to wait until the nineteenth century for a great benefactor. The original manor of Moreton was given to Westminster Abbey by Edward the Confessor, and the connection with the Abbey continued until John Freeman, Baron Redesdale, purchased the manorial rights about 1830.

The Redesdales lived until recently at Batsford Park amidst the trees on the flanks of the Cotswolds, two miles west from Moreton. Here, flanking the main road, is the picturesque village of Bourton-on-the-Hill. Bourton Henmarsche, as it was formerly called owing to its position near the boundary, has a remarkable charm. Here in one step the green meadows and hedgerow elms of the clayey vale give way to the loose stone walls and vast quarries of the dry limestone wolds. The beauty of Bourton heightens the contrast. The steep road is hemmed in on the right with high walls crowned with tufts of purple aubretia, and white snow-on-the-mountain, and the gardens raised above the road are ablaze with sweet-williams and stocks; on the left are small sunken courts where hollyhocks and sunflowers, ramblers and climbing plants blend so perfectly with the mullioned windows and grey-stone work.

The small lichen-covered church of St. Laurence has a comely appearance and is a real child of this unpretentious village. There is a little Norman work while the carved font and main part of the building are of Decorated and Perpendicular style. A 'Winchester Bushel', so called from the new Act of weights and measures, given by Queen Elizabeth to Winchester, may be seen near the pulpit; it is inscribed with the date 1816 and resembles a brass preserving pan. A fine old dovecote stands near the church, and at the foot of the hill is Bourton House with a large tithe barn near by; the initials R.P. over the entrance stand for Richard Palmer, the patron of the living in 1570. A near relative of this Palmer became the wife of Sir Nicholas Overbury, who acquired one of the two manors here in the reign of Elizabeth. The children of this marriage have their names connected with two famous murders. Old Sir Nicholas, who lived to be a hundred, had a son named Thomas, a highly-cultured man and a great friend and adviser of Robert Carr, the first favourite of James I. Now it happened that Lady Frances Howard, who, at the age of thirteen, had been forced into a thoroughly unhappy marriage with the youthful Earl of Essex, set her heart upon marrying Carr. Sir Thomas Overbury, as a true friend of Carr, strongly opposed the idea of marriage, and bluntly told the wanton Countess that she might do for a mistress but not for a wife. Thereupon the infuriated woman offered £1,000 to have him assassinated and, after much contriving, eventually persuaded Carr to have him put into the Tower (1610). Here he was slowly poisoned with aqua fortis, mercury, powder of diamonds, great spiders and goodness knows what else, probably placed in tarts and sweetmeats sent by the Countess. For months he lingered on in agony—his warder protesting to the impatient woman

that he had given his prisoner enough to poison twenty men
—and eventually, after a strong injection, he expired on
September 14th, 1613. A few days later Lady Essex obtained her divorce, and on the day after Christmas she was
married to Carr, who was made Earl of Somerset and was
now enjoying an income of £90,000 a year. Three years
later the apothecary's apprentice who had been employed
to poison Overbury babbled his secret. Soon the con-
spirators were arrested, and although Carr and his wife,
after spending five years in the Tower, were pardoned,
their four accomplices went to the gallows. For years
afterwards the murder was the talk of England and the
name Thomas Overbury was anagramed as 'O a busy
murther'.

Old Sir Nicholas outlived his unfortunate son by some
thirty years and was succeeded by a relative, the Sir Thomas
Overbury who wrote *The True and Perfect Account* of the
Campden Wonder. But these thoughts of Court intrigues
and unsolved murders seem out of place in the humble
village where men love their gardens so much.

THE SWELLS AND THE SLAUGHTERS

From Stow-on-the-Wold it would be difficult to find a
happier day's walking than that to the Swell and Slaughter
villages which lie on streams furrowing the limestone table-
land east of the Windrush. The River Dikler and its tiny
tributary the Ey have attracted settlement to them away
from the bleak wolds, which are almost devoid of habita-
tions save for a few isolated farms, a few lonely cottages and
the hamlet of Condicote.

There are two Swells and two Slaughters, upper and

lower, but all have something in common; each is small and stands on a tiny stream; each is built of Cotswold stone with a 'big house' and a church built on a knoll, and disastrously 'restored' in Victorian times; each 'Upper' village lies about a mile from its 'Lower' sister, and at each there is abundant evidence of continuous settlement since the Neolithic Age. Yet the hamlets have their individual differences according to the cunning variations in their setting and shape or in the grouping and gardening of the houses. They will afford much pleasure to the visitor who seeks to discover perfection in the little homely aspects of villages rather than a wealth of legend and history or of ancient buildings.

The Tewkesbury road near Upper Swell is planted with ash, sycamore and elm except where it leads through the village, which is smaller and more compact than its neighbours. The houses are comfortably spaced above the west bank of the Dikler, overlooking the rush-fringed mill-pond that has been cut out of the narrow strip of meadow-land along the river-bank. We are immediately attracted by the great barns, for here the arable downs are close at hand, and even the old manor is now a farm-house. A clump of great barns dwarf the tiny church which consists mainly of twelfth-century work.

Near to the church stands the gabled manor-house, an exceptionally attractive building of about 1600, whose grey symmetrical face has been adorned by a large two-storied porch built in the Renaissance style with pillars and light decorations.

Upper Swell parish has many things of interest for the archæologist, and for the person who likes rediscovering objects that are not easy to find. The name Swell is probably derived from the O.E. 'Swelgan' meaning a spring, and it was to the waters here that the Neolithic herdsmen drove their flocks and herds from the dry pastures near Condicote

and Kineton Hill. Buckle Street along the heights is as dry
as a bone, and the Dikler and Ey afford the only running
water on the wolds east of the Windrush. The valleys of
these two streams are dotted with Long Barrows and entrenchments, or to be more precise there are thirty Round
Barrows, ten Long Barrows, and three camps. Roman
remains are equally plentiful, and, although in many cases
the barrows are merely grass hummocks, there is much
pleasure in coming across these ancient sites.

South of Upper Swell the Dikler runs through the lovely
grounds of Abbotswood House and past Bowl Farm, once
the residence of Sir Robert Atkyns, the great historian of
Gloucestershire. Many Roman remains, including masonry
and the sites of two villas, have been found near the farm,
and a cowshed is built partly of stones from a Roman
building.

The present highway scarcely affects the arrangement of
houses at Lower Swell; for a few hundred yards from the
bridge, buildings occur only on the southern side of the
road so that the sunny houses, with their lovely gardens,
can face the meadows traversed by the flowery banks and
clear waters of the Dikler. But the main part of the village
has grown up at right angles to this thoroughfare, and the
church stands on a knoll almost as far as possible from it.
St. Mary's was erected in Victorian times about a small
Norman predecessor which, fortunately, partly escaped
destruction: the north porch and the tympanum, figured
with a Tree of Life sheltering a Dove beneath its boughs,
belonged to the original church as also did the six-shafted
chancel arch which is elaborately decorated with figures and
patterns. The upper of the two incised dials to the east of
the porch may be Saxon in date, while the many fragments
of pottery found here indicate that the site was a burial
ground in Roman times. The churchyard actually encloses a small tumulus, and about ninety years ago, when the

soil was being levelled for the foundations of the new nave, evidences of frequent early cremations were discovered.

At the same time a monolith, known locally as the Whistlestone or Whittlestone, which stood a few furlongs to the north of the church, was hauled down, and many bones were found at its base. The stone, which no doubt formed the only surviving fragment of a Long Barrow, has been preserved in the vicarage paddock. The Horestone, a similar monolith, still stands in a ploughed field half a mile from Lower Swell on the right-hand side of the pretty road to Upper Slaughter.

The way to Cheltenham, although a main road, passes through pleasant Cotswold scenery, and near Eyford Park crosses the valley of the Ey brook which rises at Swell Wold Farm amidst many deep, dry folds of the downs in the slate-quarrying region. All lovers of rural quiet will delight in the walk to Cow Common, a desolate, hummocky grass field whose vast, thorn-dotted surface used to be considered commonable waste. The uneven nature of the ground is increased by a Long Barrow and at least nine Round Barrows, and one of these contained a cist with a form of entrance that has been thought to represent the transition from the Long Barrow to the non-chambered tumuli of the Bronze Age. Near Eyford Hall some rough, grassy islands in a ploughed field mark the sites of four round tumuli and two Long Barrows, one of which contained parts of the skeletons of twenty people and a dog—just as if they had succumbed when mowing a meadow.

In summer the Ey contains little water until near Eyford Park, where the intermittent 'Roaring Wells' burst forth after heavy storms, and help to fill a long, ribbon-shaped lake. Rudder says that Milton may have written part of *Paradise Lost* sitting beside a well in this deep ravine. Seventy years ago the well was stone-lined and covered with a tall canopy on iron supports, but we fear that its inscription

—'Beside this Spring Milton wrote *Paradise Lost*'—is even more erroneous than Rudder's supposition. The spot lies within a thicket amidst the private grounds of Eyford House, a fine modern mansion which replaced the smaller house where Charles Talbot, the only Duke of Shrewsbury, retired at the close of the seventeenth century. According to Atkyns, the Duke liked the 'solitariness of the Place, and the pleasantness of the neighbouring country for recreations.' In 1695 William III, then on a progress from Warwick to Oxford, dined with the Duke, 'and was pleased with his entertainment, for he thought himself out of the world.'

The Ey valley is still narrow and steep-sided at Upper Slaughter, below which it is usually known as the 'Slaughter Brook'. Here the Brook makes a loop about a large circular mound, some 80 feet in diameter, which seems to be part of a Saxon camp. The village took shape around this mound and along the meander of the stream, hence to-day it assumes a roughly circular plan. The curving willow-lined stream almost separates a crescent of barns and cottages from a cluster of gabled houses perched half-way up its other bank, but a hump-backed bridge humbly takes on the task of spanning the mass of willow herb that almost conceals the tiny watercourse. Upper Slaughter possesses a quiet dignity and an air of peaceful seclusion which make it at times preferable to its more obviously attractive neighbours. The much-restored church of St. Peter retains only a few fragments of the original Norman fabric, and you will find little of real interest in it except the handsome Perpendicular font which, after a long relegation to the churchyard, now occupies its proper position. The chief glory of Upper Slaughter must be sought at the southern end of the village in the lovely Elizabethan manor-house which in many ways resembles that at Upper Swell. The twelve-gabled mansion was adorned in Jacobean times with a two-storied porch whose simple ornamentation blends most harmoniously with the quiet dignity of the Elizabethan building. The present house was erected upon a vaulted basement that formed part of the fifteenth-century manor belonging to the Abbey of Evesham. After the Dissolution the estate passed to the Slaughter family, who built the house we see and happily lived for nearly 300 years in the village from which they took their name.

Country-side well shaded with hedgerows and elms divides the two Slaughter villages, for here we are away from the porous limestones and upon the alluvial soils of the stream mouth. At Lower Slaughter, however, the stream is still limpid and reflects in its shining waters the low dry-wall banks and the footbridges crossing it. The village composes itself gracefully about the brook, which is bordered on each side by a grass sward and a roadway. Most of the big trees stand among the houses at the outskirts save for a few aged elms which shade the drinking fountain on the green. The farms and their adjoining barns are tucked away up broad alleyways, and being endwise on to the main street they cannot dominate the stone-built cottages, each with a quaint slate porch projecting above its doorway. Nor is the attractive village too exactly arranged as the pretty cottages stand at different angles to the stream and at varying distances from its sunny banks. The mill with its shallow pool adds more reflection to the scene, nor should we forget to mention the Slaughter ducks that dabble about so noisily and spend half their days stern uppermost in midstream. Lower Slaughter has been called smug and self-conscious, but in sunshine or in rain its winsome manners have an ever-growing charm.

CHAPTER III: *The Valley of the Upper Windrush*

THE BIRTH of a river can be majestic, as witness the Axe emerging from Wookey Cave in the Mendips, or it may be impressive as at Seven Springs, the source of the Churn. More often, however, a river simply comes into being as a mere trickle from a marsh, or a tiny upwelling from a spring, and so Cotswold rivers usually begin, but unlike streams on clay lands they are born in valleys already tremendous, big enough to take a full-grown river. Even the Windrush, which is 30 miles long and the largest feeder of the Thames, rises in this way. South of Snowshill its head valley deepens and widens but it is quite waterless save in time of heavy rains. Although a spring enters the valley near the tiny hamlet of Toddington, even at Ford the stream is still insignificant.

It is open to question if the rolling waterless valleys near Snowshill would have been more beautiful if they held running water, but the dry wolds are ideal for walking and the lover of plants and animals will always find much of interest. In March the lolloping hares are 'as mad as they make 'em' and scarcely deign to move off at a clap or a shout. When Justice Shallow in the *Merry Wives of Windsor* asks 'How does your fallow greyhound, sir? I heard say that he was outrun on Cotsall' we feel he must be thinking of the bleak days of winter. There is an old reddish fox which slinks about in the daytime and only the cries of the plovers betray his movements; the woods are teeming with rabbits who will scamper along the top of the walls or if the stones are decayed you may even hear them rumbling along inside the stonework. Their enemy, the white-fronted stoat, loves a home in old walls and will hiss a menace when you draw too near to his retreat. The badger is found in these woods and I have seen an old brock trundling along in front of the headlamps of a car until he came to the gap in the wall which he had helped to enlarge for his use. Hedgehogs seem to thrive here away from the traffic so fatal to them. There is a continuous murmur of rustic enjoyment. The plover's incessant 'peewit', the skylark's continuous tirade, the restless wheeling of starlings in twittering flocks, all add to the sounds, while the 'whirr' of the partridge never fails to be startling, as it rises suddenly to skim over the nearest wall and stall swiftly past the thorn bushes. The grey-green colour of the wolds is brightened by glimpses of goldfinch and wagtail, yellow-hammer and whinchat. The huge barns are beloved of white barn owls, who screech so weirdly at twilight that the beech boles become ghoulish and you wish heartily that the bloodcurdling noise would cease. All these and many others live near the young Windrush.

At Cutsdean the tiny Windrush flows beneath splendid barns and stone houses, and thence to the south a road running parallel with the stream makes an interesting car-ride for those who would trace a river in the North Cotswolds. Minute inspection is by no means desirable, and the homely villages with their manor-houses and parks should be regarded only as elements on a wider 'canvas'. They are not show-places, not miniature Campdens, for man's work here is but part of Nature's scheme to beautify a bare wold.

At Ford, where the Stow-Tewkesbury road crosses the river, the houses have shunned the steep valley slopes, and here you will find the only inn and, indeed, almost the only house in the last nine miles of the journey from Stow to Stanway. 'The Plough' is picturesque and roomy as becomes its three hundred years. Over the doorway a good example of persuasive advertisement runs as follows:

THE RIVER WINDRUSH AT SHERBOURNE

'Ye weary travelers that pass by,
With dust and scorching sunbeams dry
Or be be-numbed with snow and frost.
With having these bleak cotswold crosst
Step in and quaff my nut-brown ale
Bright as rubys mild and stale,
Twill make your laging trotters dance
As nimble as the suns of france,
Then ye will own ye men of sense,
That neare was better spent six pence.'

The invitation is well worth accepting, for whereas the larger Cotswold towns have half a dozen inns to each place of worship, some of these small Windrush hamlets have more churches than public-houses. One mile to the south a beautiful bend of the river brings us to Temple Guiting, lying in the deep-wooded valley screened by thick beech strips. The name of the village comes from the military order of Templars for whom in the twelfth century Gilbert de Lacy founded a preceptory where a knight or preceptor would take command of a few serving brothers. In 1308, Edward II suppressed the order and gave the holding at Guiting to their rivals, the Hospitallers. Some two hundred years later the manor was purchased by Bishop Foxe of Winchester, the same who baptized Henry VIII, and he gave it to Corpus Christi College which he had just founded at Oxford. At the dissolution of the Hospitallers Henry VIII gave their estates here to Christ Church, so the village became much linked up with Oxford and to-day the Lords of the Manor and owners of most of the parish are the Corpus Christi Society. The picturesque Elizabethan farm-house in the park was formerly the manor-house and the summer residence of the Bishop of Oxford. To-day only the name Temple Guiting remains to remind the traveller of the Templars.

THE GREAT HALL, BERKELEY CASTLE

Across the river, high up on the bank opposite to the mansion, stands the little church of St. Mary. Although the Norman doorway is very fine, more unusual are the three fragments of fifteenth-century glass depicting the Virgin Mary, St. James and Mary Magdalen with her box of precious ointment.

Guiting Power or Lower Guiting, farther down the river, has grown up a short way from the now placid waters of the Windrush. Here the church of St. Michael retains two Norman doorways, one of which has a chequered tympanum and a chalice carved in the centre of its elaborately sculptured lintel. The chancel was built about 1200, and some two centuries later, with wealth accumulated from the wool trade, the tower was added and the walls of the nave were raised. The community flourished anew with the coming of enclosures and so once more the church was enlarged, and this time a Norman arch in the chancel had to go in the restoration. Towards the end of the nineteenth century falling wheat prices and a marked agricultural depression caused empty houses in the village, and consequently the church became so ruinous that, when it was finally restored about thirty years ago, the chancel had to be rebuilt. At the restoration all that could be preserved of the old church was retained, and the man carved on the shaft of the north Norman doorway has many reasons for defiantly thrusting out his tongue at fate.

Continuing downstream we pass the entrance to the Grange, and soon afterwards climb up the steep valley side to the Stow-Cheltenham highway. Down below us lies Naunton, a place to be loved for its beautiful setting. The grey string of houses is set out along the winding stream, and beyond it the smooth valley side rises majestically to the bare grey-brown wolds. The church stands on the near side slope, but the grey houses forsook it to follow the sunny south-facing bank where they straggle along a sandy terrace towards a picturesque old mill.

The cyclopean dovecot makes a fine picture just where the stream widens into a silvery band of light. Naunton has a serene and lovely aspect, but at close quarters her face looks very homely. The by-way to the village is discouraging enough, and once launched into Naunton the houses do not beam a welcome as they usually face away from the street displaying an expressionless stretch of grey wall and roof unbroken by window, doorway or gable.

A little way below Naunton the Windrush becomes wildly meandering; the 'devious coils' twist and turn for all the world like a gigantic eel writhing, and before you have ceased to wonder at it, the river has waltzed under Harford Bridge. From here we will follow the footpath to Bourton-on-the-Water, and looking ahead we can see the gorge-like valley attempting to copy in more clumsy fashion the wild twistings of its river. This is an isolated world quite distinct from the exposed wolds. The flash of the solitary kingfisher replaces the glittering speckles of the gregarious starling; the swift buzzing dragon-fly is more at home here than the brown and blue butterflies, and the plaintive cry of the snipe is less startling than the whirr of the partridge. The shining fish-scales left on the bank by the secretive otter are more intriguing than the blood-stained feather left by sly reynard on the wold. The water vole is as common here as rabbits in upland brambles, and beyond the yellow mimulus and pink willow-herb the reeds shiver as their stems are gnawed noisily through near the water-line. The river seems to give with us a sigh of regret as it leaves its shady valley in the limestone hills to take up its lazier course over the clays of the Vale of Bourton.

THE WINDRUSH VALLEY

'From the troubles of the world
I turn to ducks,
Beautiful comical things
Sleeping or curled
Their heads beneath white wings
By waters cool,
Or finding curious things
To eat in various mucks,
Beneath the pool . . .'

—F. W. HARVEY

Four miles from Stow-on-the-Wold, where the Fosse Way crosses the Windrush by a well-designed stone bridge, a by-road leads along the sparkling river fringed with rushes and pollard-willows into the village of Bourton-on-the-Water. It is a smug and tidy place, 'swept and garnished', but very cool and refreshing to remain in for a while. The small town has a most prosperous air with its well-stocked shops and well-groomed inns, and the broad, rippling river that flows down the middle of the street is spanned by graceful stone bridges, and skirted with trim green sward. Everything looks so calm that we become placid too. Intrusions of red brick pass unnoticed, the proximity of the railway is not even guessed at, and the relative ugliness of the church of St. Lawrence seems of little consequence to us. For here the river claims all our thoughts, and we could stop and ponder by the rustling stream, content to watch the ducks on its shining waters, and the reflections of the poplars and grey archways. The lover of old buildings will find little in Bourton to attract him. Men come because of the river, but the village is by no means as new as it looks.

Just to the north lies Salmonsbury Camp, an ancient

British stronghold, built on the gravel terrace overlooking the Dikler stream. Here sixty acres were enclosed by tall ramparts to form a refuge guarded by the swamps of Dikler and Windrush. Near by, the Fosse Way is joined by the more ancient Buckle Street, so that the Romans took over the camp and partly destroyed the huge ramparts that might have threatened their highway.

In Saxon times it was probably the site of a victory of Northumbria over Wessex in 626. Sections of the ramparts are still standing, and recent excavation has revealed much of the ground plan of the dwellings. In the British Museum may be seen a delightful model of a Saxon weaver's hut unearthed near the camp, one of the five finest Saxon dwellings yet discovered in England.

Bourton had therefore an early beginning, and possessed most of the amenities lacking at Stow-on-the-Wold; plenty of water from wells in the gravel, a flowing stream for the grinding of corn, and easily accessible arable fields. Yet what has become of the old houses like those to be found at Chipping Campden or Stow? Stow-on-the-Wold drew towards her all the roads and captured the markets, thereby leaving Bourton, except for the Fosse, isolated in a clay vale, difficult to cross and even to-day not traversed lengthwise by so much as a footpath.

The great historians of the county have little to say of the hamlet that grew up slowly along the banks of the Windrush. The railway, however, came right to the village, and soon it was hailed as 'Venice of the Cotswolds', a name worth a score of architectural treasures.

The ancient and gabled manor-house, with its secret chamber and priest's room, has long since been destroyed; the Gothic rectory was pulled down and replaced by a large three-storied building; what may once have been a pleasing Georgian church has been largely reconstructed as a pseudo-Gothic structure surmounted by the original ugly cupola tower.

The public-spirited inhabitants of Bourton-on-the-Water have done much to beautify their church: the windows have been filled with coloured glass, and one ceiling has been elaborately embossed, but we long for the pale green glass of Sapperton and for the grace of the lovely decorated lantern at Kempsford.

Harrington House remains as a good specimen of the Georgian type of domestic architecture, and near the Victoria Hall is an older Cotswold building with sun-dials dated 1698. At the 'New Inn', an interesting sun-dial shows the quarter hours, and in the garden there is a large model of Bourton which gives a splendid idea of the plan of the village. We are, however, scarcely justified in being over-critical of modern buildings in Bourton, for many of the newer houses are stone-built in the old Cotswold style, and the hospital (1861), said to be the third village hospital erected in England, is exceptionally well built.

Near Bourton the Windrush is joined by the Dikler, and the damp, soggy vale through which it flows southwards has been avoided by man. The only large gravel patch was seized upon by 'Bourton-under-the-Water', as the people dryly call it, and the other tiny hamlets had to be content with a precarious footing on steep slopes of the valley sides. To the east lie the Rissingtons, Great, Little and Wyck.

Wyck Rissington is an easy walk past Salmonsbury Camp and by footpath across the Dikler at the mill and so up the slope to the village. The lovely little church of St. Lawrence retains a Norman nave and, although the windows are mainly fifteenth-century, the restorers did not destroy the thirteenth-century priest's doorway with the fine east window above it, nor the stone bench along the walls of the chancel. The twelve wooden carvings hanging here are Flemish work of Elizabethan times, and they represent scenes in the life of Our Lord.

Little Rissington may be reached by the winding road out of Bourton which leads down the Windrush past the fine cricket pitch and clean watercress beds. The charming village twists and clings to the slope as if liking the vale, but wanting the hills. Although several blue-slate roofs spoil the greyness of the hamlet it possesses at least one old cottage with a fine stone porch, and a small church which retains a Norman arcade.

Beyond the village the road climbs on to Wyck Beacon (over 800 feet), an arable land, where beech and ash are abundant, and Traveller's Joy lines the roadside. Stone walls are few, and the landscape is not quite 'Cotswold', but the winter snow lingers long in the hollows, and the isolated ashes lean away from the biting winds. Near by on Westcote Hill, where the road to Burford is about to leave Gloucestershire, an interesting relic of pre-enclosure England may be seen. The arable fields, over a considerable acreage, are divided by balks of turf called 'meres' into long narrow strips which are cultivated on the old system by a few small farmers, each owning up to about a hundred acres. Here strips of wheat are bordered by strips of turnips and oats; none of the land is enclosed, not even along the roadside, and some of the old stone landmarks still remain.

Our route takes us over the open trackway to the south toward the Windrush valley and Barrington Park. In this district a cluster of villages has grown up near the river where it begins to leave the watery vale of Bourton to enter once more a narrower valley cut in the limestone downs. Great Barrington is dominated by its vast deer-park, and behind the tall wall, speckled with rock plants and lichens, stands the huge house built by Charles Talbot, Lord Chancellor in George II's reign. Charles Talbot bought the estate from the Brays in 1734, after they had held it for two hundred years.

A remarkable piece of horseplay took place here in 1682. Sir Edmund Bray, then master of Barrington Park, entertained among his guests the two middle-aged sons of Philip, fourth Lord Wharton, a zealous Puritan who had brought up his family on the strictest Calvinist principles. It appears that Thomas, the elder son, rebelled against this stern discipline, and early acquired a most unenviable reputation.

The village of Barrington was soon made aware of the presence of this 'most universal villain'. After dinner one night the two brothers led a merry, drunken remnant of the party in quest of adventure. They woke up the sleeping village and broke into the church, ringing the bells, then cutting the bell-ropes, mis-using the font, smashing the pulpit, and tearing the Bible. When they started to create further havoc in the village the people, now thoroughly aroused drove the rabble back to the Park. Bishop Frampton of Gloucester forced them to meet him at Stow-on-the-Wold, where he exacted from them 'a handsome fine' which went towards the repairs of the church there.

To-day Great Barrington church seems none the worse for desecration, and, although mainly of the Perpendicular age, it has a beautiful Norman chancel arch. At the east end of the aisle is the recumbent effigy of Captain Edward Bray (1620), whose sword hangs on his right side. Robert Atkyns says that having killed a man, and been pardoned by Queen Elizabeth, Captain Edward swore never to draw sword again with his right hand. Perhaps, however, Captain Edward may have been left-handed.

A much more beautiful memorial is that to Jane Bray and her brother, victims of small-pox. A guardian angel leads the children, who are dressed in brocaded petticoat, laced coat, cravat and peruke as if about to go to a ball.

Jane, so the pathetic inscription runs, died aged eight in 1711, and her brother 'In the fifteenth year of his age' on Christmas Day 1720, 'and the Beautys of His Person were equal to those of His Mind'.

A high causeway, erected by Thomas Strong of London, Freemason, traverses the damp plain of Windrush and links up Great and Little Barrington. Many of the pretty grey cottages of the smaller village are scattered around a quarry-like combe from which a copious spring issues. The buildings are all of stone as deep quarries occur on the hill-top, and here was dug and mined much of the stone for Barrington House.

The grey, rather squat little church of St. Peter, over-looking the Windrush, possesses a fine Norman doorway, and in the north wall has been placed an ancient tympanum representing Our Lord enthroned between two angels.

Passing below Barrington House, we follow along the deep Windrush which forms a world of its own, bright with water crowfoot and yellow water-lilies, and sinuous with tentacles of green ribbon-like leaves which will writhe and curl round an intrepid bather. On sunny days the speckled trout play by the bridges, and dart swiftly away as they feel the coolness of shadows thrown by the on-lookers.

A pleasant mile brings us to Windrush, a pretty place whose tiny church, dedicated to St. Peter, has a south doorway with remarkably fine beak-head ornamentation, and a decorated chancel arch, both of Norman age. The skill of this stonework is equalled by the woodwork of the oak Jacobean pulpit which is cleverly carved with roses and dragons.

Another short walk leads to Sherborne, which nestles between its great Park and the Sherborne brook. Cottage No. 88 at the east end of the village claims our attention first for the small rounded window and the fine Norman archway forming its doorway. Sherborne was formerly a rich manor of Winchcomb Abbey, and Father Abbot used to stay at Sherborne House on sheep-shearing festivals and other important occasions. Since the Dissolution it has been the home of the Duttons, who twice entertained Queen Elizabeth and who built the present great mansion about 1830. The village itself straggles out for a mile, and is quite dominated by the fine park and much beautified by the lakes made along the stream. Except the charming gabled houses near the church, few of the cottages are much more than a century old, but all are uniformly built in the Cotswold style. Everything in Sherborne points to the care and attention of a beneficent landlord, and here you may see how a central authority can beautify a village and secure it from individual eccentricities. Each cottage faces a well-tended garden stocked with the reddest of English roses and the very biggest of dahlias, while many a household here can almost sit under its own vine-tree.

CHAPTER IV: At the Sign of the Golden Fleece

NORTHLEACH, FROM whatever direction you approach it, is something of a disappointment, if you have seen the lime-trees at Burford or the lovely reflections at Bourton and Bibury. The rolling downland, with stone walls and streamless hollows, seems interminable, and when the shielding strips of beechwood no longer line the road, the dry fields spread out before us still, and there is no sign of a village.

Suddenly the hills fall away and reveal a mighty valley whose steep hill-sides dwarf a cluster of houses which huddle round a tall church tower. Such a valley, after the waterless miles, gives hope of a sparkling river, of willows and lush water-meadows, but there is no gleam of water, no winding ribbon of light to reflect the church and the grey walls of the stone-built houses. We enter the long, narrow street, whose line is broken by the market square, but the town does not rise up challenging and lovely as at Chipping Campden.

Domesday Survey records four manors called 'Leece', which is the Saxon word for a stream, and they all take their name from the River Leach on which they are situated. Of these manors, Eastleach Martin, Eastleach Turville and Lechlade lie near the edge of the Cotswolds, whereas Northleach has grown up in the deep combe at the head of the valley amidst rolling, open hill-country, where, with limestone underfoot, the soil is dry and the grass is close and sweet, and man has herded sheep for many hundreds of years. The Cotswolds have even given their name to a breed of sheep that is one of the oldest recorded native breeds in England. The Cotswold sheep of to-day are probably descended from the flocks which roamed these hills in Neolithic times, and are the type from which all our domesticated sheep have sprung, so that they can truly be called "as old as the hills'.

Cotswold sheep were a hardy and prolific breed with lambs that quickly put on fleece and became hardened to the bracing cold of the wolds, where budding is a month later than in the sheltered vale. The meat, too, was not of inferior quality, and Marshall says it used to rank among the first in Smithfield Market. The true Cotswold sheep is white-faced, and, in Drayton's words, has

> 'A body long and large, the buttocks equal broad
> As fit to undergoe the full and weightie load.'

Farmers will tell you that the ewes will 'live on almost nothing in summer if they have water and quiet'. This famous breed, which for many generations made Chipping Campden and Northleach the centre of the English wool trade, have nearly all disappeared, yet in their day they were a source of national pride and importance. Here is Drayton exulting in his *Polyolbion*:

> 'Cotswold that great king of shepherds
>
> .   .   .   .
> T'whom Sarum's plain gives place, tho' famous for her flocks
> Yet hardly doth she tithe our Cotswold's wealthy locks.'

As early as the twelfth century Flemish traders were coming to Cotswold for wool, and in the fourteenth century Florentine merchants were active competitors in the same markets. In the early fifteenth century both sheep and wool were largely exported, but in 1434 it was enacted that no sheep should be exported without the King's licence, and there is no record of any licence being requested except for Cotswold sheep.   The King of Portugal, in 1437, approached Henry VI for liberty to import sixty sacks of Cotswold wool to make cloth of gold for Court ceremonial dress, while some thirty years later Edward IV presented twenty ewes and five rams to John of Aragon.   And so Cotswold was the talk of kings, and the 'Golden Fleece' to many a Merchant of the Staple. Cotswold wool was the prize for which wealthy merchants travelled down to the factors of Northleach, where the great barns were filled with wool and fells brought in from the neighbouring wolds.   Fortunately a faithful picture of the lives and habits of the merchants exists in the pages of the *Cely Papers*, in which a series of letters (1475–88) describes the transactions and more homely doings of the Celys, wool merchants of Mark Lane, London.   The Cely family, Richard the father, and his three sons Richard, Robert and George, did their buying chiefly at Northleach, and dealt mainly with William Midwinter.

The family made so much money out of wool that they were able to own land, to buy hawks and horses and give expensive presents, to turn over £2,000 worth of wool a year and negotiate with rich gentlemen for their daughters in marriage. They even owned their own trading vessel, the *Margaret Cely*, of some 200 tons, which carried the wool to Calais and also voyaged to Zeeland, Flanders and Bordeaux.   They had purchased her, without rigging and fittings, in Brittany for £28, and she was duly armed with cannon, bows, bills and 'V dossen dartes'. Yet they were hard bargainers, for we find Midwinter complaining that he had sold wool to them cheaper than he could buy it, and Richard writing to George to the effect that Midwinter is come to town, adding 'God ryd we of hym', and, since he mentions unpaid debts in the same letter, it is not improbable that Midwinter had come for money.

Here is Richard Cely writing to his son George who rode always with Meg his hawk on his wrist, and of whom it is also told that he rode with another merchant for ten miles in gloomy silence and then confided that 'his grey bitch had whelped and had fourteen pups and then died and the pups with her'.

'Your letter came to me the Sunday before All Hallows Day and Will Easton, mercer, and Will Midwinter of Northleach dined with me . . . and the comfort of your letter caused me for to buy of the foresaid Will Midwinter 60 sacks of Cotswold wool the which is in pile at Northleach. . . .'

Elsewhere, Richard the younger writes to his brother George at Calais: 'I have been in Cotswold these three weeks, and packed with William Midwinter 22 sarplers (a sack or bale of wool enclosed in coarse canvas and weighing about a ton). . . . William Britten says it is the fairest wool he saw this year: and I packed at Campden of the same bargain 4 sarplers . . .' The Celys had to face keen competitors, and in the summer of 1481 'wool in Cotswold is at great price, 13s. 4d. a tod (28 lb.), and great riding for wool in Cotswold as was any year this 7 year'.

Besides the wealth of business details, the Letters also reveal a romance. Richard Cely writes to his brother George: 'The same day that I came to Northleach on a Sunday before matins from Burford, William Midwinter welcomed me and in our conversation he asked me if I were in any way of marriage. I told him nay, and he informed me that there was a young gentlewoman whose father his name is Lemryke, and her mother is dead, and she shall dispend by her mother £40 a year, and there have been great gentlemen to see her and would have her. And ere matins were done William Midwinter had moved this matter to the greatest man about the gentleman Lemryke, and he sent and informed the aforesaid of all the matter and the young gentlewoman both. And the Saturday after William Midwinter went to London. . . . When I had packed at Campden, and Midwinter parted, I came to Northleach again to make an end of packing, and on Sunday next after, the same man that Midwinter brake first to, telled me that he had broken to his master, and he said his master was right well pleased therewith: and the same man said to me, if I would tarry May day I should have a sight of the young gentlewoman, and I said I would tarry with a good will. And the same day her father should have sitten at Northleach for the King, but he sent one of his clerks, and rode himself to Winchcombe. And to matins the same day come the young gentlewoman and her step-mother, and I and William Britten were saying matins when they to the church. And when matins was done, they went to a kinswoman of the young gentlewoman, and I sent to them a bottle of white romnay, and they took it thankfully for they had come a mile afoot that morning. And when Mass was done, I come and welcomed them and kissed them, and they thanked me for the wine and prayed me to come to dinner with them, and I excused me and they made me promise to drink with them after dinner. And I sent them to dinner a gallon wine, and they sent me a heronsew roast. And after dinner I came and drank with them and took William Britten with me; and we had right good communication and the person pleased me well . . . she is young, little and very well favoured and witty. **Sir,** all this matter abideth the coming of her father to London and we may understand what sum he will depart with and how he likes me; he will be here within three weeks. I pray send me a letter how ye think by this matter.'

In ten days Richard writes that he is 'to goo and se Rawsons dowttyr' so the proposed courtship must have come to nothing. Apparently Richard's affections are as fickle as his spelling, and we wonder if this young gentle-woman also pleased him well and if 'Sche ys zewnge lytyll and whery whell favyrd and whytty'. At least we can sympathize with him when he writes: 'I hawhe many thyngs in my mynde byt I hawhe ne laysar to whrytte, ze may wyndyrstond partte be my letter that I sente yow before thys.'

Other merchants there were, the best known of whom were John Fortey, whose house is still to be seen upon the Green with his merchant's mark upon a corbel, and Thomas Dutton, who gave the charming row of alms-houses to Northleach and in his will left one thousand sheep to his second son. But the finest memorial of all to these wool merchants is the stately fifteenth-century church and its famous brasses.

The magnificent church is a true child of the old town, for the stone was probably cut and quarried in what is now the Market Square. Built in the Perpendicular style, with a high, embattled tower, it is one of the noblest parish churches in Gloucestershire. The chief glory of the build-ing is its south porch, the finest of its type in England, which has a simplicity and grandeur in its conception that make it appear at once both massive and graceful. Within, the porch consists of two bays beautifully vaulted and contains an upper chamber, with a large open fire-place, an oven and candle-brackets, formerly used by the priest on the eve of great feasts so that he might be astir in time for the early masses attended by those anxious to be about their business.

The interior of the church is most impressive on account of its spaciousness and exceptional grace of the vaulting. It contains several fine examples of the mason's art, such as the original stone pulpit, a finely carved Perpendicular font and the remains of an exceptionally beautiful reredos, but much of the interest of Northleach lies in the brasses commemorating the wool merchants who rest now in different parts of the nave. Here we may find the names of men already familiar to us.

The brass to John Fortey, who so successfully rebuilt the nave to make it 'more lightsome and splendid', has lost much of its inscription, but it still bears the date 1458 and is one of the best of this period in the country. One foot rests upon a sheep, the other on a woolpack, while his merchant's mark, the initials J.F. with cross and banner between them, surrounded by a wreath, occurs at the end of his girdle and six times in the bordure. Beneath is the couplet (as translated):

> 'Behold, what is the good of anything in this life
> All of which is nothing unless to love God.'

Will Midwinter of the Cely letters probably lies at the foot of the pulpit steps for the brass bears the initials W. M. The pathetic inscription on the border reads:

> 'Farewell my frendes the tyde abydeth no man,
> I am departed hence and so shall ye.
> But in the passage the best song that I can
> Is Requiem eternam now Jhu graunte it me
> When I have ended all myn adversitie
> Graunte me in Paradise to have a mansion
> That shed Thy blode for my redemption.'

Behind the organ is the brass to Thomas Fortey (ob. 1447) and Agnes his wife, and her first husband, William Scors, probably a tailor from the scissors at his feet. Agnes' two families are also shown and, although one portion has been lost, the naive inscriptions remain—'Pray for the children of Thomas Fortey' and 'These are the children of William Scors VI'. Presumably Thomas Fortey's children were more in need of Divine guidance than those of the tailor. A free translation of the verse inscribed below the three is as follows:

'Underfoot lying dead is Thomas Fortey
And his bride Agnes pleasing to him. A Counsellor,
A merchant worthy upright and true kindly
Not conspicuously known as an unpleasantly self-
    satisfied man. . . .'

The fragmentary inscription on the border says that Thomas was a repairer of roads and churches, and the words are interspersed with quaint stops representing a fighting cock, a pig, a hedgehog, a pair of greyhounds and so on.

A highly ornamented and exquisite brass remembers Thomas Bushe who died in 1525. He and his wife are represented under a double canopy, with their feet resting on a woolpack, and a sheep with long, curling horns. In each canopy there are other horned sheep under a large bush, an obvious rebus, and the arms of the staple of Calais. His merchant's mark, a cross springing from a monogram, appears below, and the inscription, 'Off yr charitie p'y for the soulls of Thomas Bushe, m'chant of ye staple of Calys and Johan hys wyfe . . .' On the border is the addition 'for whos soulls of yr charite say a pr noster and a ave'.

In the Lady Chapel, a brass dated 1490, depicts John Taylor and his wife. Below the parents are their fifteen children, eight sons and seven daughters, and at the foot of the brass a sheep stands on a woolpack bearing the merchant's mark, two shepherds' crooks in the form of a cross.

The church possesses three more fine brasses; one, rather small but beautifully executed, commemorates Robert Serche (ob. 1501) and Anne his wife and their four children. Another, the oldest in the church and probably dating back to about 1400, is to an unknown wool merchant and his wife. The details of the clothes are most interesting, and the trader, whose feet rest on a woolpack, has a dagger hanging from his decorated girdle. Like her husband, the lady wears a flowing gown and cloak, but at her feet sits a little dog with bells about its collar. For all the world they might have stepped straight out of the pages of the *Canterbury Tales*. Finally, near the altar, is a brass to one interested in sheep of another kind, a former vicar who died about 1530. The inscription warns us that death may come when least expected, and in fancy we might read it also as a warning for the flourishing Northleach the vicar knew.

Unhappily for Northleach the days of her prosperity were numbered. The age of the Golden Fleece was passing, for the export of Gloucestershire sheep, chiefly to Spain where they were crossed with Spanish breeds, produced so strong and fine a fleece that Cotswold wool no longer headed the market. The town kept a trade in wool for another two hundred years, but the price of local wool was always dwindling and in like proportion the greatness of Northleach decayed.

The lapse into the common place was, however, incomplete. Little spurts of history illumined her doors occasionally and the Court Book records conjure up for the reader a pleasant tale of English village life. The records of the local Court cover the period from the reign of Edward VI to that of William III, and the details reveal how minutely the life of the people was regulated. The officers consisted of a bailiff, six 'arbitrators', two constables and two wardsmen, but representatives of each of the major trades of the town were co-opted on to the council and the bailiff was attended by a Sergeant at Mace who rang the bell to summon the meetings.

Every one trading in the town had to be licensed by the

bailiff—a shilling to cut men's hair and half a crown to cut their cloth—and the standard of goods sold in the market was scrupulously maintained. More than once we read of 'faggots to burn the measley piggs', while bakers from Stow, Burford and Northleach are fined for 'wanting in the peny lofe'. The Winchcomb butchers were so contumacious that they were denied stallage altogether, and we wonder if this explains a peculiar expression often used locally. When any person not wanted enters a room, or when any one leaves without closing the door, the company yells 'Winchcomb', which in literary English signifies either 'Come back and shut the door' or 'Clear off and close the door after you'. The Court even fined itself because the town bushel proved to be wanting. Disorder, in manner or dress, was frowned upon severely. The arbitrators had to attend Court 'in gowns or other decent upper garments', and any man or child going to church on Sunday without a cap, 'knitte or fulne', was fined 2d. Apprentices who had failed to return to their master's house when the town bell rang at nine o'clock in the winter and ten in summer were laid by the heels all night in the stocks. We can imagine the talk of the town when William Launchbury, a narrow weaver, was fined 6d. for playing 'coytes' during Divine Service or when, in 1577, a certain Thomas 'ffouler' assaulted the watchman 'with his sword and dagger drawn'. We wonder why Richard Bysshop and his wife broke 'the dore of the stock house'—they had to repair it or pay 10s.—and how many folk were fined five shillings for using other than the forestreet door of an inn.

The parish still had its *metae sagittales* or butts where, on specified occasions, all inhabitants had to assemble for practice 'with sufficient bows and arrows' or be fined 6d. In 1600, Northleach provided two soldiers for the local militia and also paid for powder, for 'the match, and for bringing the pykes from Syssiter (Cirencester) and a pair of soldier's shoes XXd'.

The fortunes of Northleach, however, seem to be already somewhat depressed, for within three years the brothers Thomas and William Dutton, in 1615 and 1618 respectively, left substantial sums of money to the poor. Thomas Dutton founded and endowed the six pretty alms-houses which are still to be seen in the main street, and William left the Great House and £200 to be used by 'some honest tradesman in frestains or stuffs or in any other such trade as may keep the people from idleness. . . .' The rental for house and money was to be only £4 a year, which sum was to be used to help sick and needy parishioners and had to be faithfully accounted for at churchwardens' meetings.

Perhaps more picturesque than a glimpse of this shrewd and kindly merchant apportioning his wealth is the passage of King Charles's army in the September of 1643 after the siege of Gloucester had been raised. The King passed the night at Northleach, as tradition has it, at Dutton House on the Burford Road. The following entries concerning the event are in the Court Book:

> 1643   Received of Widow Westmacott rent four and twenty shillings deducted for oates which the Constables had for the King's use.
> Paid for bread for the soldiers 3s.
> Paid for the Prince's footmen 14s.
> Paid one peck of oates for a souldier 4d. (A Scotsman surely!)

Very different was the temper of the detachment of Fairfax's troops which came to Northleach after the Battle of Naseby. The soldiers broke open the Town box, probably in search of money, cut several pages out of the

Court Book and carried off parchments for no obvious reason.

Again relapsed into rural quiet, Northleach was yet 'home' to at least one of her sons as the last entry under 1652 proves:

> 'Edward Barnard Armiger bequeathed to the town £40. He had been consul at Smyrna and Aleppo XVI years, deceased at Clerkenwell, near London. Corps brought thence hither.'

But that, apart from the growth of the sixteenth-century Grammar School, is practically the end of the story, for, up to about 1750, the main London to Gloucester road crossed the Thames at Lechlade and traversed the Cotswolds at Cirencester, far to the south of Northleach. After 1750 the crossing of the Thames' marshes was effected by a road bridge near Eynsham (where the toll-gate is to-day), and thereafter the most direct road from London to Gloucester lay through Witney, Burford and Northleach. Arthur Young, in 1768, thought 'the road from Witney to North-leach the worst turnpike I ever travelled in', and complained bitterly of the 'barbarous method of mending their capital road' by filling in ruts with loose stones 'as large as one's head'. It is highly probable that at this time the 'Flying coaches' took the high road, now mainly a grass-grown track, which avoids the Leach valley and keeps to the hills just north of Northleach and Hampnett. In 1779 road surfaces on the turnpike stretches had been so much improved that coaches preferred to tackle the drive into and out of Northleach, and so the main road passed through the town and was 'pretty much frequented'. Even at this time some of the old wool warehouses remained, and part of one had been converted into the 'Lamb Inn'. The return of prosperity from the transit traffic lasted for a century or so until the building of railways ruined the coaching trade. The town, to-day seven miles from the nearest railway station, assumed once more its rural character, and its inhabitants had little to excite them save horse-racing and politics. Arthur Gibbs describes a political meeting held in this 'very Radical town' about fifty years ago. Gibbs took the chair and, the Unionist member being unable to attend, found himself facing 'two hundred "red-hot" Radicals' with only one other speaker besides himself to keep the ball a-rolling. His companion, a professional politician of the baser sort, ranted away for three-quarters of an hour, but the audience, instead of being convinced, was fairly rabid when Gibbs stood up to speak. As he himself puts it—'After a bit they began shouting "Speak up". The more they shouted the more mixed I got. The din became so great I could not hear myself speak. In about five minutes there would have been a row. Suddenly a bright idea occurred to me. "Listen to me," I shouted; "as you won't hear me speak, perhaps you will allow me to sing you a song." I had a fairly strong voice, and could go up a good height; so I gave them "Tom Bowling". Directly I started you could have heard a pin drop. They gave me a fair hearing all through; and when, as a final climax, I finished up with a prolonged B flat— a very loud and long note, which sounded to me something between a "view holloa" and the whistle of a penny steamboat . . . their enthusiasm knew no bounds. They cheered and cheered again. Hand shaking went on all round, whilst the biggest Radical of the lot stood up and shouted, "You be a little Liberal, I know, and the other blokes 'ave 'ired you".'

Northleach improves considerably upon acquaintance. In addition to the grand barn, with a fine columbarium, near to the church, you will find several half-timbered buildings and a few lovely gabled houses; the 'Blind House', a windowless room once used as a lock-up, retains its stone ceiling and crude wooden bed, while the old school building near Oak House is not the only haunted house in the town. Old customs linger on; the mummers flourish, and each householder possesses common rights on Farmington Downs. Once a year the town throbs with excitement upon the election of the High Bailiff, who then presides at parish meetings and at a Court Leet dinner held in the 'Wheatsheaf'. During the feast, the children troop into the courtyard and proceed to kick up a hullaballoo on tin trays until they have extorted the customary reward. So it happens that, with the coming of motor transport, the fortunes of Northleach have risen again, and the narrow street is once more busy with tourist traffic. To-day Northleach folk can sing with ever-growing amusement the couplet in an ancient local ballad:

> 'While vools gwoes scramblin' vur and nigh,
> We bides at whoam, my dog and I,'

DOWN THE LEACH

Maps show the Leach rising near Hampnett, but the valley is quite waterless save in time of heavy rains when floods collect near the prison. Hampnett, before the coming of turnpikes, stood on the main coaching route between Oxford and Gloucester, yet it always remained a tiny hill-top hamlet. The small church, in spite of restoration, contains a fine Norman chancel with a groined roof and much good Norman work besides. Recently the interior has been covered with mural paintings which look rather startling at first sight.

The grim-looking prison standing near the Fosse Way has been partly dismantled, and a few hundred yards from it, just south-west of the church at Northleach, the Seven Springs or Wellings form the source of the Leach. In spite of water supplied to the town a considerable stream flows southwards past the last house in Northleach, the new Grammar School, which has given the lie to the old saying that Northleach began at the workhouse and ended in the prison.

All the way to the Eastleach villages the valley is pastoral and lonely, scarcely a cottage being visible from its green floor. The large Lodge Park, a private deer-park of the Sherborne Estate, was enclosed by 'Crump' Dutton, a member of the great Sherborne family who stocked it with deer brought from Wychwood Forest with the special permission of Oliver Cromwell. The hunting lodge here, a real gem of renaissance architecture, was built for 'Crump' Dutton about 1642 to the design of Inigo Jones. The exquisite building, which fortunately can be fully seen through the lovely gates on the road-side, is truly worth 'all the great houses near it thrown together', and has no rival for its type in Gloucestershire. Immediately in front of the Lodge stretch vast portions of a paddock one mile long where deer used to be let loose at one end and then greyhounds sent after them. A closable aperture admitted any deer that outran the dogs whose speed was thus tested.

A bleak typical Cotswold hill-road leads from the park at Larket Hill southwards through arable fields and well-stocked grasslands. Occasionally, the brilliant hue of a field of sainfoin attracts the eye, a blotch of startling sunset pink amidst the sober browns, greys and changeable greens of the Wolds. It is a very rural country-side, which we can well imagine to be the home of the eighteenth-century Gloucestershire song, 'The Turmut Hower', of which two stanzas are given overleaf:

'I be a turmut hower,
Vram Gloucestershire I came;
My parents be hard-working folk,
Giles Wapshaw be my name.

The vly, the vly
   The vly be on the turmut,
   An' it be aal me eye, and no use to try
   To keep um off the turmut.

Zum be vond o' haymakin',
An' zum be vond o' mowin',
But of aal the trades thet I likes best
Gie I the turmut howin'.
   The vly, etc.

We soon come to Aldsworth, a remote village although
skirted by a main road. The church of St. Peter, for it once
belonged to Gloucester Abbey, should be visited by all who
admire skill in stone carving. The building is perched high
above the elms and firs of the village green, and the steep,
yew-shaded path up to the porch brings us almost face to
face with a buttress decorated with a magnificent niche.
Above may be seen three carved roses and a large, life-like
head of a bearded man, one of twenty-five grotesques
spaced round the exterior of the aisle and tower. Other
carvings in this remarkable gallery of nightmares represent
a griffin, a man with his mouth stretched wide in a bursting
guffaw, a fierce-looking pig with an orange or lemon in its
teeth and a most miserable-looking fellow with a gudgeon-
like mouth that welcomes us into the porch. We wonder
if they represent the curious old folk who came to gawk
at the masons or are they caricatures of the persons whom
the workmen particularly disliked? We enter the church
through the fine north porch which shelters the original

twelfth-century door, a massive structure with foliated iron-work. The interior contains a late Norman arcade of three arches, an aisle of the Decorated Period and much work in the late Perpendicular style. Two lovely niches occur of which that with a carved wheel and the letters S.K. probably once held a statue of St. Catherine.

Aldsworth village commends itself to us on account of the lovely symmetrical Tudor house near the church and the many well-built stone cottages, some of which a century ago formed the home of a trainer, lodgings for jockeys and stables for race-horses.

This part of the Cotswolds has long been famous for horse-racing and training. In 1775, when enclosures stopped the races which had been held annually for a century on Upton Downs near Burford, the famous meeting was transferred to the 'Bilbury Race-course' near Aldsworth, where it flourished until ninety years ago. George IV, when regent, was a frequent visitor, and he used to stay as a private gentleman with Lord Sherborne's family. Two miles east of Aldsworth, adjoining the Burford road, a square field surrounded by beeches marks the site of the paddock, while some barns a little farther along the road once formed the jockeys' changing rooms. To-day the training of horses continues in the Leach valley south of Aldsworth, and it only ceased at Northleach within living memory. In 1841, Coronation, the winner of the Derby, was trained here.

Aldsworth is also noted for the flock of some 300 Cotswold sheep, probably the only pedigree Cotswold flock left on these hills. The sheep resemble young bullocks in size and are tall enough to look over the hurdles. The thick, curly fleece enhances the broadness of their backs, while the face is further lengthened by the long pointed ears which protrude from the locks of wool falling down over the eyes and brow. Cotswold hoggets have been known to weigh 16 stone, and the fleece alone will scale anything up to 25 lb. The sheep look crude and cumbersome when compared with the small crossbreeds which yield the small joints needed by the present-day housewife who would look askance at a leg of mutton weighing 30 lb. Improvements in the fleece of other breeds, especially the merino when crossed with Gloucestershire rams, led to the decline in the importance of the old Cotswolds.

About 1850 some 5,000 Cotswold rams were sold annually in Gloucestershire alone, and ten years later, when the number was 4,000, there was still a large export, rams fetching as much as 70 guineas apiece in Canada and the States. The *Cotswold Flock Books* show the decline; in 1892 there were 45 pedigree flocks in the Cotswolds, in 1914 only 19 flocks and 8 only in 1922 when the export of rams had practically ceased. The wool from Cotswold sheep had begun to decline in comparative value ever since the sixteenth century, and this was one reason for the introduction of new stock. In 1560 Hugh Westwood the founder of Northleach Grammar School, in his will requested his wife to pay Margaret and Walter Yate 'eche of them fortie pounds or elles CC (200) sheep apece', which works out at only 4s. a sheep. To-day clean wool fetches more a pound than Cotswold wool did in its heyday, but allowance must be made for depreciation in the value of our money. Although there was a Golden Fleece, it is as well to remember that the merchants had to do much trade to get rich. There are many thousands more sheep on the Cotswolds to-day than in the great wool-ranching days, but it us due to wealth accumulated from the ancestral breed that we owe so many of the old buildings, ancient monuments, charities and markets of east Gloucestershire.

From Aldsworth, a quiet road branches off on the left to Cold Swyre where the Leach appears as a sparkling stream, but if you follow it a short distance it dwindles into pools and finally disappears altogether. For walkers, however, there is an even quieter and more rural way along the white road to Ladbarrow Farm, and thence by green trackways through fields bright with wild flowers and down valley slopes capped with trees to Sheepbridge. In the whole four miles scarcely a house will be seen and Sheepbridge itself is a delightful spot; the stream bed in its wide valley remains dry for at least six months of the year, and the arch of the bridge was obviously built for a much bigger stream than it spans even when heavy rains flood the valley. Isolated hawthorns dot the old stream course, and at the lip of the valley appear beautiful hangers of beech which look denser and cooler than any in the Leach valley. The Leach seems to have fallen on evil days. In the past, leases contained a clause compelling riparian tenants to walk their oxen for a certain time along the stream bed to puddle it. On the Churn above Barton much of the water of that river used to sink into the porous limestones, so the millers used to go upstream as far as Rendcombe to stop up the seepage holes. In addition teams of working bullocks were driven up and down the stream, and especially the mill-ponds, to consolidate the bed. But to-day the working oxen, like the Cotswold sheep, have lost their place in Cotswold farming, and here only survive on Earl Bathurst's estate where five oxen are still used. Oxen, however, were working on several farms in the North Cotswolds during the present century; slow, cumbersome beasts who eat less than horses and have much stamina, but Arthur Young preferred speechlessness to profanity on seeing eight of the great beasts yoked to a plough near Stow-on-the-Wold. Probably even the Leach valley at Sheepbridge would gain in beauty by the presence of a permanent stream kept above ground by the broad hooves of oxen.

Just south of Sheepbridge, springs gush out from below Smerril Plantation and within two miles have formed the strong stream which beautifies the Eastleach villages. Eastleach Martin, the larger and the prettier village, lies in a small dell surrounded by elms on a ledge above the stream. The stone-built cottages, each with a setting of climbing plants and fruit-trees, are comfortably spaced facing each other across a steeply-sloping central green. Near to the lovely willow-lined stream a fountain spouts forth its cooling waters but a slight bank or terrace conceals the river from the houses and only a huge barn keeps watch over the church in the valley floor. From the twelfth century the manor belonged to Malvern Priory; hence the name Eastleach Martin and the former dedication of the church to SS. Michael and Martin. The church attracts more attention for its fourteenth-century transept with three lovely Decorated windows than for the Norman work in the south doorway and chancel arch. It retains also a few Tudor benches and the small Jacobean pulpit so often used by John Keble.

Just across the broad limpid river which is spanned by a picturesque stone-slab bridge still known as 'Keble's Bridge' stands the tiny church of Eastleach Turville. Two great elms shade St. Andrew's which is smaller but perhaps more beautiful than its brother on the Martin bank. Here you will find a Norman doorway enriched with spirals and zigzags and a fine tympanum depicting Christ enthroned in majesty. The Early English chancel is illumined with a graceful triple lancet while the clear green glass and old stone paving give the building a cheerful unspoilt appearance. The canopied recess in the north transept contains a floriated cross slab to the memory, no doubt, of an abbess, as when the coffin was opened a century ago an exquisitely-fashioned rosary was found within it. The low saddle-backed tower of the fourteenth century forms the complement of the equally short pyramidal structure of the twin church on the opposite bank.

Both Eastleach Martin and Turville have a quiet rural charm which remains undisturbed by motor traffic; here the pig and fowl are still an integral part of the cottage economy, and we feel sure that the cottagers still enjoy slices of home-cured bacon for breakfast. Nowhere else in Gloucestershire will you find two such charming and attractively-situated churches within so short a compass.

Still travelling southwards, after a mile we enter Southrop which, althought built of stone, lacks the lovely setting of the Eastleaches, for we have now entered upon the low-lying soggy Thames plain where the villages are at once flatter, bigger and less picutresque. Southrop, however, has many compensations to offer for its plain setting, as its buildings are typically Cotswold and its manor-house near the church has twelfth-century work in its cellars with deeply-splayed narrow lights and a doorway with zigzag moulding.

The small church of St. Peter proves interesting in spite of considerable alteration and restoration. The nave has much herring-bone masonry and two Norman windows, whilst the graceful doorways, that on the north with a lozenged tympanum, and the chancel arch belong to the same period. Most of the remainder of the building was erected a century later and it has two objects well worth seeing. The beautiful tub-shaped font of the twelfth century is richly carved with an arcade of eight arches, five of which hold figures representing Virtues triumphing over Vices. The Latin inscription shows that these signify Mercy defeating Hatred, Moderation vanquishing Lust, Charity overcoming Greed, Patience scourging Anger, and Temperance trampling on Self-Indulgence. The other three arches bear figures of Moses carrying the Tablets of the Law, of Ecclesia, the new Law, who carries a Cross and chalice, and of Synagoga, the old Law, who has no crown, no sight and no oil in her lamp. This remarkable font was discovered built into the south doorway by John Keble when he was curate here.

In the chancel, low stone slabs support the slightly defaced effigies of Sir Thomas Conway and his lady (ob. 1606), who owned the manor here in Elizabethan times. The knight is depicted in armour with a small ruff round his neck and elegant ruffles at his wrists. A long sword hangs from the belt at his waist, while a pleasing touch is the signet ring on his thumb. Lady Conway is dressed in a full-pleated gown over a scalloped kirtle and neatly-pleated bodice. The sleeves terminate in narrow cuffs and she, too, wears a ruff which partly hides the big collar turned back on her shoulders. A loose hood keeps her hair in place and she holds a small, very lady-like book in her hands.

Southrop and the Eastleaches are closely connected with the 'Oxford Movement', for John Keble's father, Vicar of Coln St. Aldwyn, lived in his own house at Fairford and many generations of the family had been lords of the manor of Eastleach Turville. John Keble, after a most successful career at Oxford, was ordained in 1815 when twenty-three years of age and began work as a curate at the Eastleaches. He lived in Oxford until 1823 when he came to stay for sometime with his family at Fairford, and later as curate lived for two years at Southrop Rectory. Here he wrote much of *The Christian Year:* which before his death in 1866 reached nearly 100 editions. In 1831 Keble was elected professor of poetry at Oxford, and the little Leach villages lost their most illustrious preacher.

HISTORIC WINCHCOMB

WINCHCOMB LIES between the jaws of Salter's and Langley Hills where the small River Isbourne comes down into the Vale from the well-wooded heights of the Cotswolds. The small tongue of lowland, rich in poplars and elms, opens to the north, and thence the town looks for its present-day connections with the rest of Gloucestershire. Three main roads converge on the town from the north and then proceed through Gloucester Street and climb over the mighty flanks of Cleeve Cloud to Cheltenham. The town has expanded along these ways and has grown up above the valley floor of the Isbourne, but charming side roads, such as Castle Street and Duck Street (a delightful name) lead down to the stream.

Owing to its star-like plan the town is not easy to befriend, but the three rather narrow well-packed streets of low houses and frequent shop windows seem to focus naturally on the wide Abbey Terrace near to the church. You will probably smile at Gloucestershire people when they protest that Campden is a town, but of Winchcomb's prestige you are in little doubt as you set foot in the narrow streets. Antiquity is in the very air of Winchcomb, and you can feel in the atmosphere of the town that it has been the seat of kings.

A tour of the place might well begin at the Abbey Terrace. The large church of St. Peter, although much restored, is a fine example of later Perpendicular style. At its western end is a lofty tower, adorned with battlements and eight crocketed pinnacles. The numerous clerestory windows still run in almost continuous series, and the gargoyles outside the church, some forty in all, are skilfully carved and are often exceedingly grotesque. The porch is worth noticing for its graceful vaulting, and a chamber above it, with a stone fire-place, which is used now as a museum. The exhibits range in age from Neolithic flints found at Belas Knap tumulus to the implements used on Cotswold farms previous to the coming of enclosures and mechanical aids. Here you may see a shepherd's crook, a breast plough of the type once much favoured on the shallow oolitic soils, a flail bound with eel-skin and two Winchcomb "dollies' or large elaborate plaitings of straw which were formerly occasionally fashioned on the Wolds as a sign of 'harvest-home'. The church also contains a beautiful embroidery composed of fragments of a mediæval cope with a border bearing the emblem of Catherine of Aragon.

The building was begin about 1485 when Abbot William, with the help of Ralph le Boteler, lord of Sudeley, and the people of Winchcomb, had it erected to replace the old church which had fallen into decay. The interior of the church is spacious and well-illumined. Attached to a pillar is a quaint alms-box with three locks dated 1547. The triple sedilia in the chancel are unusually well made and have niches for statues of saints between the seats and canopies over them on which are the arms of the abbey of Winchcomb, the abbey of Gloucester, and Ralph Boteler of Sudeley.

The relics placed here from old Winchcomb Abbey include numerous moulded stones, mainly with ball-flower ornamentation, some tiles and two stone coffins, supposed to be those of King Kenulf and his son Kenelm. The site of the abbey is next to the present church and consists to-day of a park-like green space facing Abbey Terrace. It was this great building which rendered the first small church at

Winchcomb unnecessary and caused it to fall into decay. The stonework stored in the church to-day indicates that the main parts of the abbey were of late Norman work, and it must have been an imposing building. The nave lay just to the east of the present church and here excavation has revealed a large central tower. Tablets have been set up to mark the limits of the length of the abbey church and a cross marks the central point beneath the tower. To-day all that remains of the building is a doorway built into the parish church, and perhaps some of the ornamental stone-work in the walls of a few cottages in Gloucester Street.

The story of the abbey goes back to Saxon times when Winchcomb was the capital of a 'county' called Winch-combshire, which formed part of the kingdom of Mercia and was at one time the residence of its kings. The abbey was founded for 300 Benedictine monks in 798 by Kenulf, King of Mercia, on the site of a nunnery built by Offa ten years before. Kenulf was succeeded in 821 by Kenelm, his son who, being then only seven years of age, was left to the care of his sister Quenride (Quendrida). What happened to the boy has been told with slight variations by many authors, and especially by Caxton in the *Golden Legend of Saint Kenelm,* Chaucer mentions the story in the *Nonnë Preestes Tale*:

> 'Lo, in the lyf of seint Kenelm, I rede,
> That was Kenulphus sone, the noble King
> Of Mercenrike, how Kenelm mette a thing;
> A lyte ere he was mordred on a day.'

Kenelm, it appears, was warned in a dream of his fate but was too young and innocent to tell it. Other chroniclers tell how the ambitious Quenride, entertaining hopes of the kingdom for herself, committed the little boy to the care of a tutor Askobert, whom she induced to kill him. Under pretence of hunting, Kenelm was decoyed into an unfrequented wood, where the wicked Askobert cut off his head and buried him beneath a thorn tree. At the moment of death a white dove is said to have flown from the boy's neck heavenwards. A year or two later when the Pope was celebrating Mass in old St. Peter's, Rome, a dove dropped near to him a parchment scroll on which was written:

> 'In Clent cow-pasture, under a thorn,
> Of Head bereft lies Kenelm, king born.'

Luckily an Englishman was found at hand who could interpret the message, and the Pope duly informed the 'Kings of England' of its contents. A wise white cow which had loved the boy guided the searching monks to a thorn, over which, some say, a heavenly ray was shining. The body was found in the presence of a numerous assembly and a miraculous spring issued forth from under the thorn. The journey from Clent in Worcestershire to Winchcomb was accomplished without adventure until the monks were overcome with thirst on the hills near Sudeley, about two miles outside the town. Where the body was rested on the ground a spring gushed forth which later healed many people, and, in due course, was covered with a well-house and a chapel was erected near by. The chapel was pulled down in the last century, but the water-house over the spring still contributes to Winchcomb's water-supply.

The procession continued into the town and the wicked Quenride, hearing the noise of the multitude, looked out of the window of her chamber. Now, by chance, she had in her hands a psalter and, 'for I know not what charm', she read the 109th Psalm backwards, endeavouring to drown the song of the choristers. At that moment her eyes dropped from their sockets and scattered blood upon the verse which runs to-day: 'This is the reward of mine adversaries from the Lord and of them that speak evil against my soul.'

The early twelfth-century chronicle of William of Malmesbury continues the tale: "The marks of blood are still to be seen proving the cruelty of the woman and the vengeance of God. The body of the saint is venerated by all, and there is scarcely a place in England held in greater respect, or where more persons attend at the festival; and this is due to the long-continued belief in his sanctity and the constant happening of miracles.'

The magnificent abbey which enshrined the bones of the saint suffered many vicissitudes. The Danes burnt it down and in 985, Oswald, Bishop of Worcester, recovered the lands which had been alienated, reformed the discipline of the monks and dedicated the house to St. Kenelm instead of the Virgin Mary. In Norman times the abbey, in spite of the walls surrounding its precincts, was again burnt to the ground, and the stones in the parish church show that most of the last magnificent building was of late Norman work. The thousands of pilgrims coming to pray at the shrine greatly enriched the town, especially as equally great multitudes came here on their way to Hailes Abbey near by.

The old 'George Inn' was the pilgrims' house and it must have been busiest in mid-July and mid-September, the times of the great feasts. The initials 'R.K.' on the spandrels of a doorway leading into the courtyard stand for Richard Kyderminster, who probably founded the house. Richard was abbot in the reign of Henry VII and 'he made the monastery to flourish so much that it was equal to a little university'. This celebrated abbot had studied at Gloucester (later Worcester) College, Oxford, and had the right to represent the abbey in Parliament.

At the 'George Hotel', above a fine stone water-trough, is a Pilgrims' Gallery running along one side of the court-yard, but it is probable that the gallery completely encircled a much bigger yard at one time, like that at the 'New Inn', Gloucester.

The abbey grew rich and famous until its revenue at this time was something like £300 a week of our money. In 1539, when the abbey was granted to Thomas, Lord Seymour, there were 29 monks and nearly 100 servants and lay officials. Lord Seymour left not a trace of the great buildings above the ground. It is said that 'the last abbot was a great stickler for church privileges', so perhaps a feeling of revenge for annoyances in Parliament might help to explain the extraordinary thoroughness of the destruction.

By the time of the Stuarts, Winchcomb had fallen on evil days, but the 'inhabitants made great profit of planting tobacco'. This continued in the teeth of Parliamentary opposition, and attempts to suppress it caused much rioting. In 1667 Pepys records that the Life Guard was sent to Winchcomb 'to spoil the tobacco there, which it seems the people there do plant contrary to law, and have always done'.

The tobacco growers also resorted to pamphleteering, and a tract of 1655 entitled *Harry Hangman's Horror*, or *Glostershire Hangman's Request to the Smokers and Tobacconists of London*, humorously relates how the trade of hanging has declined since the planting of tobacco, 'in Glostershire, especially at Winchcomb. . . . Indeed before tobacco was there planted, there being no kind of trade to employ men . . . necessity compelled poor men to stand my friends, by stealing of sheep and other cattel, breaking of hedges, robbing of orchards and what not'. The planting was restrained, according to Defoe, 'in the twelfth year of King Charles II from which time the town decayed little by little, and is now poor and inconsiderable'. (300 houses.) To-day the name of a field, called Tobacco Close, is all that remains to tell of the industry.

Winchcomb is to-day aptly called 'historic'. The old

smallish houses in Gloucester Street curve gracefully like
a miniature Campden. The gabled Jacobean house opposite
the church belonged at one time to the town and was
probably the Guild House and was subsequently used as
the King's School. There are, too, some pleasing old inns
such as the 'Pack Horse' and 'Old Pack Horse', and the
ancient gabled hostelry in Gloucester Street known as 'The
Corner Cupboard' which still flourishes, and deservedly so
with such an attractive name. 'The Gate' public-house
has the following verse upon its sign:

> 'This gate hangs well and hinders none,
> Refresh and pay and travel on.'

The Tudor House is well worth noticing, and occasional
pieces of stone work, a lintel here and there, especially in
Gloucester Street, or a fine doorway. Opposite the old
Corner Cupboard is a string course in the wall carved with
roses and a fleeing hare, and there are some fine old buttresses in the main street as well as the stocks near the
Town Hall. Here, as at Chipping Campden, the curfew
is rung, though at Winchcomb it sounds only in winter
when the bell tolls for ten minutes before the tenor bell
rings out the date of the month.

Hales Street in Winchcomb leads from the 'Pilgrims'
Inn' northwards, and where the road turns sharply to
bridge the tiny Isbourne rough routes lead off on the right;
one climbs up towards Stancombe Woods and to Monk's
Hole; another, just beyond the farm-houses, is called Puck
Pit Lane and continues as a direct footpath along the foot
of the hills across the sloping pastures which belong neither
to Hill nor Vale. This pleasant walk, formerly the paved
Pilgrims' Way, is the most direct path between Winchcomb
and Hailes and leads, as one would expect, directly to the
site of the old Pilgrims' Tavern.

The small cluster of ruins at Hailes forms a striking picture rising in lonely majesty from a flat green plain at the foot of a small well-wooded combe. Vast overhanging woods look down on the ruins and tiny streams flow to it through fine hazel-nut plantations.

Hailes Abbey was probably more magnificent even than that at Winchcomb, and although its great church, gatehouse and precinct-walls have all gone, enough remains to give an idea of its splendour. The abbey was a Cistercian House founded by Richard, Earl of Cornwall, second son of King John and brother of Henry III who gave the manor to him. Richard had vowed an abbey to the Virgin Mary when he was in dire peril of shipwreck on his way home from Gascony; and in 1246 a colony of twenty monks and ten lay brothers came to Hailes from Beaulieu in Hampshire and the foundation began under Prior Jordan. Five years later the main buildings were completed at a cost to Richard of some 10,000 marks. In the November of 1251 Walter Cantilupe, Bishop of Worcester, consecrated the great church with the assistance of thirteen other bishops, each consecrating an altar in what must have been a scene of great splendour. Among the vast assembly were the King (Henry III) and his Queen Eleanor, Richard and many of the English nobility, as well as three hundred knights. The abbey was already well endowed with the manor and church of Hailes and 1,000 marks when it came suddenly to fame.

In 1270, Richard's son Edmund brought to Hailes one-third of a relic of Holy Blood which he had obtained on the Continent and which had been guaranteed by Pope Urban IV. On Holy Rood day in mid-September the relic was placed with great ceremony in a grand shrine behind the High Altar in the presence of the communities of both Hailes and Winchcomb. Recent excavations have laid bare the great platform, 8 feet by 10, on which the shrine stood.

In the following year, after a great fire, the eastern end of the church was rebuilt by Earl Richard, now King of the Romans, so that five semi-octagonal chapels radiated from the shrine in the form of an apse where the pilgrims could kneel when the Holy Blood was shown at appointed times. According to Leland, 'God daily sheweth miracles through the virtues of that Precious Blood'.

By the middle of the fifteenth century, the monastic buildings were much dilapidated, but successive Popes gave financial help towards rebuilding the cloisters and other parts of the fabric. Even in 1533, Hugh Latimer wrote rather scornfully to Thomas Cromwell, 'I dwell within a mile of the Fosse Way (at West Kineton), and you wonder to see how they come by flocks out of the West Country to many images . . . but chiefly to the blood of Hayles.'

In 1538, the Commissioners, under Hugh Latimer, now Bishop of Worcester, destroyed the shrine and took away jewels, ornaments and money.

On Christmas Eve, 1539, Hailes was surrendered, and the abbot and twenty-two brothers were pensioned. The abbey then was valued at about £350 a year. The same ruthless destruction occurred as at Winchcomb, but the abbot's lodgings were used as a residence. The Tracys held this portion in the time of Sir Robert Atkyns, but it, too, was destroyed less than two hundred years ago. As for the relic, Latimer and the Commissioners say that 'it was enclosed within a round Beryl', garnished and bound 'with silver, being within a little glass'. After much testing, in the presence of a great multitude, the Commissioners came to the conclusion that it was 'an unctuous gum coloured' and that the glistening red tint was due to the glass. There is apparently no truth in the frequent assertion that the Blood at the Dissolution was found to be the blood of a duck, renewed every week. The relic was destroyed in 1539 at

London, and the saying 'as sure as God's in Gloucestershire' lost much of its significance.

All that remains to be seen to-day are seven lovely arches of the old cloister garth, most of which belonged to the original abbey. In the south walk are the remains of a lavatory and entrances to the refectory, a parlour and stone stairs to the dormitory. On the east are three fine archways of the chapter-house which stand out isolated yet very impressive. Recent excavation has outlined the ground plan of most of the buildings, and in the case of the great church, which was 341 feet long by 140 feet across the transepts, an evergreen tree has been planted on the site of every pillar and groups of shrubs to outline the shrine of the relic, and the five chapels round the high altar.

The little church, with its curious bell-turret tower, consists only of a nave and chancel, yet it is one of the most interesting small churches in Gloucestershire. It dates back to the twelfth century, when Ralph de Worcester built some sort of fortified residence here. The earthworks and moat may still be traced in the field adjoining the churchyard. Of the original church, the shafts of the chancel arch and the two pilasters supporting the south chancel wall still remain. As soon as the abbey was founded the monks took over the church and added the Decorated windows and priest's doorway in the chancel. The nave was probably built a century later by William Hobby, lord of the manor, who died of plague in 1603 at the ripe old age of 103.

In the chancel are old encaustic tiles probably from the abbey, many of them decorated with heraldic devices. There are many remains of medieval (*c.* 1300) wall painting, notably in the splays of the chancel windows where the one depicting St. Catherine of Alexandria trampling on the Roman Emperor Maximin is especially well preserved.

The chief heraldic decorations on the south wall refer to Richard, as Earl of Cornwall, and King of the Romans, and the devices are repeated in part on some of the three hundred tiles. Admirers of ancient woodwork will notice the roof, the handsomely carved box pew in the west end, the oak panelled seats in the. chancel arranged for communion in Commonwealth days, and also the medieval screen delicately carved in oak and quite unspoilt by any subsequent restoration.

Altogether the little church is most pleasing with its quiet green meadow and woodland background, and it should be regarded as part of the abbey for which it was probably a *capella ad portas*, a gateway chapel of ease for the use of strangers and visitors.

CHAPTER VI: *The Country around Winchcomb*

LANGLEY AND SALTER'S HILLS

'No Everest is here, no peaks of power
Astonish men. But on the winding ways
White in the frost-time, blinding in full June blaze,
A man may take all quiet heart's delight
Village and quarry, taverns and many a tower
That saw Armada beacons set alight.'

—IVOR GURNEY

THE HIGH wooded hills encircling Sudeley Castle are full of surprises for the strong walker, and may even be tackled by motorists who do not mind rough, narrow roads and steep, twisting gradients.

The road past Sudeley Castle[1] leads straight up the hills, and on the left of the road where the great sweep of woods clothe the lower slopes of Salter's Hill are the water-house and site of the chapel connected with the story of St. Kenelm. After obtaining the key at the solitary house half-way up the steep hill ahead, you will find the well-house in a haw-thorn-dotted meadow just beyond some cottages on the side of the Wold. The little building is truly Cotswold and its stone roof terminates in two carved finials. A modern sculpture of St. Kenelm, reproduced from the fourteenth-century Cottenham manuscript, adorns the front, while also on the external walls are inscribed tablets telling the history of the conduit which was built by the third Lord Chandos to commemorate one of Queen Elizabeth's three

[1] The key of the chapel containing the magnificent tomb of Catherine Parr is available at the Lodge on Tuesdays and Saturdays, 11 a.m. to 5 p.m.

visits to the castle. Mrs. Dent's *Annals of Winchcombe and Sudeley* (1877) contains verses translated from a Saxon document which aptly describe the original foundation:

'These men towards Winchecombe, this holy body bear
Before they could it thither bring, very weary they were,
So they came to a wood a little east of the town,
And rested, though they were so near, upon a high down.
Athirst they were for weariness, so sore there was no end,
For St. Kenelm's love they bade our Lord some drink send.
A cold well and clear, there sprang from the Down,
That still is there, clear and cold, a mile from the Town.
Well fair, it is now covered with stone, as is right,
And I counsel each man thereof to drink, that cometh there truly.
The monks, since, of Winchecomb have built there beside,
A fair chapel of St. Kenelm, that men seek wide.'

The well is still cold and clear, but the fair chapel was demolished about 1830 and only a window inserted in the adjoining farm-house remains of it to-day.

The motorist must now take the precipitous stony hill which leads up past the larch plantations and along the ancient White Way around the outer park wall to Roel Gate: the walker may follow what proves to be an even rougher gated way which leads to the old Sudeley Lodge and on to Spoonley Wood. Here, after a little searching, you will find the remains of a fine second-century Roman villa built in the shape of a courtyard with the sides of the square about sixty yards long. Along three sides were rooms, and on the fourth a wall enclosed the courtyard.

The central room of the buildings looking out upon the open courtyard is the library, which faced the main entrance in the precinct wall. Near by, and protected now by restoration of the walls and the roof, is the dining-room which was used in winter-time and heated by a furnace. Part of the floor was covered by tables, but the portion that would have been most visible is covered with an elaborate mosaic. The larger range of buildings, also restored and roofed in by tiles actually excavated on the site, formed the bath wing. There were six bathrooms with hypocaust floors covered with fine mosaics and heated by two furnaces.

The wing facing the bathrooms had no internal connection with the rest of the house and no heating arrangements, so here presumably were the working and living-rooms of the household slaves, of which it appears the owner possessed enough to cultivate a farm of considerable acreage. The large building on this side is the granary, measuring 54 by 34 feet, and in plan like a church with nave and aisles. The roof of the veranda was supported by columns with very delicately-moulded capitals and bases. In the kitchen was a water-well, neatly lined with stone, and two stone uprights that once formed a table with a crosspiece. The villa was probably still in existence in the fourth century, and it needs but little imagination to conjure up what a magnificent building it was and how carefully the owner selected its site commanding a fine view and abundant water. Here a self-contained community tilled the land, tended animals and made the requirements of the household. The owner had taken good care that the rooms were well heated to keep out the inclement weather, and his journeys to Corinium, and more rarely to Glevum, no doubt made him appreciate the efficiency of the central heating. To-day the restored portions over the best mosaics are kept locked and the keys are to be got from Sudeley.

From Spoonley Wood trackways lead along the bleak

ridge-road with fine vistas of rolling downs and occasional great thorn trees to Charlton Abbots. The tiny grey village hides away from the road usually followed by travellers and looks down upon the wooded valley at the source of the Isbourne. The monks of Winchcomb Abbey kept a leper-house here which is said to be still represented by an old thatched cottage close to a bubbling spring flowing into a roundish basin large enough for a bath. The church of St. Martin, in spite of much recent rebuilding, has retained a little Early English work as well as the thirteenth-century bowl of its original font and one of its medieval bells. Adjoining the western end of the churchyard is a beautiful old Elizabethan manor-house, whose varied gables and dark-grey facings make a pleasing picture in its rural setting.

We will follow the winding road towards Winchcomb, one of the most pleasant in the Cotswolds. The white roadway is hemmed in with low stone walls until the fir trees of Humblebee Wood come down to the left of the roadway. On the right lies the whole sweep of the Isbourne combe, mottled with dark patches of woodland and flanked by the towering buttress of Salter's Hill. The aisles of fir trees recede from the trackway, and above them, where the slopes are steeper, is a forest of oaks and dense undergrowth where the stinking garlic forms a beautiful carpet in summer.

Following the edge of Humblebee Wood, we may climb the steep hill with the close turf underfoot for one of the best sights in Gloucestershire. It must be earned, however, for the hill is a stiff one, and as the summit is neared the grass becomes drier and the air keener and away in the distance Sudeley Castle looks like a child's toy. Just over the stone stile at the second wall is a sight that never fails to be impressive and always catches one unawares, for in front lies a huge whale-shaped mound of earth with two mighty projections enclosing between them a great slab of stone.

This is Belas Knap, the celebrated Long Barrow, one of

the two finest in Gloucestershire, which is almost the same as saying in England. The tumulus has been carefully repaired by the Historical Monument Society and the four chambers may be entered with safety. This burial-ground was built about 1,900 years before Christ and belongs to the late Stone Age. The elongated, heart-shaped mound was surrounded at one time by a wall seven feet high but it is now seldom more than five. The dry-walling was skilfully done with slates half an inch thick such as are used on the roofs of Cotswold houses even to-day, and which may have been dug near the spot. The perfectly laid walls rise gradually in height towards the north end, where they turn gracefully in a faultless ogee curve inwards to the entrance. The Long Barrows form the nearest approach in England to a Pyramid, for they too were gigantic houses of the dead. The main portal of Belas Knap consists of two uprights near 6 feet high bordering a vertical slab which is nearly 4 feet square and a foot thick. Resting on the uprights is a lintel nearly 3 feet wide and 9 inches thick; it had fallen when the tumulus was first excavated, and under it were the remains of five children and the skeleton of a fairly young man, in addition to many bones, tusks and teeth of pig and horse, a little flint and a few fragments of coarse pottery. It seems that these relics were secondary interments of victims sacrificed in honour of the buried dead and were probably folk whose territory lay south and east of the Cotswolds. The doorway is false and leads nowhere, and apparently it was used as the scene of sacrifices. The four chambers are equally interesting. The five great wall slabs in both the east and the west chamber seem originally to have been roofed with over-lapping slates; the former chamber contained fourteen skeletons of all ages, the latter twelve of middle-aged persons squatting on flat stones round the walls. The large number of skeletons confined in such a small space has been explained by the fact that the bodies were exposed to decay in the open and only their skeletons were interred there.

The small passage on the east side with corbelled roofing held four human skeletons and many bones, including a bone scoop. The long narrow passage at the south end of the barrow was originally closed by a vertical upright slab and contained nothing but a skull and a few animal bones. Right in the centre of the mound was a circle of flat stones with evidence of the fire lit nearly four thousand years ago to mark either the site of the future burial-ground or to incinerate a native chief.

Around these ashes a huge mound was built containing the chamber and encompassed by the wall, and to it were brought thirty-eight more dead as partakers of a signal honour or as victims of sacrifice to the departed. The tumulus was used over a long period and was entirely covered with soil, the earth being removed for fresh burials, and so it remained until the recent excavation and careful restoration.

It is not very obvious why the barrow is at this spot on the flanks of a hill-top nearly 1,000 feet high. The wide-reaching view may have had something to do with it, or perhaps here amid the dry scrubland was a clear view of the sun.

'Here—Here's his place, where meteors shoot, clouds form,
    Lightnings are loosened,
Stars come and go! Let joy break with the storm,
    Peace let the dew send!

Lofty designs must close in like effects:
    Loftily lying,
Leave him—still loftier than the world suspects.
    Living and dying.'

THE HAMLETS NEAR STANTON AND STANWAY

The mighty bastion which the towering twin headlands of Nottingham and Langley Hills thrust out into the Vale of Severn is continued northwards by the isolated hillocks of Dumbleton and Oxenton, and by the larger block of limestone forming Bredon Hill. This imposing headland and its 'island' continuation thus separate the Vale of Gloucester from the Vale of Evesham, where, to the north of Winchcomb, the edge of the Cotswolds is equally majestic and less sinuous than in the south. Wherever the wooded wall of the high rampart is furrowed by a tiny stream, forming either a sheltered combe or a dry patch of gravel in the clay vale beneath, a hamlet has arisen. Between Winchcomb and Broadway, half a dozen such tiny settlements may be found: peaceful Hailes, rural Didbrook and isolated Wood Stanway, Stanway major and well-preserved Stanton, little known Laverton and cul-de-sac Buckland. With merely a few score of houses between them, these hamlets are quiet, homely places and unspoilt by modern 'improvements' and quite unaware of their own prettiness. As in most of the smaller Gloucestershire villages east of the Severn, the great barns dwarf the greystone cottages.

A footpath from Hailes leads to Didbrook, which naturally came under the influence of the neighbouring abbey, its manor being part of the original endowment of Hailes. The last abbot, Stephen Sagar, was allowed the use of their summer residence, long since rebuilt as a farm-house, at Coscombe, which is high up on the hill slope in Didbrook parish. This abbot was a personal friend of Thomas Cromwell, and in writing to thank him for a pension of £100 a year he mentions, incidentally, that he suffered from ague every summer at Hailes.

William Whitchurch, also an abbot of Hailes, rebuilt the church of St. George at Didbrook in 1475, four years after its predecessor had been desecrated by the massacre of some Lancastrian fugitives from Tewkesbury. It is said that the holes in the ancient door were made by some of the first bullets ever fired from a hand-gun. The church is entirely late Perpendicular in style and can only be entered through the door under the square western tower. The east window contains a little old glass, portraying two angels and a head above an inscription asking your prayers for "Willi Whytchyr".

The church, in addition to the seventeenth-century altar rails and oaks seats, has more woodwork than is usual in Cotswold churches, while an ancient-looking cottage near the western end of the straggling village has a gabled end constructed about two stout 'crucks' or two big curving pieces of rough-hewn timber which curve inwards from the base of the wall and meet at the apex of the gable, like the upturned keel of a boat. It has been thought that the upper part of these 'crucks' formed the roof, which was thus merely a continuation of the walls, but, of course, even the Romans built roofs as we do to-day and these 'crucks', not uncommon in the Midlands or even in Gloucestershire for that matter, seem an easy labour-saving method of using big curved pieces of timber for building gable ends.

A short walk past Wood Stanway brings us to the main Tewkesbury-Stow road which here winds down the escarpment edge. After the great quarries near Stumps Cross the road soon dips below a high bank clothed in magnificent beeches and made impressive by outcrops of lichen-tinged rock. Fir plantations on one side of the road face evergreen bushes interspersed with ancient and large laburnum trees whose cascades of yellow gold overhang the road and form in May an unforgettable picture. At the base of the hill, where the hedgerows and oak-trees begin, a few grey houses with well-stocked gardens nestle beneath the woods. Here may be found two of three factors which have made Stanway: a copious, bubbling spring and a steep stony trackway which goes straight to the top of the hill, to the very summit of the escarpment.

This cluster of houses, the humble part of Stanway, is almost swallowed up with the fine woods clothing its small combe. Just off the main road slightly nearer the vale is the other part of the village standing in a magnificent park where horse-chestnuts make the way unbelievably beautiful in June.

Stanway was given to Tewkesbury Abbey by Odo in 715, and here the Benedictines founded a cell which proved such a pleasant change after the foggy vale of Severn that it later became the abbot's country house. Here he was able to enjoy the stag-hunting on the hills, and his 'fayre mannour place', as Leland called it, is now represented by Stanway House. This fine gabled mansion was built in the reign of James I by Sir Paul Tracy of Toddington, the Tracy family having acquired Stanway Manor at the Dissolution. The building stands in fine grounds with beautifully terraced gardens, while the hall has a remarkable oriel window rising almost to the height of the eaves and divided by stonework into sixty panes. The magnificent gateway near to the road is attributed to Inigo Jones. In 1771 the family of the Earl of Wemyss came into the manor by marriage, and it is still in their possession.

The house faces the small church of St. Peter which is largely fifteenth century, but was probably erected on the site of a Norman building. In the well-kept churchyard in a vault of the Tracys, Robert Dover lies buried. Dover had built himself a house in the village shortly before the accession of James I, and here he died in 1641. This part of Stanway contains a great tithe barn built about 1600, and into it was incorporated a doorway of much earlier date.

Stanton village is more compact and lovelier than Stanway. It is approached by ways lined with oak, chestnut and elm, and the two ancient barns near the entrance, one of half-timber and the other thatched with Norfolk reeds, are its only buildings not of stone. Here is almost a model Cotswold village, each cottage flower-fringed, and well kept, with trees lining the alleys; nothing out of place, and even the street lighting done in the old-world style. The manor was given to Winchcomb Abbey by Kenulf its founder, and at the dissolution, Henry VIII gave it to Catherine Parr.

About this time the Warren family settled here from Snowshill, and Thomas Warren built the lovely vine-clad house that bear his initials and the date 1577 over the doorway. Within, on an elaborate plaster ceiling, the Warren arms, Tudor roses and fleurs-de-lis are repeated, and they also appear on a monument to John Warren (d. 1728) in the church. The local belief that this was Catherine Parr's house seems without foundation.

The grey church of St. Michael, owing to frequent alterations, is architecturally a very composite structure, but the clear, bright-looking building has retained two Norman archways and a little old glass. The curious fifteenth-century panel in the south aisle, showing a bird, probably a raven, encircled with the words 'Mauritius Wraybury, Lawyer', is apparently a copy of the seal of the Wraybury who added this aisle to the church. Traces of frescoes representing the Presentation and Purification have been recently uncovered, and the room over the church porch has been made into a small museum. Some of the pews in the church are worn at the ends as a result, so they say, of the tethering of shepherds' dogs during the service. The older pulpit, although of wood has survived since the fourteenth century, and, taking all in all, although many Gloucestershire churches are more interesting, few are more pleasing than Stanton's, especially on Sundays when the choir maidens are decked in their bonnets and gowns.

Stanton Court, a fine Elizabethan house, was recently acquired by the late Sir Philip Stott, who became largely responsible for the present unspoilt and well-kept, almost idyllic, appearance of the village. The head has been added to the Tudor base and shaft of the village cross, and a similar diligent restoration of the cottages where necessary has made the hamlet a model of harmonious orderliness and of natural tidiness. The houses, with their tiny flower gardens, are almost a museum of the characteristcs of Cotswold architecture, and the Jacobean round-headed windows, the variations in the number of windows on each floor, the finials, stone ornaments, bay windows, dormers, lintels and fire-places with inglenooks can only be matched in places three times the size.

Less than an hour's walk to the north, lies Buckland, one of the most out-of-the-way and one of the best built hamlets in the whole of the county. The secret to Buckland is in its isolated position, for the road to it ends at the dwellings which are almost hidden in the great elms and poplars of a small combe. Anciently it was a 'Buckland' or manor held by charter or book, and the King of Mercia gave it in 709 to Edburga, Abbess of St. Peter's of Gloucester before the Benedictines came there. Later the villeins and bordars had to wash and shear the abbey sheep for two days each year, in return for which each man, at harvest, was given a *shorn* sheep. In such isolated spots old customs died hard, and Buckland retained much of its Saxon character as late as 1266, when there were no freed men in the manor. Perhaps this lingering-on of old customs will partly explain the love for the church and the ancient treasures still to be found in the village.

The little church of St. Michael, according to Dr. Cox

'the most interesting church on the Gloucestershire side of Evesham', is perched on a knoll facing the green, wooded slopes of the Cotswolds. A good deal of Early English work remains although most of the structure belongs to the time of Edward IV. In the well-tended churchyard may be seen the base of an old cross, now lovely with rock plants, and at least two ancient tombs, of which that near the north porch till recently formed part of the church-yard wall. The interior is remarkably interesting. Two doorways and stairs remain to indicate the former presence of a large rood-loft with an altar. The fifteenth-century work includes many oak benches, the font and the old painted glass in the east window, where three modest lights depict the Sacraments of Confirmation, Matrimony and Extreme Unction. The first-named sacrament is most easily distinguishable, and in it a Bishop in cope and mitre is anointing a child with the help of a tonsured attendant. In addition small fragments of the Sacrament of Baptism remain to emphasize further how beautiful the complete window must have been. William Morris visited Buckland when living at Broadway Tower, and he was so impressed with the beauty of the window that he paid for the re-leading of it.

On the wall hangs a fifteenth-century pall, of English workmanship, made of parts of three velvet vestments, richly embroidered in gold and silver thread and coloured silks. The blue velvet centre is thickly worked with flowers and pomegranates, while the lower portion of red velvet, is embroidered with a small Crucifixion and several figures. The top portion bears a rebus of the letters W.H.Y. and a perspective view of a church which may refer to William Whytchurch, Abbot of Hailes (1464-79), in which case the pinnacles of a monstrance between the rebus and the church could be taken as a reference to the Holy Blood of Hailes.

The famous Buckland Bowl may be seen on the opposite wall. Made of maple wood, which was embellished with silver in 1507, the bowl bears a tiny silver disc beautifully engraved with a picture of St. Margaret. In the sixteenth and seventeenth centuries it was used as a bridal bowl for the parish.

Worth noticing, too, are the old encaustic tiles, now much faded, and traces of mural paintings. In the south aisle are three Jacobean seats with testers while the panelling over the back of the seats in the north aisle is inscribed 'Thomas Izard and James Sowthorn of theyr own charg have given this benchin and wainscot to church in yere of our Lord 1615'. The west gallery, also of this age, has kept its original pegs in the panels. Three fifteenth-century stones, probably from Hailes, may be seen on a window-sill, and in the south aisle it is pleasing to notice a brass tablet to John Foster, a tobacconist of Westminster, who died in 1733. Surely one of the few brasses to a tobacconist in England.

Not far from the church stands the ancient rectory, which can be distinguished by its symmetrical stone front and by a quaint addition to the roof, terminating in a cross finial. The hall here reaches right up to the roof timbers, and in one of the tall windows is a tun with the graft of a tree rising out of it, which was the rebus of William Grafton, who built the rectory and gave the lovely east window of the church during his rectorship about 1480. The fine old manor-house adjoining the churchyard had a similar hall, but this has since been partitioned.

At Michaelmas 1518 the manor of Buckland was inventoried for purposes of a lease, and among the goods of this rural estate were, in the words of the inventory:

Quicke catall prisid

Sixteen oxen . .	12£
sixteen Keen and heifers	8£
A bole . . .	10s.
Three young heifers and bullockes . .	9s.
Eleven store shepe .	18£
five horsis for the cart ⎫ A mare with a fole ⎭	3£ 3s. 4d.
six storing pyggis . .	6s.
Six other pyggis . .	3s.
eight bakyn pyggis .	13s. 4d.
four store hoggetis .	4£ 6s. 4d.

quycke stuf unprisid

A boore
fourteen dookes and drakes
three gese and a gander
six capyns and hennys
A sow for store
two cockes
four poyhens and a pecoke

The list forms an interesting commentary on Tudor spelling and farming economy; the 'bole' and the 'pyggis' seem cheap at the price compared with the 'store shepe' and 'hoggetis' or yearling sheep, but it should be remembered that the Michaelmas slaughter decreased the number of sheep to the minimum necessary for a flock in the ensuing year.

Buckland was given at the Dissolution to Sir Richard Gresham, Lord Mayor of London, from whom it passed to his son, Sir Thomas, the founder of the Royal Exchange. It is difficult to imagine a more incongruous partnership than this old-world dreaming manor in the hands of the able son of the busy metropolis.

CHAPTER VII: *The Coln Villages*

A MILE from Northleach the great Fosse Way, which pursues a direct and undulating course to Cirencester, is lined on its western margin with beeches which may be seen stretching right away in the distance to Puesdown Hill as a ribbon of green six miles long. We pass on the right-hand side the grey-stone lodge gates guarding the fine parklands of Stowell House, and soon afterwards the Roman road plunges directly down the Coln valley.

From here, at the 'Fossbridge Hotel', the narrow lane going northwards towards Chedworth Villa undulates above the green meadows bordering the willow-lined Coln. The hedgerows, bright with wild flowers, are, after a mile, gradually replaced by stone walls whose sombre grey fades into the dun colour of the distant fields, except where broken now and again by the dark green of overhanging bushes.

Past the cross-roads and keeping straight on down the slope towards Chedworth woods and so into the lovely valley of the silvery Coln, you come at last to a house and a mill alongside the stream where a choice of ways lies open to you. The walk through the white gates traverses the edge of the woods and keeps quite close to the river through twelve furlongs of shade and quiet; cows standing in the shallow stream flick their tails automatically, rabbits scamper about their burrows in the green riverine strip which they have shaven so closely, and occasionally a brilliant pheasant walks leisurely off into the undergrowth. Beneath the great oaks a dense carpet is spread of lilies of the valley and Solomon's seal, while in the height of summertime the masses of tall willow herb make a glorious sight. Beyond the dignified gamekeeper's lodge rise stately rows of dark firs, free from undergrowth and heavy with scent, their roots covered thick with pine needles and cones of surprising length. Soon the road leaves the woods and begins to twist uphill to the villa.

Those with no leisure for this walk may continue by car along the narrow lane past the mill and follow the white trackway overlooking the Coln and Chedworth Woods. The vast expanse of dark conifers interspersed with the more varied greens of deciduous trees looks at its best when autumn has transformed the woods into a chequerwork of flaming reds and bluish greens. The way is rough and winds downhill through parkland. The numerous pheasants peck on unconcernedly as you pass, although the grand cock on the wall may turn his bedizened neck inquisitively, and the rabbits may show a sudden desire to play hide-and-seek among the ant-hills. Straight ahead, across the valley in a combe almost surrounded by dense woods, may be seen a half-timber building, the house of the caretaker of Chedworth Villa.

The villa, with seven acres of wood near it, including majestic beeches and fine hazel bushes, belongs to the National Trust and is open to the public. Here, in the second century after Christ, a wealthy Roman built a magnificent house which flourished for at least another two hundred years. Ten miles to the south lay Corinium, which could be reached by the local Whiteway, and less than four miles to the east was the great Fosse. After the Romans left Corinium the Chedworth Villa fell into disuse, and for 1,400 years the wind and the rain washed soil and leaves upon the site until great trees flourished where once slaves had toiled at the fulling vats. Then in the fullness of time the keeper of the woods lost a ferret, and in digging for it came across tesserae, and so in 1864 the building was discovered. To-day the villa, one of the four finest in the British Isles, has been so carefully excavated that the remains do not give one a sense of ruin. Owing to the exigencies of the slope the great landlord chose an almost unique site facing the cold east, but here, by way of compensation, a strong spring issued from a bed of "Fuller's Earth', which was itself used later in the fullery. The villa was built on a courtyard plan, the rooms enclosing three sides of the square and the other being open to the east.

Of the south wing, which consisted largely of offices and servants' quarters, little remains. The west wing, comprising the main living and bathrooms, opened into a corridor that faced an inner courtyard. The remnants of the original walls have been roofed with slates found during the excavations, and the pavements have been covered with pleasant wooden shelters. The mosaic in the original dining-room, for the most part a formal design of leaves and flowers, depicts the four seasons, and three of these corner figures remain almost intact. Spring is shown as a girl with a basket of flowers and a swallow on her free hand; summer is a merry, naked Cupid and Winter a thick-set peasant, in hood and cloak, holding a leafless branch. The figures are skilfully outlined by using tesserae of various shapes while the subdued, carefully-graded colours give the limbs an appearance of solidity. The tesserae probably came from Gloucestershire, the grey and cream from the oolite, the red and russet from the sandstone and the blue and dark green from a lias limestone of the Severn valley.

The well-worn steps of the almost perfect bathroom tell of its constant use, and adjoining the 'Turkish Bath' is the cold plunge, a custom not eagerly revived in Britain since Roman times. The villa derived its water-supply from a well-constructed reservoir near by, now shorn of its rich decorations and of the little altar that stood in the curved apse behind the well.

The north wing consisted mainly of workshops, store-houses and living-rooms. Here two semi-circular buildings paved with cement probably housed the anvil and blast of the smithy while two huge vats near by may have been used for fulling. Another room retains the stone pilae that supported its hypocaust floor, and here, too, you may see the box-tile flues for conducting the hot air into the building.

The probable appearance of the villa is shown in a sketch hanging on the wall of the little museum which also shelters the objects found on the site. The collection includes such varied exhibits as sculptured stones, large 'pigs' of iron and little penates, compasses and a perfect pair of curling-tongs. Some of the larger stones were brought from the site of a temple, a fine structure that stood overlooking the Coln some 600 yards away near the keeper's lodge.

You may also walk freely in the woods upon the slope above and find fragments of age-old pottery and the huge snails introduced, so they say, by the Romans. From the depth of these coppices a tumulus and small camp dominate the site of the Roman settlement just as Belas Knap looks down upon that at Spoonley. The road near the villa leads eastwards over the dry hills through Yanworth to Stowell Park, where the gardens of the house surround the pretty church of St. Leonard, a small Norman building with additions of the Decorated period. Careful modern restoration has revealed a fine twelfth-century Doom painted on the plaster wall of the nave; the workmanship shows considerable skill and the svelte figures of the Apostles are gracefully arranged in an arcade of pairs on either side of the Virgin Mary. The actual Doom scene below the figures has become very indistinct.

From Fossbridge a narrow road winds between stone

walls to the peaceful little hamlet of Coln St. Dennis, a cluster of ivied cottages and box hedges lying in a small tributary combe of the Coln. The village owes its name to the fact that the parish church of St. James, so prettily placed near the river, once belonged to Deerhurst, a cell of the Abbey of St. Denis of Paris. The quaint little building is almost dwarfed by a giant tree and seems to be fully occupied in supporting its squat and heavy tower. Its Norman ancestry is visible in the south doorway, the tower arch and the font, but there are many later additions, in particular a fifteenth-century belfry.

Only a meadow of rough grasses and thistles separates the way to the south from the clear Coln with its fringes of willow-herb and white spiraea. Coln Rogers closely resembles Coln St. Dennis, even in the position of its church. The name is derived from the Norman baron, Roger de Lacy, whose father came over with William the Conqueror, and of whom it was said,

'The Tracys, the Lacys and Fettiplaces
Own all the best manors, the woods and the chases.'

The church of St. Andrew belonged formerly to the Abbey of Gloucester and is one of the oldest churches in Gloucestershire. Much Saxon work remains in the nave and chancel, including several Saxon pilaster strips and a Saxon window. The south doorway, chancel arch and tub font are Norman, while the north doorway is said to be Saxon within and curious Early English without. The chief Perpendicular additions to the plain fabric comprise the panelled stone pulpit and the triple-light east window. Among the few fragments of old glass may be seen a tiny fourteenth-century figure of St. Margaret with a book and rosary in her hands and the head of a dragon beneath her feet. Non-ecclesiologists will humbly admire the lovely approach to the churchyard and its charming setting amid the water-meadows of the Coln. The lovely Elizabethan vicarage, with its grey-weather gables and large windows is also well worth noticing.

Leaving the Saxon church we pass by the grey stone houses of Coln Rogers and through Winson with its massive stone barns and numerous farm-buildings to the better-known villages of Ablington and Bibury. In 1726 Alexander Pope found the prospect at Bibury pleasing, and one and a half centuries later William Morris thought it 'the most beautiful village in England', but the village became better known following the publication in 1898 of *A Cotswold Village* by Arthur Gibbs, and the hanging of Leslie's picture of Arlington Row in the Academy.

To-day motor transport has made the place famous, but no amount of traffic seems to spoil Bibury; if you would prove this, visit Bibury and mercenary Broadway on the same Sunday afternoon. Notwithstanding its popularity, very few people really know Bibury, although many are familiar with the sparkling Coln and the never-to be-forgotten Arlington Row. The small homely cottages on the south bank mount the straight hill leading to Cirencester at whose foot a large mill with stout buttresses overlooks the valley floor.

Here on one side, between the mill-stream and the Coln, is the fish farm where rushy banks separate the various ponds that supply trout to most of the Cotswold rivers. On the other side lies a flat, swampy field encircled by the mill-race and the river, while ahead the 'Swan' appears in its new plumage, and from its grounds pours a tremendous spring forming a river in itself round the rose garden, and joining the Coln at the bridge, just where the big trout float lazily among the reeds. Separated from the river by the main road is a line of well-spaced houses which in many cases have been built right into the bank of the valley slope so that trees grow close to their chimneys. The famous Arlington Row stands beside the mill-race, a Row at once so prettily irregular and diminutive that it compels you to stop and look and wonder what whim took the builders that they should have produced this crooked row of win-dowed gables. Perhaps the crooked man with the crooked smile of the nursery rhyme was a real person after all. The smoke from the cottages rises up against the densely-wooded cliffs of the Coln, so completing a picture of contentment and spontaneity that has few rivals in the Cotswolds or in Britain.

On the north bank, above the damp valley floor, you will find a lesser-known Bibury, where lovely cottages spring out of a border of flowers and creepers surround a tiny green. 'Not a cottage is in sight that is not worthy of a painter's brush; not a gable or a chimney that would not be worthy of a place in the Royal Academy.' This beautiful group holds the church of St. Mary which has considerable remains of Saxon work, including parts of four pilaster strips, two windows and the jambs of the lofty chancel arch. One of the doorways forms a good example of Norman architecture, while five of the arches are Transitional, and the square arcaded font with octagonal pillars belongs to the late thirteenth century. The chancel contains no less than nine almeries and a small oblong window with thirteenth-century glazing. Under the tower you will find a single stone inscribed with an early Maltese cross, and in the churchyard, against the north wall of the chancel, there has been placed a pre-Norman stone decorated with Scan-dinavian design, similar to three others sent from here to the British Museum. More modern art is represented by the stained glass depicting a lively scene of the coach used by Rowland Cooper when he lived at Bibury Court, and by two early eighteenth-century brasses, the one with a skull and cross-bones, and the other with a baby lying on a mattress. The carved wooden roof compensates somewhat for the reddish colour-wash on the walls, and the church-yard with its finely carved eighteenth-century tombs is delightfully well-kept.

A memorial in Latin commemorates the Rev. Benjamin Wynnington (ob. 1673), a painstaking minister here of whom it is said 'that after he had preached an hour by the glass he would turn it, assuring the congregation that he meant to continue in his sermon *only* one hour longer. During the second hour Mr. Sackville, then lord of the manor, usually retired to smoke a pipe but always returned in time for the benediction.'

The Sackville family are remembered by many inscriptions in the church and by the lovely manor-house near the Coln just below it. Bibury Court may date back to Henry VIII's time, but the greater part of the house was built by Sir Thomas Sackville in 1623, and one wing was added sixteen years later, in the Renaissance style, by Inigo Jones. Embattled bay windows, two stories high, project from the many gabled stone front and face a spacious elm-bordered garden. The house with its wide lawns and green park-land overlooks the silvery and placid Coln and makes a lovely picture when seen from the road to Coln St. Aldwyn.

Ablington, really a hamlet of Bibury, lies near the Coln not a mile to the north. It centres upon a picturesque bridge over the river and a charming row of large cottages over-looking the road from a terrace. Not far from the gigantic pollarded elm stands a huge barn, one of three in the village, and near by a wall hides the secluded manor-house where Arthur Gibbs wrote *A Cotswold Village*, which has been reprinted ten times since 1898. No other book describes the life of the people in Cotswold villages with more sincerity or more sympathetic insight. Arthur Gibbs, who died when only thirty-one, combined a love for all outdoor life and sports with a scholarly taste for literature. The old manor house where he wrote is a low rambling house with a dignity and position rather inferior to many elsewhere in the county, but Gibbs loved it from his first visit.

He lived here for many years, taking a keen interest in everything around him. 'The wild flowers by the silent river pleased me best of all. Such a medley of graceful fragrant meadow-sweet, and tall, rough-leaved willow-herbs with their lovely pink flowers. Light blue scorpion-grasses and forget-me-nots there were too, not only among the sword-flags and tall fescue-grasses by the bank, but little islands of them dotted all over the brook.'

He always took a kindly and sympathetic interest in the villagers and went as a friend among them. He noticed the cleanliness of the cottages, the marked honesty of the cottagers, and how well dressed the children were on fourteen shillings a week. He regarded his carter, the father of twenty-one children by the same wife, 'as a kind of hero', and says that 'to watch a boy of 14 years managing a couple of great strong cart-horses, either at the plough or with the waggons, is a sight to gladden the heart of man'.

Country cricket was the same good fun then as now. In a neighbouring village the field was marked by a large red flag, and 'it was the fat butler, I think, who after sailing about in a sea of waving buttercups . . . first discovered the stumps among the mowing grass'. The scene following is re-enacted on scores of local cricket pitches almost every summer Saturday afternoon. I caught the ball 'just as it pitched on a rabbit-hole and sent it straight up into the air like a soaring rocket. "Right, right, I have it!" yelled bowler and wicket-keeper simultaneously. "Catch it in your 'at, Bill!" screamed the Edgeworth eleven. I was already starting for the second run, whilst my stout fellow-batsman was halfway through the first, when the ball came down like a meteor, and hit the ground with a loud thud

about 5 yards distant from the outstretched hands of the
anxious bowler, who collided with his ally the wicket-
keeper, in the middle of the pitch. Half-stunned by the
shock . . . the bowler yet had presence of mind enough
to seize the ball and hurl it madly at the stumps. But the
wicket-keeper being still *hors-de-combat*, it flew away
towards the spectators, and buried itself among the mowing
grass.'

Gibbs had a rare, kindly sense of fun—'Let us be optimists
in literature even though we may be pessimists in life'—
and in his gentle way tells of the old lady who went to the
stores to buy candles and was astonished to find that owing
to the Spanish-American war 'candles was riz'. ' "Get
along," she indignantly exclaimed. "Don't tell me they
fights by candlelight." ' His verses on 'grammar' for the
Gloucestershire dialect have never been excelled:

> 'If thee true "Glarcestershire" would know,
>   I'll tell thee how us always zays un;
> Put "I" for "me", and "a" for "o",
>   On every possible occasion.

> When in doubt squeeze in a "w"—
> "Stuns", not "stones". And don't forget, zur,
> That "thee" must stand for "thou" and "you";
>   "Her" for "she", and vice versa.

> Put "v" for "f"; for "s" put "z";
>   "Th" and "t" we change to "d",
> So dry an' kip this in thine yead,
>   An' thou wills't talk as plain as we."

Two of Gibbs' saying should be remembered by all who
are interested in the welfare of the Cotswolds:

'It is a sad thing when the big-house of the village is empty.'

and:

'The great attraction of this country lies in its being one of the few spots now remaining on earth which have not only been made beautiful by God, but in which the hand of man has erected scarcely a building which is not in strict conformity and good taste.'

Any parishioner will vouch for the truth of the first, and the last should be the text of every Cotswold settler.

THE FAIRFORD NEIGHBOURHOOD

Coln St. Aldwyn is scarcely three miles from Fairford and lies near the spot where the ancient Salt Way crossed Akeman Street. The name may be derived from St. Aldwyn, a Bishop of Worcester about 844, as most of Gloucestershire was in that diocese until the Reformation. The stone cottages of the pretty village pleasantly group themselves within a big loop of the Coln near to which stand the church and a fine spacious manor-house of Elizabethan times. The church of St. John the Baptist has a beautifully carved late Norman doorway with the original studded door and a skilfully wrought-iron latch. The main part of the building and the two lower stages of the tower belong to the Early English period, but the uppermost stage, which bears the arms of Neville, Clare and others, is Perpendicular. The two large lancet windows in the chancel have been filled with good glass to the memory of John Keble, vicar here from 1782 to 1835, and to his better-known son who occasionally assisted him in this church.

Quenington is at once both more picturesque and irregular than Coln St. Aldwyn. Its gardens are equally lovely with roses and phlox, and the cottage walls are bright with flowering creepers. The name, according to Rudder, was originally Colnington, but ever since Domesday Survey, when Roger de Lacy held the manor, the hamlet has been known as Quenintone or Quenington. The small church of St. Swithun, in addition to interesting carved fragments of Norman work built into the west wall, contains two exceptionally rich Norman doorways with elaborately carved tympana. The tympanum above the south doorway depicts the Coronation of the Virgin and bears on either side an angel, lion, bull and eagle, the symbols of the four evangelists. One of the beautiful courses of the doorway consists of beaked and other strange heads; man occupies the lower places beneath the ox and ass and a lovely crouching rabbit. The sculpture over the north door is an older, more vigorous carving depicting Christ triumphing over Satan and Death; Satan lies prostrate, bound hand and foot, pierced in the mouth by the cross of Christ who leads the adoring Adam and Eve and Abel out of the gaping Maw of Hell. Above, a sun, probably enclosing the face of God the Father, shines brightly, and near by is a Ram's head, perhaps a crude representation of the Lamb of God. This tympanum forms the nearest approach in Gloucestershire parish churches to the exquisite 'Burning Bush' in the chapel of Burford Priory. What a pity it is that such a glorious church should be saddled with such an ugly little bell-turret!

In 1193 the de Lacy family founded at Quenington a preceptory of the Knights Hospitallers, but the community never grew large and in 1338 consisted only of two knights and a preceptor. At the road-side close to the church stands its lofty gatehouse with a canopied niche and postern door, a graceful, well-preserved structure now part of Quenington

Court. Traces of the moat also remain, but little else survived the seventeenth century.

The Coln flows southward to Fairford, whose life still centres upon the market square near to the fine bridge over the river although the houses have spread to the other bank. The town arose on the dry healthy gravels at the threshold of the flat Thames Valley, and only a few miles from the Round House guarding the junction of the stripling Thames with the Coln and with the Severn Canal. At the Conquest King William seized the manor and so, in *Domesday Book*, Fairford is described as 'Terra Regis'. The purchase of the manor from Henry VII by John Tame, a wealthy wool-merchant, proved the turning-point in the history of Fairford. This 'praty uplandisch towne' according to Leland 'never florished afore the Cumming of the Tames onto it'.

John Tame immediately set about rebuilding the church and no doubt witnessed its consecration in 1497. On his death in 1500 he was succeeded by his son Sir Edmund Tame, thrice sheriff of the county, who probably completed the handsome, well-proportioned structure, planned in imitation of the nobler church at Northleach.

Although the lovely church is mainly late Perpendicular, distant traces of the older building may still be seen, for example, in the ball-flower ornament of one of the tower piers. The noble edifice stands on a knoll not far from the Coln and amid a large churchyard bordered with gardens and tall trees, so that it shows up to the best advantage. The tower cannot compare with that at Campden or Kempsford but is pleasing both in proportion and strength and is adorned externally with corner figures and with the arms of Clare and Tame, Beauchamp and Neville. The church is said to lack spontaneity but it has a handsome appearance which only the wealthy woolmen could have afforded to give it, while its twenty-eight painted glass windows are the finest and most numerous specimens of sixteenth-century work in existence. A wealth of literature and legend has sprung up concerning these windows, and much research has yet to be done before the question of their origin is finally settled. To-day experts agree that the paintings were made in England for the windows they now occupy and that the contractor was probably the famous glazier Barnard Flower, who worked on the windows for Henry VII's chapel at Westminster and King's College Chapel, Cambridge. It is said that the total cost of the glass was probably about £200, or nearly 2s. per square foot. The obvious traces of Flemish work can be explained by the presence of foreign craftsmen, one of whom T. Aeps (*floruit* 1480–1528) left his monogram (T. Aeps Vitrifex) on the sword of an executioner and a rebus picture of an ape. It is pleasing to think that the generous Tames were not pirates and that the glass is English. More remarkable is its survival when that in neighbouring churches was almost utterly destroyed.

During the iconoclastic outburst of Edward VI's reign, Alice Verney, daughter of Sir Edward Tame, was Lady of the manor, and she probably induced her husband, Sir Thomas Verney, to see that the church was protected. During the Civil War it is said that Mr. Oldisworth, the worthy rector, had the glass removed and carefully concealed. The Fairford people believe that it was buried near the obelisk on the Quennington road, but no documentary evidence has been found to support their view. More care, however, was taken to conceal the glass than to replace it, and until recently some of the quarries were out of their original order and actually upside down. The windows could have been empty for a few years only for they were complete when Wood visited Fairford in the summer of 1660, and a poem written about 1656, making a satirical attempt to account for their preservation, includes the following lines:

> '. . . then Faireford boast
> Thy Church hath kept what all have lost,
> And is preserved from the bane
> Of either war or Puritan . . .'

The two aisle windows at the west end were badly shattered by the hurricane of 1703, and the upper parts of these are now mainly modern restoration work, while all the windows have been carefully restored and releaded with slight additions, where necessary.

That the paintings have vigour and beauty none will deny, although many will probably disagree with Sir Anthony Van Dyck's assertion 'that the pencil could not exceed them'. They form a remarkable harmony of skilful design and realistic portraiture, and each face, be if of angel, saint, persecutor or devil, has a distinct personality of its own. The paintings can be easily studied in groups as they are nearly all placed in a consecutive order forming a connected story. They form a great illuminated book intended to teach by appeal to the eye in the days when the Bible was not available for reading by the congregation. On the north side, near the Lady Chapel, the series is introduced with a retrospect of the Old Testament showing the Fall, and later scenes from the life of the Children of Israel during the 4,000 years of waiting for the coming of the Messiah. They include a picture of Moses and the Burning Bush, Gideon and the Fleece, and the visit of the Queen of Sheba to King Solomon. The next three windows in the Lady Chapel show scenes from the life of the Blessed Virgin Mary and the coming of the Redeemer, beginning with a picture of SS. Joachim and Anna, the parents of Mary, and continuing with pictures of her birth, presentation in the temple and her marriage to St. Joseph, and ending with her Assumption.

The chancel windows illustrate the Redemption of Man. The Passion and Death of Christ are portrayed and His Descent into Limbo, while St. Michael and the heavenly hosts are shown thrusting the fallen angels into Hell, where Beelzebub is already imprisoned within a fiery gate.

Other incidents in the life of Christ occur on the south side. In the windows of the south chapel appear the Transfiguration, while one of the best of the series shows the Appearance of Christ to the eleven apostles in the upper room after the Resurrection, with Thomas shown disbelieving. The Ascension scene is followed by a series of three windows depicting the twelve apostles which are all carefully differentiated. St. Peter is seen holding the keys of Heaven, while St. John, with silken hair and beautiful, youthful face, forms a perfect contrast to the grave look and heavier build of St. Mark.

The thirteenth window commences the series dealing with the history of the church. At first we see the four Fathers, SS. Jerome, Gregory, Ambrose, Augustine, and then, in the north clerestory windows, twelve persecutors of the church, Herod, Caiaphas, Judas, Nero, Diocletian and so on, each being surmounted by hideous devils. Ranged opposite to them on the south side are twelve martyrs or confessors with angels above them; they include St. Dorothea with her bridal basket of roses and apples and St. Agnes with her lamb, both very beautiful figures with lovely faces.

The western windows form a great triptych of Judgement. The central window contains a masterly representation of the Last Judgement, with Christ enthroned in great power and majesty, seated on a rainbow and encompassed with ruby cherubim. Below, St. Michael, a noble figure, weighs a person in one scale and though a red devil with yellow eyes endeavours to turn the scale, the good outweighs the evil. On one side the good are ascending into Heaven, with on the other the wicked are being thrust by grinning demons into Hell. In another part is a representation of Hell with colours more glowing than those of the neighbouring heaven, with its angels of sapphire and ruby. The myriads of devils, some red, some blue, others dark green, have faces like dogs, lions and monkeys, expressing fiendish enjoyment as they torture the damned, which are mainly women. The naked females are being pinched and mischievously pricked as the gloating fiends carry them off shoulder high to hurl and toss them into the fiery furnace. A horned, blue devil with white webbed feet pulls a bright yellow handcart containing a lost soul seated clasping her knees. Another devil with blue body also draws a handcart holding a damned person, who is being pushed from behind by a dark green fiend with a red-hot poker. Satan himself broods menacingly with his hands on his knees and his long green tail coiling about his scaly legs. He has three staring round eyes, and enormous red-and-white teeth; two rows protrude beneath the ape-like nose in his belly, whilst the third, in his fish-like head, has hooked fangs which suck in damned souls amid licking flames. In one light is a mill of the type once used for grinding materials for glass-making, and a ruby demon, with flaming hair and yellow eyes, turns the handle, so mincing up the damned, one of whom, with arms extended, is seen upon the hopper in process of being crushed.

No brief account could give an adequate impression of the skill and versatility of the craftsmen, as it is only from the incidental details, such as the exquisite backgrounds and beautiful landscapes, some no doubt of the Coln, that the perfection of the windows may be fully appreciated.

Although the glass has made St. Mary's famous there is much else of considerable interest in the church. Under the chancel arch, a large handsome tomb of grey-polished marble covers the bodies of John Tame, the founder (ob. 1500), and Alice, his wife; the brass plates engraved with their effigies are placed at the head, and this pathetic inscription at their feet:

> For Jhus' love pray for me:
> I may not pray, nowe pray ye
> With a Pater noster and an Ave:
> That my paynys relessid may be.'

Another large, flat marble stone on the floor, near the altar steps, holds the brass effigies of the founder's son, Sir Edmund Tame (ob. 1534), his two wives and family, while against the north wall, brasses depict the same persons kneeling. Near by may be seen the freestone effigies of Roger Lygon and Katherine his wife, who was formerly married to Sir Edmund Tame the younger.

The screen work of the choir and chapels is beautiful, although much repaired, and there are considerable traces of old mural paintings. The fine oaken roof should be noticed, especially for its finely-carved stone supports. The choir stalls have interesting misericords representing the lighter side of family life in fifteenth-century England. A married couple are drinking home-made brew from a barrel, and the husband urges on his rather tipsied spouse to further excess by kicking her with his foot. A fat lady spins as her dinner cooks in a large iron cauldron, but the flax on her distaff hides from her view a dog stealing the contents of the pot. Probably the carvers recalled their youth in the scene showing a woman bending over a boy whom she clutches by the hair and soundly belabours with a thick bat.

The old-fashioned town of Fairford centres upon its High Street, which towards the south opens out into a large square faced on one side by the 'George' and the 'Bull', old coaching inns, and on the other by a row of pleasant commodious houses, built largely of stone and usually gabled.   The picturesque 'George' has bay windows right to the eaves, a fine Gothic archway and a high-pitched slated roof.   The 'Bull' appears less charming but has acquired greater fame as the trout-fishing inn of the Coln at Fairford.   Here may be heard and told, in-season and out-of-season fishermen's tales and local anecdotes, such as the following, all equally veracious.

Serious rioting took place at Fairford in 1830, partly owing to the introduction of new agricultural machinery. A large body of farm-workers armed themselves with home-made weapons and proceeded to smash up the machines, whereupon the military was summoned. Just as the captain came face to face with the mob he happened to notice that one of his gaiters was partly unbuttoned, and turning to the leading rioter he sharply ordered him to button it up. The rustic was so flabbergasted that he dropped his pole with a scythe on the end and meekly obeyed the command. It is said that the rioters were so impressed with the incident that they dispersed peaceably to their homes.

The damp, floodable meadows south of Fairford still harbour the dainty spotted fritillary.   The roads are flat and lined with rhines or streams, each shaded by tall hedge-rows dense with greater bindweed and woody nightshade, with hemp agrimony and purple loosestrife.   Yet the meadows only predominate near the watercourses and many fields are thickly cropped with corn.   It is a refreshing land of many shadows, a land where horses look sleeker and errand boys grow fatter than elsewhere in east Gloucestershire.

Kempsford, the largest and most attractive village in this flat vale, stands on the Thames some three miles from Fairford.   Its stately church tower rises high above the encircling trees and a few trim gardens descend to the river from the old grey houses at the southern end of the one long street. Many of the smaller cottages are thatched or colour-washed, but all are arranged in rows and groups so that their doors open on to the road. The village green breaks the length of the street near the bridge over the old Thames-Severn canal, now a sorry sight and pitifully choked with reeds. Occasionally a pretty garden is fenced with stone slabs set endwise in the ground, and what could be out of place in any village with an 'Axe and Compass Inn'?

The noble, aisleless church of St. Mary retains much Norman work in its nave such as a flat buttress, extensive string-courses, several deeply-splayed windows and two fine doorways. In the early Perpendicular period the stately grey tower and the clerestory together with various windows were added, since when the church has suffered little change. The tower, built about 1390 by John of Gaunt, 'time-honoured Lancaster', consists of three stages with four tiers of windows, the greatest being in the upper stage. The structure is supported by pillars and arches while its massive corner buttresses terminate in crocketed pinnacles that extend ten feet above the leaden roof.

The tower space, perhaps the most graceful in any Gloucestershire parish church, has a lovely ceiling tastefully decorated with the arms of Edward the Confessor, the first builder of the church, and of the Earls of Gloucester and and Lancaster. The big window contains some fine modern glass by Kempe. The vestry hides not only the fine south doorway and a scratch dial, but also the benefaction board that tells of an anonymous gift of hay annually to adorn and beautify the church. The lofty chancel retains an old beam for the lenten veil and a few fragments of old glass. Near the altar a finely-executed brass depicts Walter Hickman (ob. 1521) dressed in flowing gown that is girdled with a belt ornamented with Tudor roses. Corystan, his wife, and their four sons lie beside the wool-stapler. There is, too, a fine effigy (*c.* 1450) of a priest in full choir dress, probably a member of the Church of St. Mary of Leicester to whom the manor was given by the Plantagenets.

Kempsford, although not mentioned in *Domesday*, was according to tradition the site of Saxon earthworks or of a palace of Saxon kings that stood in Mercia facing Wessex across the river. At the end of the thirteenth century it formed the dower of Maud, daughter of Sir Patrick Chaworth, on her marriage to Henry Plantagenet, third Earl of Lancaster and grandson of Henry III. Maud then owned the castle which guarded the ford at the head of the village street and enclosed the stately church within its precincts. Here Lancaster entertained Edward I and brought as his prisoner the ill-fated Edward II. The villagers tell a tragic story about Henry Plantagenet and Maud. Against the will of his newly-wedded wife, Henry joined the barons in their struggle with the King and suffered several reverses. Lady Maud helped many of the stragglers who crossed the Thames at Kempsford, and among them her brother-in-law, whom she lodged secretly as there was a price on his head. She used to carry his food to him in a room at the end of the terrace, but a jealous guest discovered her habit and told the Earl of Maud's apparent infidelity. The Earl secretly witnessed the meeting and in a fury struck down his brother and hurled his innocent young wife over the ramparts into the Thames. When he found out his mistake he was overcome with remorse and returned to the wars and his death. Since that day sad Lady Maud has haunted the terrace, while the traitor guest became a monk and rests, so they say, under one of the sculptured tombs in the church.

Henry, the first Duke of Lancaster, who succeeded to the manor in 1355, left Kempsford, never to return, when his only son, a mere child was drowned in the ford. As the

Earl rode away from the scene in his grief, his horse cast a shoe which may still be seen nailed to the door of the church.

His daughter and heiress was Lady Blanche, the first wife of John of Gaunt, who built the fine tower in her honour. Lady Blanche was a patroness of Chaucer, who composed several poems in her honour, and probably attended her wedding, which took place at Reading, and the famous joustings held afterwards in London. About this time (1359), Royalty and the young poet were no doubt frequently entertained at the castle of Kempsford.

The earliest works of Chaucer include an A.B.C., a hymn in honour of the Virgin, written, according to Speght, 'at the request of Blaunche, Duchesse of Lancaster, as a praier for her private use, being a woman in her religion very devout'. Chaucer's first great original work was produced in 1369, when the beautiful Blanche died of plague at the age of twenty-nine. This, the *Book of the Duchess*, contains the funeral poem entitled *The Deth of Blaunche the Duchesse*, and describes Lady Blanche:

> 'I saw hir daunce so comlily
> Carole and sing so swetely,
> Laugh and pleye so womanly,
> And loke so debonairly,
> So good speke and so friendly,
> That certes I trow that nevermore
> Nas seyn so blisful a tresore.
> For every hair upon *hir* head
> Sooth to say it was not red,
> Nor yellow neither, nor brown it was
> Methought more like gold it was.'

He writes a few whimsical lines on her name:

'——goode faire White she hight[1]
Thus was my ladye naméd right
For she was both fair and bright.'

and adds:

'joye get I never none,
Now that I see my ladye bright,
Which I have loved with all my might,
Is from me dead and is agone.'

It is sometimes said that *The Assembly of Fowles* or *The Parliament of Birds* was composed in honour of Lady Blanche's wedding, but the work is thought by authorities to have been written at least twelve years after her death.

The ancient manor-house, the old home of the Lancasters, was rebuilt in the reign of James I, but nothing remains of it to-day, save the haunted terrace, now a green walk, and a tall, solitary stone wall set with a fine mullioned window overhanging the Thames. The church at Kempsford had one notable vicar at least in Dr. Woodford, afterwards Bishop of Ely, a remarkably absent-minded man, and astonishingly ignorant of country matters. Locally, he is always fondly remembered as the Doctor who thought ewe was pronounced 'ee-wee', and who, wishing to purchase a horse, suggested that one 'some fourteen or fifteen feet high' might perhaps do. Let us hope the worthy Bishop did not ride his 'high horse' at Ely.

[1] was called

CHAPTER VIII: *The Valley of the Churn*

THE UPPER CHURN

THERE ARE at least eight Seven Springs in Gloucestershire, but none is more picturesque than that at the head of the Churn, where copious springs gush forth into a clear pool beneath aged trees beside the main Andoversford-Gloucester road. An enthusiast, overcome perhaps by the strength of the bubbling water, has placed a tablet here, inscribed

Hic tuus O Tamisine Pater Septemgeminus fons.

Leland would have it otherwise when he writes that 'the head of Isis in Cotteswolde riseth about a mile on this side Tetbyrie'. The source at Trewsbury Head near the Fosse Way, not four miles south of Cirencester, is the only spring to bear the name of the river. This 'Thames Head' consists of four or five springs which trickle into the green mead, and, although yielding more water, lack the surprise and majesty of the upswelling waters at the source of the Churn.

The Churn differs from the Windrush and Coln in more than the majesty of its source, for its impetuosity and its well-wooded, gorge-like valley have more in common with the streams near Stroud. In addition, since it is faithfully followed by a main road, it lacks the quietude of its northern neighbours. The place names Cubberley, Cowley, Colesborne, Cerney and Cirencester are alliterative and pretty enough, but we miss the interesting personal appendages, the Saints Aldwyn and Dennis and Rogers of the Coln.

This valley is a land of picturesque, aisleless churches, usually with low saddleback towers as if the builders knew how hopeless it would be to compete with the cathedral-like dimensions of Cirencester church.

Coberley or Cubberley, on the west bank of the stream, lies but a short walk from Seven Springs. Save for an old barn and the battlemented wall with Tudor doorways adjoining the churchyard, the ancient Court has entirely disappeared. A branch of the Berkeley family lived here in the reign of Edward III, and among the effigies in St. Giles' Church are those of Sir Thomas Berkeley, who survived Crécy, and of Joan, his wife, who later married Richard Whittington of Pauntley and became the mother of the famous 'Dick'. All the fourteenth-century effigies in the church probably represent Berkeleys; they include, to use a quotation, 'an ancient female figure' and two armoured knights, one of whom lies with his legs crossed, while the other defends himself with a sadly-defaced escutcheon.

A by-road leads to Elkstone, a bleak, lonely hamlet at the head of a small combe which plunges down to the Churn. The small aisleless church of St. John the Evangelist, a simple, dignified building dates mainly from about 1130, but the exterior was considerably altered a century or so later, and a few windows as well as the sturdy tower were added in the Perpendicular period.

The handsome grey tower was built with large shaped blocks of local stone and forms a noted landmark. It carries some interesting gargoyles, two of which represent dwarf-like men, the one playing a guitar, the other blowing a horn. The external wall of the nave is ornamented with sculptures of human faces, greyhounds, stags and ghoulish mythical beasts, which, however, are much smaller than similar carvings at Aldsworth. The south doorway consists of very fine Norman work, surmounted by a tympanum showing Our Lord in Majesty, with one hand raised in blessing. Even the beak heads of this rich doorway have been carved into weird monsters.

The interior of the church proves equally interesting. The solid-looking nave retains its fine old timber roof, while the Norman chancel is an architectural puzzle owing to its division into two parts, both with groined vaulting. The richly carved Norman arches terminate in hungry-looking wolves and form a suitable frame for the splendid ornamentation of the east window.

Originally the first half of the chancel supported a tower while the sanctuary was vaulted at the usual level, but the tower proved too heavy for the supporting arches and soon after its erection either collapsed or had to be removed. The groined vaulting beneath the tower was therefore roofed in and at the same time the sanctuary walls were raised up to keep the outer roof of the church at one level. Thus between the vaulting of the sanctuary and its new outer roof there was space for a room, and the old tower staircase was used as an approach to it. This room was used as a columbarium, or pigeon-house, and the nesting-holes of forty-three pigeons remain, although to-day the small entrances from the outside are blocked up.

From Elkstone a quiet road descends steeply to Colesborne and southward to Rendcomb, which is healthily situated on a projecting headland and almost moated around by the Churn and a narrow tributary combe. The pretty village hides itself away from the main road which skirts its fine beech-woods and green park-lands. The church of St. Peter, which stands on a hillock overlooking the Churn, was entirely rebuilt by Sir Edmund Tame, whose initials may be seen on the corbels and on some old glass in one window of the nave. There are many fragments of lovely old glass here which may have been brought as surplus from Fairford, but some of the panels are probably Flemish work of about 1600. The small detailed Biblical scenes are beautifully executed. Sir Edmund did not destroy all traces of the original Norman church and he also spared a circular font skilfully carved with ornamented arcades containing eleven Apostles, and a shapeless figure intended for Judas. The elaborate screens, now partly restored, and the roof of the nave with its restrained colouring are good examples of sixteenth-century work. The present Rendcomb Park, a modern building standing amid the well-wooded undulations of the old deer park, is used as a boys' school, and the militant tradition of its former owners has been succeeded by that wondrous, unnatural calm which emanates from studious classrooms.

Woods and parklands line the way to North Cerney which for centuries was under the same ownership as Rendcomb. The secluded village is pleasant enough without containing any cottages out of the ordinary. All Saints is a typical Churn-valley church, an aisleless structure perched on a hill-side, with a slate roof and a low saddleback tower. The south doorway has a star-diapered tympanum and lintel and holds an ancient door with skilfully wrought-iron work. Three windows are filled with very fine fifteenth-century glass; one asks for prayers for the soul of William Whytchurche and another for John Bicote, who is depicted very artistically as a tonsured priest kneeling in a girdled red robe. Another window shows the Madonna with St. Catherine and St. Dorothy, and again with two bishops all in blue, gold-embroidered robes.

A Perpendicular stone pulpit, deeply undercut with wreaths of lilies, and a wooden figure of the Virgin and Child by no means exhaust the treasures of this church. The exterior is noted for its two large 'manticoras', or fabulous beasts of Abyssinia with human heads, the swift body of a lion, a scorpion's sting in the tail and a cannibalistic appetite. You will find them incised in outline on the wall of the south transept and near the ground on an angle of the tower. But why they should be here we cannot imagine, unless someone in North Cerney had been reading Pliny or a seaman had brought back strange yarns from 'vurrin parts'. The fourteenth-century churchyard cross with a restored head made of an ancient Maltese cross that was found in the wall of the churchyard, makes a worthy companion to one of the prettiest churches in rural Gloucestershire.

At Perrot's Brook south of Cerney, those with leisure would do well to follow the Welsh Way westwards up the hill-side to Ermin Street and so to the hamlets upon the Duntisbourne stream, a small tributary of the Churn and the last of the Cotswold streams to follow a wide-open depression as distinct from the deep gorge-like bottoms of the Stroudwater Hills. The pretty village of Daglingworth, with its houses, all of stone, straggles in picturesque fashion along the tiny stream which is wisely preferred to the bleak, high ridge near Ermin Street. Lustrous evergreens and conifers brighten the grey cottages, and even the new car park at the church has its fringe of flowers.

The most striking building of all is a large circular dovecote, with two small dormers in its conical roof, standing in the grounds of a pretty gabled farm-house, once probably the manor. The lovely old dovecote retains its revolving ladder, which is similar to that preserved at Izod's House, Chipping Campden.

There were actually 550 nesting-holes in the cote, so it seems highly probable that the farmers of Daglingworth spent large sums on bird-scaring. Nearby, a few ruined arches also remain to tell us of the cell of Godstow Abbey, Oxfordshire, the refuge of Fair Rosamund. The nuns held an advowson and a small pension out of the rectory at Daglingworth from 1156 onwards, and they built a cell here owing to a superfluity of sisters at Godstow.

The lichen-covered church of the Holy Cross is bright and cheerful and retains its stone-slab floor. Traces of Saxon work may be seen in the long and short quoins of a nave angle, perhaps also in the narrow south doorway with a sun-dial and in the fairly large sculptures of the chancel walls. When the chancel arch was taken down about a hundred years ago the jambstones were found to be sculptured, but at some time they had been reversed. These rude Saxon carvings have been placed in the walls; one represents the Crucifixion, Christ being depicted clothed; another Our Lord in Judgement, and a third, St. Peter as a beardless youth. Another ancient carving in the outer chancel wall representing the Crucifixion also shows the figure of Christ clothed.

A little Roman votive altar now in the vestry wall was found in the fabric and bears a Latin inscription telling that Junia dedicated this altar to the goddess Mother *et genio loci*. The three 'Norman' arches are imitation, being only a century old, but a small Norman window existed here until it was given to Barnsley church. A fine scratch sun-dial may be seen over the porch, and within it a curious brass on which the quaint inscription reads:

'The Dissection and Distribution
of Giles Handcox
Who Earth Bequeathe to Earthe to Heaven His Soule
To Friends His Love to the Poor a Five Pound Dole
To Remaine For Ever And Be Imployed
For Their Best Advantage And Releefe
In Daglingworth.
April Th9, 1638.'

The little hamlet of Duntisbourne Rous lies scarcely a mile upstream. Shortly after the Conquest it came, according to Rudder, into the hands of the family of John Rufus, from which the village gained its surname, for Le Rous or Le Rus meant red-headed just as Blount or Blond meant white hair and fair complexion.

This tiny picturesque village is more attractive than the other Duntisbourne settlements, Middle, Lear and Abbots, which are strung out along the upper course of the wall-partitioned valley. Its grey cottages and few farm-houses cluster in the deep green valley near the ford, but the almost perfect Norman church, a quaint, small aisleless structure, is perched charmingly on a cliff overlooking the stream. From the outside only its height and the low saddle-backed tower prevent it from being mistaken for a tithe barn. The herring-bone work on the north of the nave, although possibly Saxon, is less arresting than the chancel which is illumined by two narrow Norman windows and enriched with a most elaborate arch. The church was built on a slope sufficient to allow a crypt under the chancel, and this small barrel-vaulted room, formerly used as a chapel and entered from the chancel, has a deeply splayed Norman window. The nave retains its old black-and-white roof and the walls are panelled with what looks to be old pew ends. Even the two bells are medieval, and four misericord stalls, carved with a vine leaf on either side of a lion, will be found here, as well as a fine Jacobean pulpit. The entrance to the churchyard is by means of a quaint scissor-like device in iron which when opened admits thin people only, a very remarkable piece of work which should successfully warn church-going parishioners of oncoming obesity.

CIRENCESTER

Cirencester, 'capital of the Cotswolds', has a dignified and commercial air, not so much an attitude of persuading you to buy something or anything regardless of cost, as an impressive, benevolent, 'value-for-money' spirit which says, 'We cater for well-to-do farmers and hunting gentlemen'. Here are the best shops, the largest estates, the finest hunters and the biggest markets on the hills. What is more important, the town has always held this position in the eyes of Cotswold folk. A word first on the name; the Roman town was called Corinium, which later became known as Cirenceaster, and so changed to our present Cirencester. Written records show that for at least five centuries the 'common appelation', I quote from Rudder, has been 'Syssiter', 'Ciseter' or 'Ciceter', which is its present pronunciation, 'Cirencester' being totally inadmissible. It is a great pity that the lazy abbreviation 'Ciren' should have found its way recently into print, as it tends to perpetuate a modern slang expression at the expense of a name of such long-standing.

Of Caer-cori, the ancient British town on this site, and a stronghold of the Duboni tribe, very little is known, but its successor, the Roman Corinium or Corinium Dobunorum, became the administrative capital of the vast tribal territory of the Dobuni, and was destined to become the second largest town in Roman Britain, London (Londinium) alone exceeding it.

Here upon the gravels near the Churn, the great Fosse Way from Exeter to Lincoln was crossed by Ermin Street, which linked Winchester to Gloucester and Caerleon. The Roman road-builders favoured the dry limestone hills and Corinium was placed by nature to control an easy east to west crossing of the Cotswold. Nor was this all. Near to this point Akeman Street came in from St. Albans and Bicester, and later half a dozen minor Roman roads converged on Corinium. The eight highways and half as many secondary roads of to-day which meet in the town are based largely on the Roman route system.

Corinium probably first came into being about A.D. 60, during the reign of Nero, and was a flourishing town within a few years. There are two large and well-preserved tombstones in the Museum, each carved with the figure of a mounted soldier whose foe lies prostrate, pierced by the cavalryman's spear. The Latin inscription beneath indicates that Corinium was a Roman military station forty years after its foundation. 'Pax Romana' soon prevailed over the Cotswolds, and, as the Roman armies steadily advanced westwards, Corinium became a great civil and commercial centre. It became the greatest and most civilized of all the dozen tribal capitals of Britain, and at the end of the third century, when Diocletian reorganized the administration of the country, Corinium became the capital of the large subdivision Britannia Prima.

The Cotswolds have been called 'The Dukeries of Roman Britain' and rich men must have been as common as weeds round Corinium during the Roman age. On the east side of modern Cirencester portions of a long low mound from The Beeches round to Watermoor, and especially visible in the Town Playing Fields, mark the course of the Roman Wall. Other traces are visible on the west, especially near the workhouse. The city wall was two miles in circumference enclosing 240 acres or an area twice as large as Silchester and five times that of Roman Gloucester. It was intact in the reign of Henry IV, but in the sixteenth century very few vestiges of it remained, although Leland traced the site of the wall along its entire length. The frequent Roman remains discovered at this time included a broken shank bone of a horse, stopped up with a peg, which, upon removal, let escape numerous silver coins. A small part of the wall uncovered in 1774 was found to be 8 feet thick. Entrance through these walls was effected by means of four gates, of which the North Gate probably stood at the end of Dollar Street, where travellers along Ermin Street, from Gloucester, gained admittance, while the South Gate, near Watermoor station, opened on to the same road from Silchester.

Just outside the site of the West Gate, at the end of Querns Lane, may be found The Querns, a field covered with large grassy mounds, among which can be distinguished a large oval earthwork with banks, even to-day nearly 20 feet high, enclosing an area of level ground. This impressive wall of earth, called locally the Bull Ring, is the remains of a Roman amphitheatre measuring 50 yards by 45, of which the steep inward slope was formerly either stepped or disposed in rows of seats.

The glory of intra-mural Cirencester may be judged from the elaborate remains which have been unearthed. Tessellated pavements of exquisite workmanship may be seen at the splendid new Corinium Museum in Park Street, in the grounds of Abberley House. Other tessellated pavements have come to light in private property at Gloucester House in Dyer Street, in Ashcroft, just off Querns Lane, and at the Firs in Victoria Road. A lovely mosaic, at Barton Farm in Earl Bathurst's Park, which will shortly be removed to the new museum, shows Orpheus with his lyre charming proud peacocks, lions, leopards and more homely ducks. A round Roman pillar has been worked into the angle of a house at the corner of Park Lane, and now helps to support the garden railings.

The streets were probably laid out on the usual chessboard plan, and the main north to south thoroughfare, Ermin Street, is overlaid to-day by Dollar Street, the Church and Tower Street. The existence of newer buildings on the Roman site has made excavation almost impossible, and, although the Forum or market-place has not yet been found, a colossal Basilica or Law Courts was discovered forty years ago. It is partly overlain by the Avenue, but was proved to be 320 feet in length, while its columned nave and the two aisles measured 70 feet in width.

Portions of two columns of its giant portico are in the Museum, while part of the south wall remains in its original position within the garden gate of Watermoor House. A magnificent composite capital is now standing in splendid isolation in the abbey grounds, but most of the other finds made here and elsewhere in Cirencester are now being collected into the Museum which holds, besides the large exhibits already mentioned, a wealth of articles intended for personal use. A medicine stamp, with four prescriptions for eye diseases, belonged once to Atticus, a Corinium oculist, and similar stamps for making medicines have been found at the Roman temple in Lydney Park. Here are ranged the pots and pans, ornaments and intimate possessions of the Roman settlers. Nor should we forget at least one beautiful sepulchral urn of translucent green glass, and the famous palindrome, a secret confession of the Christian faith discovered scratched on the plaster wall of a Corinium house. Only recently has the meaning of this 'word-square' been solved, and all the ingenious translations of

```
R O T A S
O P E R A
T E N E T
A R E P O
S A T O R
```

have now become Paternoster with Alpha and Omega as terminals.

```
            A
            —
            P
            A
            T
            E
            R
A / P A T E R N O S T E R / O
            O
            S
            T
            E
            R
            —
            O
```

Every admirer of ancient Rome will find something to his taste in Cirencester, and will further be impressed by the splendour and culture brought to the friendly Dobuni by the Roman invaders.

Nearly four centuries elapsed, and Corinium still flourished with its public baths and public games until the Roman legions were recalled, and then the Dobuni found that their safety depended more on Imperial strength than on their city walls. The destruction of the town was delayed until 577, when the Britons of Mercia were defeated by the West Saxons at Dyrham, and Corinium was burnt to the ground and sacked.

Two centuries before the Conquest a Prebendal College was founded at Cirencester, and Reinbald, a Norman, was set in charge of it by Edward the Confessor. There was almost certainly a Saxon castle here, but of the pre-Norman history little remains to be said save that in 879 Alfred allowed the defeated Danes to stay in the town for one year before moving off eastwards, and that a general council of nobles was held here under Canute in 1020.

The medieval story of the recovery of the fortunes of Cirencester is best read from a history of the abbey and the parish church. The new town which sprang, as the town arms show, like the phoenix out of the ashes of the old, largely ignored the Roman plan, which was probably almost obliterated. The new streets, Dyer Street, Castle Street, Shoe Lane and Abbot Street speak of a new life here. The castle stood near the western end of Castle Street until Stephen burnt it and razed its outer defences to the ground. Just before the destruction of this fortress, the people of Cirencester witnessed a fine abbey in the building. The town's collegiate church of secular canons was replaced in 1117 by an abbey founded for Austin Canons by Henry I. Upon its consecration fourteen years later Serlo, fourth dean of Salisbury, became the first abbot. The abbey was so richly endowed by the King that during the following centuries the abbot almost completely controlled the trade of the town, in spite of violent opposition from the citizens, and he had the greater right to sit in Parliament and even to coin his own money. John Blake, the last of the line of abbots, and sixteen monks subscribed to the King's supremacy in 1534, and five years later, a week before Christmas Day, the abbey was surrendered to the King's Commissioners. John Blake was awarded a pension of £250 a year and his brethren were equally generously dealt with. And so closed the second phase in the history of Cirencester.

The abbey at its dissolution was valued at £1,051 7s. 1½d., or probably rather more than £200 a week in our money. The buildings were sold on the express understanding that they should be pulled down and the materials carried away. In 1564 Queen Elizabeth sold the site to her physician, Dr. Richard Master, and he used what fragments he could find for his house, which was replaced two hundred years later by the present elegant building, named rather appropriately Abbey House. It stands in beautiful grounds just north of the parish church marking the site of the old abbey buildings. St. Catherine's chapel in the present church has a vaulted roof which was brought from the abbey, and practically the only parts of the original building still standing *in situ* are the charming twelfth-century hospital gateway in Grove Lane and a fragment of walling in Gosditch Street.

The main events at Cirencester from the thirteenth to the seventeenth centuries are recorded in the fabric and memorials of the church of St. John the Evangelist, one of the largest parish churches in the county and larger than three of our cathedrals. Few parish churches are more interesting and fewer still have such an encumbered site, for the beautiful grey pile is almost shut in along the whole of one side with a row of undignified shops. A better but still limited view may be obtained from the green plot to the northwest, where the ancient High Cross now stands. Perhaps in the distant future the benefactors of Cirencester will enclose the noble building with a green space in keeping with the majestic dignity of their fine 'cathedral'.

The present building, 60 yards long and 35 yards wide at its greatest measurements, consists mainly of fifteenth-century work in the Perpendicular style. The original church, built upon the line of the old Ermin Street, dates back to Saxon times, but rebuilding began in the reign of Henry I. The fine tower (*c.* 1400) rises majestically 134 feet to its battlements, which may be reached by a seemingly endless flight of stone stairs. It was intended to carry a spire but proved unequal to the weight and, even before completion, had itself to be supported by flying buttresses. It houses thirteen bells, the thirteenth being used for minor peals and fire alarms, the tenth for curfew in winter and the ninth as the 'Pancake Bell' for shriving or confession on Shrove

Tuesday. Each Saturday morning, following a medieval custom, the bells are lifted one by one.

The mid-fifteenth-century additions to the church include the high-decorated Trinity Chapel, since 1775 the mausoleum of the Bathurst family, the Lady Chapel and the lovely oak screen in the south aisle erected to enclose a chantry chapel by the Garstang family who also started to rebuild the nave. The screen bears their coat of arms and merchant's mark and retains an exceptionally fine doorhandle of ironwork.

The memorials furnish abundant evidence of the flourishing trade of the town in the fifteenth century. Perhaps the three most interesting of the twenty brasses in the church, now collected together in the Trinity and Lady Chapels, are those to Richard Dixton (ob. 1438), to Reginald Spycer (ob. 1442) who lies with his four wives, Margaretta, Margarita, Juliana and Johanna, and to William Prelatte (ob. 1462), a special benefactor to the Trinity Chapel, who is represented in armour with two wives, each in a quaint mitred head-dress.

It was a prosperous Cirencester that in the reign of Henry VIII saw the rebuilding of the nave and probably of all the church west of it. Numerous legacies and donations went to the abbot, who supervised their expenditure. A note of smugness and self-complacency creeps into the early benefactions. In 1457 Henry Garstang 'honoured' the Lady Chapel 'with Worshipfull Vestmentis', and Robert Rycarde, a clothier and one-time bailiff, bequeathed his 'scarlet and crimson gowne' to be used 'to the lawde of God and hym'. Indeed some even go so far as to refer us to the Parish Catalogue of Benefactions. Although later benefactors are more humble-minded, they still have a business itch. In 1535 Hugh Norres tried to encourage the giving of legacies by leaving 'a pall of velvett' to be used free only by benefactors of the parish; a brass in the Trinity

Chapel shows an old man in a gown with a tailor's shears above his head and a dog at his feet with the words:

> 'In Lent by will a sermon he devised
> And yerely precher with a noble prised
> Seven nobles he did give ye poore for to defend
> And 8ol. to XVI men did lend
> In Cisester, Burford, Abington and Tetburie
> Ever to be to them a stocke yerrly
> Phillip Marner who died in the year 1587.'

This bequest is still in existence and the noble is now taken as being worth 6s. 8d.

The graceful cathedral-like nave and clerestories were additions of the early years of the sixteenth century while the unique south porch was erected about 1500 on the site of an older structure. Where there is now one lofty room over the porch there were formerly two, intended no doubt for various meetings of the merchants' guild. The rooms were let for public use for the first time in 1672, and were used as a County Sessions and as a Town Hall until the erection of the new municipal buildings in Castle Street. About a hundred years ago the porch or 'Vice', as the inhabitants call it, was rebuilt stone for stone, and its richly ornamented façade, with its handsome niches and six fine oriel windows, forms a constant source of interest. Not the least attributes of the building are the subdued grey tones of the stonework, and the delicate fan-tracery of the beautifully-groined vaulting.

During the sixteenth century several chapels were built within the church; that to St. Catherine is richly ornamented with arms, knots, and other devices, including the initials of Abbot John Hakebourne, who built it in 1508. It's curious, fan-traceried roof was probably added after the dissolution of the abbey, the chapel being lengthened to receive it. Scattered throughout this great museum of a church may be found numerous brass tablets and beautiful tombs and carvings. Nor should we forget the grand old oak roof nor the fifteenth-century pulpit, a fine example of the 'Gloucestershire wine-glass' type, coloured and decorated with an unusual design of open tracery. The medieval glass has 'suffered from bigots and bungling workmen', but the remaining fragments have been tastefully collected mainly into the great west window of the tower, where it glimmers beautifully but more like a homely patchwork quilt than a cathedral window. The fine fifteenth-century glass of the east window was removed from Siddington Church and commemorates the Langley family of that parish. Lovers of old needlework will, no doubt, admire the framed portions of the blue-green velvet vestments of Ralph Parsons, a chantry priest who was buried here in 1478, and is shown on one of the brasses in full canonicals. The church plate of Cirencester also attracts much attention as it includes the famous 'Boleyn' Cup that belonged to Anne Boleyn when she was Queen, and was given by Queen Elizabeth to Dr. Richard Master, who presented it to this church.

Above the clerestory windows on the north exterior wall of the nave is a related series of quaint gargoyles which are believed to represent the people who took part in a 'Whitsun Ale' or the Whitsuntide festivities common at one time on the Cotswolds. A 'Lord' and 'Lady' were chosen for the occasion, and after a mock reception the 'guests' danced, the girls being bedecked with ribbons. The carvings show the Lord and Lady, together with the steward, purse-bearer, and several musicians and all the mock-officers of the Whitsuntide merry-making. A pictorial key to these gargoyles and most praiseworthy photographs of the great west window hang in the tower space.

Many of the houses of Cirencester are interesting, especially the small cottages with overhanging upper stories in Dollar Street[1], and the stately Renaissance doorway in Gloucester Street. One of the largest and most attractive of the old gabled buildings consists partly of the 'Black Horse Inn' in Castle Street, while the most picturesque is the Hospital of St. John in Spital Gate Lane, which was founded by Henry I (not Henry II as the modern tablet says) for three poor men and three poor women, each to have 20d. weekly.

This alms-house, with its charming pointed archways, was enlarged by Francis Cobham, Bishop of Worcester, in 1317 and has been in use ever since its foundation. The Gothic arches remaining probably formed part of the nave of the chapel, and the walls they support were evidently originally interior structures as they are windowless.

Two other old alms-houses remain near by; the rebuilt leper hospital of St. Laurence in Gloucester Street which was founded in the reign of Edward III, for a master and two poor women; and the restored but ancient-looking hospital of St. Thomas in Thomas Street, founded for four poor weavers by Sir William Nottingham about 1437. The latter building has quaint little windows, and a sadly weatherworn carving over a central doorway opening into a low passage that divides the lower rooms of the two small stone cottages. The old Grammar School was founded in 1464 by John Chedworth, Bishop of Lincoln, but in the early sixteenth century Thomas Ruthall, a Cirencester man, greatly increased its endowments.

Many of the newer houses in Cirencester are splendidly built, and the spacious thoroughfare, where the great fairs take place, and the twisting narrow side streets never appear suburban or dull. Even its exceptional size for a wold town (7,500 pop.) has not dimmed its Cotswold spirit, and close beside it stretches the greatest of all the eighty parks

[1]Dole Hall Street.

on the hills. This vast estate is generously laid open to walkers, and here you may tread in the steps of Alexander Pope and marvel at the beauties, both natural and artificial, of the finest estate in Gloucestershire. The park and woods cover 3,000 acres, and the chief avenue, some fifty yards wide, stretches for nearly five miles between Cirencester and Sapperton. Seven rides, terminating where possible in a view of a church, converged upon the lawn near Pope's Seat, the ornamental, rather classical shelter which the 'hermit of Twickenham' designed for himself. In Oakley Great Park no less than ten rides meet near the centre on rising ground, from where Kemble and Coates church and other villages, when the foliage is not too luxuriant, may be seen. Near here stands Aldred's Hall, a sham ruin, fitted up with black oak and rusty armour, and bearing an inscription over the chimney piece:

> IN MEM ALFREDI
> REL. RESTAUR.
> ANO   D.   1085.

So excellent is the imitation that many 'antiquaries' have been duped, and an old woman is said to have told one of the pleasurably deceived that Lord Bathurst could have built it 200 years older had he wished. Avenues in the park end with statues and masonry; here appears a statue of Queen Anne, and elsewhere a pair of classical buildings, on either side of the Broad Drive, known as the 'Horse Guards' from their resemblance to Whitehall. Of the many lovely avenues, mention should be made of the graceful 'Cathedral Firs' near Overley Lodge, but, as Pope said, 'No words or paintings, or poetry, can give the least image proportionable to it.''

Alexander Pope and Dean Swift were both deeply interested in the designing of the park, and Earl Bathurst was also on intimate terms with Steele, Gay, Prior, Congreve, Arbuthnot and Burke. Burke refers to the Earl as one of 'the most amiable, as he is one of the most fortunate, men of his age'. Sterne made the acquaintance of the aged Earl, and in a letter of 1767 writes: 'This nobleman is a prodigy for at eighty-five he has all the wit and promptness of a man of thirty; a disposition to be pleased, and a power to please others beyond whatever I knew; added to which a man of learning, courtesy, and feeling.'

Earl Bathurst was rewarded for his generosity by living to see his son made Lord Chancellor, and by winning the unstinted regard of his contemporaries. From 1715 to 1725 at least, Pope used to stay at Bathurst Park in summer, and these are said to have been the happiest years of the poet's life. The poet addressed his third *Moral Essay on the Use of Riches* to the Earl, and here is Pope praising his friends' moderation, in spite of great wealth and a pension of £2,000 a year.

> 'Oh teach us, Bathurst, yet unspoiled with wealth,
> That secret rare between the extremes to move
> Of mad good-nature and of mean self-love.'

Lord Bathurst was among the first landowners in Gloucestershire to demonstrate the value of enclosures and of the more modern methods of agriculture. We find a reflection of this interest in the *Moral Essays* (Ep. IV. 1731).

> 'Whose cheerful tenants bless their yearly toil,
> Yet to their Lord owe more than to the soil;
> Whose ample lawns are not ashamed to feed
> The milky heifer and deserving steed;
> Whose rising Forests, not for pride or show,
> But future Buildings, future Navies, grow:'

Seven years before the poet's death in 1744, the demolition of some old buildings near Sapperton, in order to extend the ducal estate, produced the following protest in the *Imitations of Horace* (Bk. II. Ep. II).

> 'Alas, my Bathurst! what will they avail?
> Join Cotswold hills to Sapperton's fair dale,
>
> .   .   .   .
>
> Link towns to towns with avenues of oak,
> Enclose whole downs in walls,—'tis all a joke!
> Inexorable Death shall level all,
> And trees, and stones, and farms, and farmers fall.'

The Earl, who is said to have 'united a sort of French vivacity to English principles', was no doubt also highly amused at Pope's answer to one of their conversations:

> 'Woods are—not to be too prolix—
> Collective bodies of straight sticks.
> It is, my lord, a mere conundrum
> To call things woods for what grows under 'em
> For shrubs, when nothing else at top is,
> Can only constitute a coppice . . .'

Many of the great trees still standing in Cirencester Park were planted by Pope, and visitors walking in its fine glades or coming unexpectedly upon the classical stone structure called by the poet his 'bower' will recall the deformed little writer who looked upon himself as 'the magician appropriated to the place, without whom no mortal can penetrate into the recesses of these sacred shades . . . . the finest wood in England'.

Chapter IX: Painswick

IN 'PAINSWICK PROUD', the most aristocratic of all
Cotswold towns, you will find trimness allied with wealth,
and precision with artistic skill, and, although the pastoral
charm of many of the Cotswold valley villages is missing,
you will see here the most perfect collection of large Cotswold houses in the country. The picturesque antiquity of
the small Gloucestershire cottages is partly replaced by
spacious, well-devised, substantial residences, of faultless
workmanship of two centuries ago.

Many of the old houses in Gloucestershire, with low
ceilings, window frames awry, sloping floors maybe, and
with steps at every door, may delight the person who does
not live in them, but here, at Painswick, are houses comforting to both inhabitant and onlooker, houses such as find
their mention in every volume on English domestic architecture. Painswick should be first viewed from Bull Cross
on that lovely road from Cheltenham through Birdlip to
Stroud; from here a vast panorama lies before us, and the
town is seen sprawling like a great grey spider upon the
tip of the sunny headland between the Washbrook and
Painswick stream. The spire of St. Mary's church gleams
white in the sunshine, for the local stone is perhaps the
whitest of all oolitic rocks, and does not fade into the warm,
rusty shades so common near Stanway.

From Bull Cross the way plunges down to the stream,
and so along Tibbywell Lane into the open space near the
great churchyard. Painswick immediately strikes one as a
considerable town, and I find the population of the parish
is over 2,500 and fifty years ago exceeded 4,000.

The Census Returns of Gloucestershire make amusing if

puzzling reading. The county as a whole has 45,000 more females than males. Cheltenham has 8,000, Minchinhampton 500 and Painswick 400 more women than men, while across the Severn the parishes of Lydney, West Dean, and East Dean are overweighted (to the extent of 2,000) on the male side and could do, at least I suppose they could, with a few hundreds of Cotswold females to make good the discrepancy. This state of affairs may, of course, be due to an ignorance of the facts, and no doubt the numbers would be more evenly maintained were the proposed bridge across the Severn at Aust ever completed.

The streets of Painswick show little sign of this female predominance; one could almost doubt even the old adage —'an Englishman's home is HIS castle'.

Of the antiquity of Painswick much has been written, and those who are interested in the Roman villa discovered at Ifold Farm near Painswick House should consult W. St. Clair Baddeley's authoritative and beautifully illustrated volume, *A Cotteswold Manor* (1929). In *Domesday Book*, Wiche has no less than four mills and a vast wood, five miles long and two broad. About the time of King John, Pain Fitz-John became lord of the manor, and the town henceforth is usually called Painswick. The pre-Tudor history also records a woollen trade at 'Wyke' or 'Wiche' as early as 1440, including yarn and 'iiij stekkyngs of woollen clothe the price xd'.

In July 1535 Henry VIII with his Queen, Anne Boleyn, visited Miserden and Painswick during their month's progress through Gloucestershire which began at Sudeley Castle and ended at Little Sodbury. The Royal pair stayed at the Lodge now Lodge Farm, near Sheepscombe. Early in the nineteenth century large portions of it were destroyed and it became a large farm-house, but more recently it has been carefully restored, and although much of the house is fairly modern, parts of the structure may be as old as the thirteenth century. The east side of the house is heavily buttressed and the present dairy has lovely old moulded windows.

It was probably Sir William Kingston who welcomed the king and his bride to Painswick Lodge. Sir William, a great man of his age, was one of the 'foure sad and ancient knightes' who were placed in charge of the youthful Henry's private chamber when the gay king became a prospective candidate for the Holy Roman Empire. This big bearded man arrested Wolsey near Leicester, and the fallen minister's dying speech was to his serious, kindly warder: 'Well, well, Master Kingston . . . if I had served God as diligently as I have done the King, he would not have given me over in my grey hairs.' Anne Boleyn had good reason to remember Sir William, for shortly after he had taken an official part in her coronation he was acting as her warder in the Tower and led her to the scaffold. No doubt these events were far removed from the minds of either host or Royal visitors during their stay at Painswick in 1535. Sir William coveted dearly Painswick manor, and after much cajoling induced Thomas Cromwell to alienate it to him. Kingston died here almost immediately afterwards and was buried at Painswick in September 1540. The table tomb to him and to Elizabeth his wife still remains inside the church, but their brasses have been replaced by the alabaster effigies of Dr. John Seaman and his wife (ob. 1623) who, clad in rich clothes and facing each other, kneel rather unconcernedly upon the Tudor minister's mortal remains.

Sir Anthony, William Kingston's son, succeeded to the manor, and was in addition created 'Admiral of the Ports' about the Severn, lord of the manors of Flaxley, Newnham, Haresfield, Stanley St. Leonard and Miserden, and Constable of St. Briavel's Castle. Sir Anthony seems to have been a much more sinister and aggressive figure than his father. He was knighted for his good services during the Pilgrimage of Grace (1537) and earned an evil reputation by his ruthless suppression of a rebellion in Cornwall twelve years later. Holinshed related how Sir Anthony dined at his own request with the Mayor of Bodmin who had been busy among the rebels. Before dinner he told the Mayor privately that he wished a pair of gallows to be erected so that an execution could take place at the end of the meal. The unsuspecting Mayor diligently saw to the matter, and after both had had their fill led Sir Anthony to inspect the gallows. 'Thinke you, maister maior, that they be strong inough? Yea, sir, quoth he, that they are. Well, then, said Sir Anthonie, get you even up unto them, for they are provided for you.'

Kingston himself, however, came to an untimely end (1556) when only about thirty-seven years of age. Conspiring with others to put Elizabeth on the throne he was betrayed and taken to be examined at Coberley Court. On his way thence to his trial he died, or more probably committed suicide; some say he plunged with his horse into the Thames at Lechlade and was drowned, possibly while trying to escape. He left little behind him save an evil reputation, but at Miserden, a few miles away, there is an altar tomb with a fine painted effigy of a William Kingston (ob. 1614), sheriff of the county, and these Kingstons were illegitimate issue of Sir Anthony.

In the seventeenth century the clothing trade at Painswick began to flourish exceedingly and there were over two dozen mills on the little streams in the parish. The wealth from the clothing trade led almost naturally to building in the town, and in 1632 the tall needle-like spire was added to the church tower. The present church dates chiefly from the late fifteenth century but has been much altered since, and in 1883 the spire was struck by lightning and crashed down into the chancel. It has a clean, bright interior with few objects of interest, which makes it seem all the more a pity that the clothiers' tombs, one dating back to Elizabeth, should be left for all and sundry to walk upon.

To the south of the church stands the beautiful stone Court House which was completed in about 1600 by Thomas Gardner, a clothier, but Dr. John Seaman added a spacious-looking wing in 1620. The house, which is named from the old Court Orchard, forms a splendid example of a gabled Cotswold House with tall chimneys, lovely terraced gardens, spacious views and many old elms. Yew Tree House and other lovely buildings in the town also belong to this period.

'Painswick Proud' enjoyed in the century following a time of peace and plenty, and many large houses were built. Dover House in Vicarage Street was rebuilt, as also was 'The Falcon Inn', so named from the crest of the Jerninghams, now lords of the manor. The famous bowling-green at the 'Falcon' is only excelled in Gloucestershire by that at the 'Bell Inn', Tewkesbury.

The prosperity of this age is also reflected in the fine tombs in the churchyard which were the work of the Bryans, a local family of stone-masons. Such churchyard tombs as those to John and Richard Poole are unsurpassed in the county for artistic skill. About 1774 the first two dozen yew-trees were planted along the paths of the church-yard, and many have been added in later years, so that now Painswick yews are noted all over England. Tradition has it that only ninety-nine will grow, but there are well over a hundred of them. Most of the trees are clipped into a neatly shaped oval or cone, the bole being left clean for a few feet, but some have grown over the path, forming a compact archway. The yew avenues became the fair weather resort of the ladies and polite inhabitants of the town in the late eighteenth century, while a traditional

'Clipping Feast' is still held in September on the Sunday following the feast of the Nativity of the Virgin (September 19th. O.S.). The ceremony has varied a good deal since 1900 and formerly it did not take place every year.

The bells ring, the 'ting-tang' tolls while a crowd of on-lookers collect in the churchyard. Usually the Sunday school children march in double file to the church, where after a brief service the procession forms. With the town band in the van and closely followed by the clergy and choir with cross and banner and the fire brigade in brass helmets, the whole congregation processes round the churchyard singing a hymn. As the echoes of the last deliberate notes of the band die away, the adults gather together at one end of the church while the children, with chaplets of wild flowers on their heads, 'clip' hands all round the building and facing it trill a hymn. The church now being 'clipped' the whole audience gathers at the foot of the steps leading to the tower door and listens to an address by the vicar. The word 'clipped' is used apparently in the sense that Shakespeare uses it so frequently, as in *Coriolanus: Act 1, Scene 6.*

"O, let me clip ye in arms as sound as when I woo'd.' Yet the word is thought by some to mean 'cleping' or naming and, in any case, the yews, always neatly clipped before the day, have no part in the 'Clipping Feast'.

Little need be said of late Georgian and Victorian Pains-wick. During this period of economic change the first four-horse coach from Stroud to Cheltenham came through the town and the old 'Plough Inn', now the 'Adam and Eve', began to flourish, and the 'Henry VIII' was patriotic-ally changed to the 'Royal William'. To-day Painswick is catering more and more for tourists, but luckily she has kept herself as yet unbedaubed with garish notices and 'ye olde worlde' effects. Due deference was paid to her pride and position when, in 1938, the fine Gloucestershire Exhibition of arts and crafts was held for the first time in Painswick.

I would not have you think that the town is entirely composed of the spacious houses of rich clothiers as there are pretty little streets of more homely dwellings leading down to the streams and the mills. Tibbywell Street is particularly charming, and so is Tibbywell Lane with its stream trickling along the base of a wall from a stone trough called Tibby Well or St. Tabitha's Well. This is recorded as Towy's Well and Tobyes Well during the Tudors when nothing unclean might be washed in its waters, while in Stuart times special mention is made prohibiting the cleansing of swines' entrails here. Vicarage Road includes a charming medley of cottages large and small, unusually gabled and placed at varying angles to each other, while the steep Bisley Street abounds in picturesque stone-tiled houses which stand a-tiptoe on the tops of steps or peep out of alleyways. There is a fine-pointed doorway in this street of the time of Richard II which was made wide enough to take a pack-horse and retains the old marks of the ring for tethering the wool-stapler's horse.

The town retains its iron-stocks (*c.* 1845) which may be found outside the churchyard near to the fine lych-gate, built forty years ago from the timbers of the old belfry.

To the north of Painswick lie the majestic beech woods of Cranham and the great Kimsbury Camp which covers the summit of the Painswick ridge and follows the natural lines of the hill-top. Here well over 900 feet above the sea, surveying a vast expanse of country, is a three-acre rect-angular enclosure, having its southern flank guarded by three successive ramparts, one of which is twenty feet high from the ditch. Three sides are precipitously steep and the fourth is reached only by a very narrow ridge. The ram-parts are now used as hazards on the golf course, and the unskilled golfer faces them to-day with as much trepidation as did the wandering tribes over two thousand years ago.

The park to the east surrounds Paradise House, and the 'Adam and Eve Inn', which is suitably placed in Paradise, named, so they say, by Charles I. We wonder if the Cromwellians would have named the pretty hotel 'The Serpent'.

THE STROUD NEIGHBOURHOOD

SAPPERTON, the gateway to the Golden Valley, is one of the few villages of the Frome to escape the marks of industrialization. At the grey Cotswold village, where the valley turns abruptly northward, the railway tunnels underground and the great canal burrows beneath the beechwoods. The gabled stone houses and barns are perched on a high terrace above the green fields and hawthorns of the deep gorge. Their crescent of pretty, walled gardens pivots naturally upon the small bluff on which, right at the lip of the chasm, the small church has been placed. No other church on the hills is dedicated to Winchcomb's saint, but St. Kenelm should be well pleased with the choice, for no Cotswold church has a more lovely view, and none, surely, a more obvious personality of its own. Its Norman origin has been completely smothered by rebuilding in Queen Anne's reign, which resulted in a squat spire on top of a well-proportioned building.

Much elaborate Jacobean woodwork was also introduced, and the two lovely old pews with linenfold panelling were given as companions carved oak from the old manor-house. The lovely panelling on the seats and the classical figures, startlingly out of place in a church, might be induced to look ecclesiastical in the dim light of painted windows, but here the charming clear green panes make it apparent that the wood work has but the soul of a dining-hall. The squire's ornate pew, bedight with carved figures, and reached by a few steps, would suit his lordship better as head of the festive board rather than leader of the psalm.

The individuality given by the bright sunshine falling upon a wealth of oak is enhanced by the magnificence of the tombs. A well-preserved freestone tomb (1574) of a knight in armour, lying with his head on his helmet, probably commemorates one of the Pooles who owned the manor in Elizabethan days. More remarkable is the finely-coloured monument to Sir Henry Poole (ob. 1616), who kneels in steel breast-plate, full breeches and an ermine-lined mantle, beside his wife, who, to add to the splendour of a ruff, is shown in long ropes of pearls and other jewels. Behind them their sons kneel, while their daughters recline languidly on their elbows. These children probably entertained Charles I when he stayed at the manor in the summer of 1644.

The largest tomb of all, perhaps in the whole county, is that in white marble to Sir Robert Atkyns, who died aged sixty-five in 1711. As in life, we suppose, Sir Robert elegantly reclines with one elbow resting upon a pillow. The right hand, which once sent a sword-thrust through the navel of Sir Christopher Guise, touches lightly his flowing robe, while the left toys with the pages of an open book, no doubt his famous history. He looks severely at you, a gentleman at ease in his great periwig and square-toed buckled shoes, the very Sir Roger de Coverley to sit in the squire's pew. A long inscription surmounted by cherub heads says that the wife erected this 'inadequate' monument to his memory although 'he left behind him one more durable, *The ancient and present state of Glostershire.*' The history is indeed a notable achievement, and Atkyns deserves unstinted credit as the first great historian of the county. Samuel Rudder, who sixty years later improved the work very considerably, was the product of another age; he lies buried in Cirencester church, where a small brass plate says: 'Samuel Rudder of the Town, Printer. Died March 15th, 1801. A man of the strictest honour and the most inflexible integrity. His *History of Gloucestershire* will establish his character as a writer.'

Atkyns was a man of many parts. He represented the county in Parliament, and at fifty was made a judge, only to be dismissed from the Bench largely because his great probity was an embarrassment to the Court. Sir Robert, lord of the manor of Sapperton, retired to Pinbury Park, where he zealously continued his history, which was issued nearly two years after his death. Pinbury Park, a mile up the valley, was long the home of John Masefield, Poet Laureate. The grey, gabled and peaceable house is beautified with much topiary work, and the well-wooded grounds contain an exceptionally tall avenue of yews, called Nun's Walk, on account of the convent which formerly stood here.

A footpath below the church leads down to the valley and to the beechwood beneath which the old canal commences its tunnel of two and a half miles. From Stroud to Lechlade, the waterway stretched for over thirty miles to link up the Severn and the Thames.

The tunnel, which cost a quarter of a million pounds, was opened with much ceremony in 1792; a tremendous triumph of engineering skill for the time, the fine stone arch was duly given an imposing battlemented entrance with two tall monoliths. There was no tow-path, and the men used to lie on their backs and push the barge along with their legs. The donkeys were luckier as they were unharnessed from the barges at the entrance and walked overland to the other end of the tunnel. The 'immense amphitheatre' imagined by Pope dwindled in reality to a widening of the stone arch where, for a short way, the barges might pass, and the men walk to relieve their limbs: you may still see the entrance to-day, a more impressive sight than ever. The canal hereabouts is largely weed-grown, save in the tunnel beyond the entrance, where the long line of murky darkness stretches away underhill unlit now by the

bargeman's lamp, and undisturbed save for the eternal drip-drip of water from the dank roof.

The high lands south of the Golden Valley, known as the Stroudwater Hills, look down from their bleak stone-walled plateau upon the furrow shared by the Frome with the canal and the railway. The occasional factory chimney is limited to the valley floor, and most of the houses cling perilously to terraces on the north bank. Hence it comes about that the high wolds south of the River Frome look away from the Golden Valley and towards Minchinhampton, the nucleus of this large flat-topped tableland. The eastern approach from Sapperton to Hampton is heralded by a solitary round barrow on which five Scots pines stand gaunt against the skyline. The roads from the west cross over the vast, open expanse of Minchinhampton Common, of which over 600 acres have been acquired by the National Trust. Spaciousness and antiquity are the keynotes of the district.

Minchinhampton itself consists of four streets crossing at right angles and terminating outwards in well-spaced new suburbs. It is a considerable town, more pleasant than dignified, and has the grey look of a wold town, but the colour wash upon a fine-pointed stone archway with Tudor roses reminds us that we are leaving the true Cotswold villages. The most striking building is the Market Hall in the High Street, built in 1698 and retaining some of its original timbers. The toll-board tells us that the town-crier charged 6d. for each crying, and we wonder if this custom was observed when Mrs. Siddons enthralled her rural audience here in the days before she became famous.

After the Conquest, the nuns of Caen, in Normandy held Hampton, hence the prefix Monachyn or Minchin. Later Henry V gave the manor to his newly-founded nunnery of Sion in Middlesex, and, at the Dissolution, Henry VIII forced Lord Windsor to take it in lieu of a manor of his

A COTSWOLD SHEPHERD

coveted by the king, and so Lord Windsor unwillingly came into the possession of a vast manor with a large church. This building, dedicated to the Holy Trinity, was much rebuilt a century ago, and retains only a little Early English work. The octagonal tower with a truncated spire belongs to the fourteenth century, but 800 years later it was given the excrescences which make it the most curious spire in Gloucestershire. Around its battlements are crocketed pinnacles above which rises a large central pinnacle so that the whole looks as if an ill wind blew away the upper 50 feet of the spire, and the original top happily settled down on the unscathed base. The south transept, with its many shallow buttresses and highly-pitched, stone-vaulted roof, remains still in the splendour given to it by Sir Robert de la Mere in 1382. He and his wife Matilda occupy a position they so richly deserve within the arcade beneath the lovely traceried window. The church possesses several early Tudor brasses; a citizen in a full-gown is shown with his wife, who wears a wasp-waisted dress; Edward Halyday, a merchant, as the marks tell, has a mantle trimmed with fur; John Hampton and his wife Elyn (ob. 1556), appear clad in shrouds, with their nine children, including a nun, Alice Hampton, who gave the town the use of the Common.

A mile west of Minchinhampton, on the edge of the Common and overlooking the Nailsworth valley, stands Rose Cottage, a modest grey house which has acquired world-wide fame, for here as a guest Mrs. Craik wrote much of *John Halifax, Gentleman* (and here, it is supposed, is the cottage where John first met Ursula March). The spacious common is known in the novel as Enderley Flat.

'Did you never hear of Enderley Flat, the highest table-land in England? Such a fresh, free, breezy spot—how the wind sweeps over it! Shouldn't you like to live on a hill-side, to be at the top of everything, overlooking everything? Well, that's Enderley: the village lies just under the brow of the Flat. . . .'

The route southwards from Minchinhampton to Avening crosses some of the greyest farm-land on the hills divided by rank upon rank of grey stone walls over which the gull wheels as often as the plover in the North Cotswolds.

The village of Avening, which lies well in the shelter of the deep Avon valley, has a history similar to that of its more exposed neighbour; like Minchinhampton, it was Terra Regis at Domesday and eventually came into the hands of Sheppard, the clothier. Its stone houses straggle picturesquely along the clear stream which worked at least two charming mills, and below Avening Court has been dammed to form the lovely Washpound. The church, also dedicated to the Holy Trinity, is older and considerably less repaired than its neighbour's. It stands a little apart from the village and is reached from the north by a steep road over the old bridge near the mill. Three windows, round-headed and deeply-splayed, belonged to the original early Norman church as did also the north doorway which is enriched with twisted shafts and carved capitals. Various windows and the north porch were added in the fourteenth century, but perhaps the most interesting addition was the vaulted chancel roof, in which the tightly packed stones are supported by ribbing. The Norman tower with its vaulted roof was raised by two stages in the century following. The panels of the ancient font, showing much defaced sculptures of the Apostles, are to be seen built into the north wall of the church and the porch. The church has at least two interesting monuments. A stone bust to John Driver (ob. 1687) shows him in a curled wig and an eccentric cravat, while an alabaster monument to Henry Brydges (ob. 1615), the fourth son of Lord Chandos, shows him kneeling devoutly in prayer although as a youth he was a notorious scoundrel. Somehow Henry managed to win the daughter of Samuel Sheppard, the lord of the manor, and obviously benefited much from the alliance.

One praiseworthy custom in Avening parish should not pass unmentioned. Years ago, exactly when or how no one knows, a terrible wild boar was killed between here and Tetbury. The village inns still remember his death by serving pig's face on 'Pig's Face Sunday' in mid-September and on the Monday following. The cheek is cooked and pressed into brawn and then tenderly put into sandwiches. I am told that many an Avening man for a week after a 'square' meal at the 'Nag's Head' or 'New Inn' cannot look a pig in the face without wanting to clap a cottage loaf round it.

THE DURSLEY NEIGHBOURHOOD

'A praty clothing town, well occupied with clothiers' —so Leland about 1540 described most of the villages near Dursley and Wotton while, a century later, King Charles sent Prince Rupert a letter which still hangs on the walls of Lodgemore Mills, which ran as follows:

'Most trusty and entirely beloved Nephew Wee greet you well Whereas We are credibly informed that at Cirencester Stroud Minchinhampton Tetbury Dursley Wotton underedge and Chipping Sudbury great quantities of cloth canvas and Locherame[1] are to be had for supplying ye great necessities Our Souldiers have of Suits. Wee have thought good to advertize you thereof And doe hereby pray you to send a competent party of Horse under ye command of some able person to visit those several places wch lye not farr asunder, and to bring from thence all such cloth, canvasse and Locherame as they shall find there to Cirencester. . . .'

[1] Coarse cloth.

To-day seven factories still make cloths, five of which are on the Frome, one on its tributary the Avon, and the last on the Cam, near Dursley. Walbridge Mill is reputed to date back as a fulling mill over five hundred years, and on the gable wall is the cloth mark carved by a mason in 1645. Here indeed are mills without grime and factory workers living in rural surroundings. The European reputation and connexions built up since the days of Elizabeth have now been extended to all parts of the world. After a visit to the great factory at Cam, one can understand better the superior grandeur of Guardsmen. The huge bales of odorous wool were grown in Australia and in South Africa on the same veldt where our grandfathers fought resplendent in this selfsame broadcloth, and on the wall hangs a telegram urgently requesting cloths for the troops at the Boer War.

Dursley is a busy town with picturesque courtyards, plenty of shops and many fine houses and the most comfortable of inns. Local writers, not content with the pottage of Edward Fox, a subservient Tudor minister, have done their best to show that Shakespeare stayed here for a short while. A Thomas Shakespeare, weaver, was married at Dursley in 1678, and the name was then well known in the neighbourhood. A tomb in the churchyard commemorates Arthur Vizar, gent., who died in 1620 and was probably bailiff in 1612, four years before Shakespeare's death. In *Henry IV, Part II*, Justice Shallow, at his house in Gloucestershire, is beseeched by Davy, his servant, 'to countenance William Visor of Woncot against Clement Perkes of the hill'. It happens that Woncot would fit the corrupted local pronunciation of Woodmancote and the the wolds hereabouts are usually known as 'the hill'. Moreover, one scene of *Richard II* is set in Gloucestershire, obviously upon the hills above Dursley:

'BOLINGBROKE: How far is it, my lord, to Berkeley now?
NORTHUMBERLAND: I am a stranger here in Gloucestershire
These high wild hills and rough uneven ways
Draw out our miles and make them wearisome;

Henry Percy meets his father:

'PERCY: There stands the castle by yon tuft of trees.'

Now it happens that Berkeley Castle stands four miles away
well hidden by trees of its park, and from the east to-day
can only be seen from the huge projection of the Cotswolds
between Dursley and Wotton. This topographical correct-
ness, however, is what one would have expected from
Shakespeare, and what else could he put beside a castle in
a plain but a 'tuft of trees'? If the poet ever knew the so-
called 'Shakespeare's Walk' in the woods above Dursley,
it must have been immediately following the poaching
escapade at Stratford-on-Avon.

The shaven crowns of the hills rising up abruptly south
of Dursley are encircled with magnificent woods of beech,
ash and fir. The walker will enjoy the fine views of the
Severn with the dark forest beyond, and the glimpses of
Dursley tower lying down below, framed in leafy tree-tops.
Plant lovers will notice the Deadly Nightshade, the *Belladonna* of botanists, which, seventy years ago, grew so plen-
tifully here that it was sent by the half-hundredweight to
chemists at Clifton. The turf-capped summit of Nibley
Knoll can only be reached by foot, but the tall gaunt tower
erected to the memory of William Tyndale yields an inspiring view. Breakheart Hill, too, in spite of its name, is a
sylvan dream, especially when shafts of sunlight gleam between the beech boles.

The road which dashes madly up Uley Hill is a mecca
of archæologists, for in this part of Gloucestershire nature

makes lovers of pre-Roman relics work hard for their day's pleasure. Opposite the woods on the summit a green track-way leads to Uley Bury Camp, the finest and most impregnable entrenchment on the Cotswold escarpment. The head of a spur has almost been severed here by two deep, wooded combes, and this isolated peninsula was used by early man as a fortress. The hillock's thirty acres were enclosed already by steep slopes which the inhabitants rendered more formidable by cutting two terraces, each with a wall of earth all round the hill-side. The narrow entrance to the north, the only vulnerable point, was strongly guarded by high mounds, by ramparts and triple ditches. The Romans occupied this fine camp a century later, when they first swept up the Cotswold edge and subdued the tribes in the Vale of Severn.

But Uley boasts a treasure more ancient than its camp. The road-side cottage at the top of the hill and close beside the entrance to the camp, has a notice informing us that the keys to Uley Bury and the requisite candle and matches are to be had within on payment of threepence. This great Long Barrow, prettily known as Hetty Pegler's Tump, lies just off the main road a half-mile to the north. Here in the corner of a ploughed field is an oval mound some 40 yards long by 30 broad at its widest. The lower end has been encroached upon by the plough, but the higher end, which even now is 10 feet high, is securely railed off. Here fine ogee-curved walling leads to the entrance, where a massive flat stone quite 8 feet by 4 feet resting on two uprights forms a portal, once closed with a stone.

Unlike Belas Knap, the portal of the slightly older Uley Bury leads direct to the chambers into which we can crawl. A dank, sepulchral smell comes from the darkness as we open the door, and as the candle burns brighter we find ourselves in a stone gallery over 20 feet long. The height is sufficient to allow us to walk about stooping and we can discern the projecting stones which divide the passage into unequal portions. Two chambers, also formed of huge blocks of stone, may be entered on the left, but the two similar chambers that probably stood on the right hand have been lost. A weird feeling of trespass, of undescribable watchful resentment at our intrusion, enhances the musty, earthy smell of this burial vault of forty centuries ago. Portions of at least twenty-one bodies were found in the chambers, and near the surface was a later burial with three Roman coins. The tribes had brought these skeletons hither to the ancestral pyramid which they built in full view of the Severn where it widens out at the Noose and Frampton Sands. Here at 820 feet above sea-level, where to-day the ash-trees barely creep to the lip of the wind-swept precipice, our ancestors wished their dead to rest.

> The men in yonder humped-up barrow
> Crouched with their mortal joys and sorrow;
> The Roman soldiers sound asleep
> By walls where English weeds slow creep
> (A thousand years are but a span . . .)
> Each dead man was a Gloucestershire man!'

From Uley Bury the road continues above the deep quarry faces and through the beech woods of Frocester Hill to the piedmont grasslands, which are here lined with a string of villages lying midway between the Frome and the escarpment.

The pleasant village of Frocester lies barely a mile from the steep Buckholt Woods and the same distance from the church. Few of the houses are old, as a disastrous fire, common enough in Tudor times when wood and thatch were mostly used in these vale villages, burnt down the old building near the church and the new village grew up farther away from the floodable stream. The manor of

Frocester was granted by Boernulph, King of Mercia, to the college of secular canons of Gloucester, which was later changed into the great Abbey of St. Peter. The abbots of Gloucester needed storage room for the tithes of the district and Abbot John de Gamage (1284–1306) built here the greatest tithe barn in England. It still stands well-preserved and unaltered save for a group of low farm buildings erected along the farmyard side of it. The measurements, 184 feet long, 30 feet wide and 36 feet high to the roof ridge, give little idea of its impressive immensity. The sweeping slope of vast roof is broken only by a tiny dormer which perches upon the thousands upon thousands of Cotswold slates, moss-covered with age. The two large porches on the other side which give easy access to loaded wagons are even wider than the traditional barn door. Within, master beams of English oak divide the vast barn into twelve bays, each of which till take a large rick and dwarf the men working on it. These huge principal beams are built into the walls which, aided by massive exterior buttresses, support the enormous weight of the roof.

Adjoining Abbot John's barn and its busy farmyard, or barnyard rather, is Frocester Court, originally a college, 'a sumptuous residence' belonging to Gloucester Abbey. Sir George Huntley in 1554 rebuilt the house, and twenty years later, according to the parish registers, Queen Elizabeth stayed the night here before progressing to Berkeley Castle. The building, with its 'Cotswold' gables and mullioned windows and skilfully-faced stonework, recalls the masonic skill of Chipping Campden. The charming gate-house is also of cut stone except for a picturesque extension of half-timber that bears quaint gables on each of its faces and actually surmounts the entrance arch.

CHAPTER XI: *Wotton-under-Edge*

THE HISTORY of Wotton-under-Edge begins with a blaze, but not of glory, for in the reign of King John the town was utterly destroyed by fire. The new and probably less congested settlement grew up slightly nearer the hills and Henry III granted to Maurice, Lord Berkeley, a market, fair, and certain municipal rights. Soon 'Wooltoun-under-Ridge', as it was called locally, derived much benefit from its markets and also from the soft waters of Tyley Bottom. The figure of a woolsack was placed in the town arms, and by Tudor times Wotton had grown into a 'praty Market Towne, welle occupyed with Clothiars, havinge one faire longe strete'. The town was governed by a mayor who was chosen annually at the court leet of the Earl of Berkeley. This position of mayor was for some reason or another much disliked by the townspeople, and in 1639 two men declined the honour of accepting it, and thereupon suffered a fine of £10 and £6 13s. 4d. respectively, a difference based, I suppose, on the excuses proffered. Fifty years later another citizen preferred to pay £10 rather than become the mayor of this flourishing cloth-making community. To-day, now that the corporation is extinct, the old silver mace has been fashioned into a loving-cup. During the nineteenth century Wotton was off the track of the great turnpike roads and found no compensation for the loss of its wool trade. At the present time, however, it is near the manufacturing centres of the Vale of Berkeley and is prosperous enough without enduring the bustle of Dursley. High fantastic knolls shelter Wotton from cold north winds and the town is built on an eminence which makes its street usually narrow and steep, although occasionally, where the roadway widens, it almost assumes that spaciousness typical of Cotswold towns. The medley of architectural styles, and especially the great variety of chimneys and roofs, the numerous alleyways and gabled houses combine to give a picturesque and pleasing appearance.

The alms-houses in Church Street, built at the expense of Hugh Perry, an alderman of London in 1632, possess a plain, dignified front with symmetrical mullioned windows, two set under each of the six gables that would be appreciated even in Chipping Campden.

Adjoining the churchyard stands Court House, which dates mainly from Tudor times and may be recognized by the old pieces of carved stonework built into it. Lisle House, the greatest building of ancient Wotton, has disappeared save for the remaining portion of the 'Town Wall'. This massive fortress-like structure was the occasional residence of the Lisle branch of the Berkeley family. The story goes that on the death of Thomas, Lord Berkeley, his daughter, the wife of Richard Beauchamp, Earl of Warwick, induced her husband illegally to seize and to hold Berkeley Castle. The feud thus commenced between the Berkeleys and the Lisles of Wotton culminated fifty years later in the pitched battle of Nibley Green, some two miles to the north-west, where, in 1470, William Lord Berkeley and his retainers put to rout Lord Lisle's men. Lord Lisle himself was shot dead by a forest archer and his great house at Wotton-under-Edge was sacked. His body was carried to Painswick and buried under the altar tomb which was later appropriated by Lady Kingston for her use.

Wotton's connexions with the Beauchamp family are still remembered in its right to nominate resident pensioners to the Earl of Leicester's Hospital at Warwick, but the great family of Berkeley left here a more lasting memorial. In 1384 Dame Katherine Berkeley founded in Wotton the first free Grammar School in England. 'Considering that the desire of many who wish to learn grammar, which is the foundation of all other liberal arts, is often frustrated through poverty,' she obtained the necessary licence from Richard II and her school is still flourishing.

In Orchard Street a house bears a tablet inscribed to the effect that Isaac Pitman worked here at inventing shorthand. Pitman came to Wotton as a schoolmaster in 1836, and his invention was largely perfected at this house where he composed his first published treatise *Stenographic Sound Hand*.

The church of St. Mary is a spacious, graceful building surrounded by a most pleasant churchyard. After the great fire in the reign of King John it was rebuilt, but few traces of this church remain owing to extensive rebuilding about 1400 in the Decorated style. The tall tower, with its restrained decorations, has much ball-flower ornamentation on the two lower stages while the two upper stages are of later date. The elegance of its embattled exterior is matched by an equally imposing interior with fine Early English arcades and a handsome fifteenth-century clerestory. The nineteenth-century restorers worked here with great energy and at least they might have spared us the white plaster roof. There are two charming windows in the east end and several capitals carved with queer faces and delicate foliage. A brass matrix on a tomb slab depicting a figure kneeling at the Cross commemorates Richard de Wotton, a rector here in the early fourteenth century. The fine marble tomb of Thomas, fifth Baron Berkeley (1417), bears splendid brasses to him and to Margaret his wife; they are shown life-size, she in a flowing gown with a dog at her feet, he clad in close-fitting plate armour, with a peaked cap and a gorget adorned with four exquisite figures of mermaids a decoration said to be unique to Wotton.

The district round Wotton-under-Edge is varied both as regards scenery and architecture. A mile to the south in the busy manufacturing centre of Kingswood the remains of a Cistercian abbey, though scanty, are well worth a visit.

The hills lying to the west of Wotton are incised by two great valleys, Tyley Bottom, accessible only to walkers, and Ozleworth Bottom, which could not be recommended to motoring novices. The Ozleworth valley is so charming and picturesque that almost all its sunny bank has been seized upon by three large estates.

A few miles to the west is Beverstone, a tiny village with typical Cotswold cottages, stone-built, and with gabled stone-slated porches, many of them creeper-clad, and a great pleasure to look at. The castle and castle farm share the upper half of the village with the church and the rectory. Beverstone Castle was built at the beginning of the eleventh century to command the narrow crossing of the Cotswolds near Tetbury, but in later centuries it also guarded the borders of the great Berkeley estate. In 1051 Earl Godwin and his sons, Sweyn, Earl of Gloucester, and Harold, used the castle as their base in an attempt to force Edward the Confessor to dismiss his Norman favourites. The king, overawed by the strength of their armies quartered in Uley Bury Camp, yielded, but later the rebels were outlawed for a year, all except Sweyn, who forfeited Beverstone Castle to the Crown. Soon after Domesday Survey, William granted it to 'Rogerus de Berkele', Lord of Dursley, and with the Berkeleys it remained until 1145 when Stephen took and destroyed it. Eventually the property came to Maurice de Gaunt, Lord Berkeley, who rebuilt the barbican in 1225, apparently without the consent of Henry III. About 1360 the castle was greatly enlarged and strengthened by Thomas, Lord Berkeley, with ransom money paid by French prisoners taken at Poictiers. As Leland says, 'After Poyters Lord Berkele buildid the Castell of Beverstane thoroughly, a Pile at that time very preaty'. During the Civil War the castle was held for Charles I until 1644 when Colonel Massie besieged it with nearly 400 men and several guns. Colonel Oglethorpe, its commander, was taken prisoner by the Parliamentarians when, so it is said, he was courting a young woman at a farm-house near by. Then the garrison soon surrendered, having been given 'faire quarter and true performance'.

In 1691 a disastrous fire gutted the magnificent banqueting hall which had been built within the curtain walls, and about eighty years later only one of the four great towers was left standing. Since then the castle was used as a quarry for building materials for the great farm-house and its outbuildings. To-day, however, enough remains to give us an adequate idea of the original lay-out and of the splendour of Lord Berkeley's rebuilding. The ruin is of great beauty, being both graceful and massive and standing among trim gardens shaded by beeches and walnut trees. Entering by the undercroft where the castle's food supply was stored, we pass, by a wincing stairway, into the dining-hall from which a narrow entrance communicated with a secret dungeon below. The great Norman tower is now cleared of ivy and contains much of interest. The first floor, originally the soldiers' room, served as a garrison chapel in the fifteenth century and has a fine groined roof, sedilia and piscina. A stone staircase winds up from it to the original living-rooms, including the priest's chamber, with a canopied piscina and squints from adjacent apartments. Steps lead up 76 feet to the battlements that command extensive views of the Cotswolds, while down below may be seen the remaining portions of the old moat which once encircled the building. Some of the outer walls are still standing as well as large parts of the fourteenth-century gate-house.

The small church of St. Mary stands almost hidden by trees at the rear of the castle. The original Norman church was restored by Thomas, Lord Berkeley, in 1361, no doubt again *ex spoliis Gallorum*, but he spared the three pillars of the fine south arcade and a doorway with foliage capitals. The chancel retains two fine Decorated windows with ball-flower mouldings and graceful tracery as well as its ancient roof. It communicates with the fourteenth-century chapel by a curious passage under the rood loft stair which also forms a squint. The rood screen of somewhat later date has been repaired and restored after its stout pillars and canopied fan-vaulting had served for a while as a pergola in the rectory garden. The pulpit, of Perpendicular age, is made of stone, carefully panelled and carved with foliage and flowers. Another interesting piece of carving may be seen on the exterior of the embattled tower where a carved panel, now much worn, depicts what appears to be a figure carrying a cross in one hand and raising the other in blessing.

CHAPTER XII: *The Vale of Berkeley*

THORNBURY is queen of the Vale. With nearly 3,000 inhabitants, or as many as Iron Acton and Yate combined, it has assumed the business of a town and retained the friendliness of a village. Its wide streets are lined with a pleasing and attractive medley of houses, few very large, but all well-preserved. Each man seems to sit under his own fig-tree, and quite rightly too, for Thornbury folk have been waiting three hundred years for the promised land. Much of the parish nearest to the Severn is liable to floods where the inhabitants used to gather wild asparagus and 'purslain' for their tables.

The lower part has always had a reputation for unhealthiness, and Rudder, who perhaps never experienced the pangs of lumbago, sceptically quotes Dr. Franklin. 'It seems strange that a man, whose body is composed in great part of moist fluids . . . who can swallow quantities of water and small beer daily without inconvenience, should fancy that a little more or less moisture in the air should be of such importance. . . .' The people of Thornbury, however, preferred to take no risks and placed their houses a few dozen feet above the marshes over which they can look to see the state of the tide in the Severn. The market was worth twenty shillings at Domesday, but the prosperity brought in following centuries by the clothing trade was destined to be short-lived. Leland tells us that the town is 'set almoste upon an equalle grounde, beinge large to the proportion of the letter Y, havinge first one long strete, and two hornes goyne out of it. There hathe been good clothing in Thornebyry, but now Idenes much reynithe there!' Yet in 1642 it was a woollen-draper, William White, who founded the Gram-

mar School, and a century later a little spinning still remained. The cruellest blow was the loss of the flying-coach traffic, for the new Gloucester to Bristol turnpike took a short cut east of the town whereas the previous road ran straight through it. But Thornbury's fortunes returned when the railway came from Yate, and above all when the motor-coaches found an assured welcome here.

Thornbury has interesting historical connexions. It probably possessed a castle in the reign of Edward II or III the Earls of Gloucester being the owners, but the castle seen from the churchyard to-day was begun on the site of the old, by Edward Strafford, third Duke of Buckingham. The Duke had permission from Henry VIII in 1510 to impark 1,000 acres within his lordship of Thornbury, and, according to Leland, 'the inhabytaunts cursyd the Duke for the lands so inclosyd'. The level park was laid out two miles from the Severn and a noble castle was started. Beneath the arms on the gateway still standing is the inscription: 'Thys gate was begon in the yere of our Lorde God MDXI, the ij yere of the Reyne of Kynge Henri the VIII by me Edw. Duc of Bukkyngham, Erll of Herforde, Stafforde, and Northampton'. The great embattled tower of smooth-faced freestone is dated 1514, and seven years later when the Duke was executed the building was still unfinished. The main hall and chapel have disappeared but the rest of the fabric was considerably improved and restored about a century ago. Much of the exterior can be seen from the churchyard, which is fenced on one side by a fine embattled wall, spaced with lovely mullioned bay windows and beautified with green creeper. Above this curtilage wall may be seen parts of the stately west front which is 70 yards long and would have been high in proportion had the founder lived. The graceful south tower is 67 feet high and the central towers over the gateway would have been on a like scale. The late Perpendicular

¹ THE IMPERIAL GARDENS, CHELTENHAM

style and the smooth-faced stonework give the castle a grace and loveliness which almost belie its defensive qualities. The grim, so-far-but-no-farther impregnability of the Norman mind has been replaced by the Tudor idea of 'stone walls do not a prison make'. The richness of the brick chimneys, the beautiful oriel windows, the length of the battlements and the pleasant spaciousness of the design can be appreciated at a glance. Here Henry VIII and Anne Boleyn stayed for ten days in the August of 1535 when the plague was raging at Bristol.

The canny representatives of the Bristol Council came to Thornbury Castle and gave the King ten fat oxen and forty sheep towards his hospitality, and to Queen Anne one cup containing a hundred gold marks, 'hir grace then promysing to demand or have noon other gifte but oonly that if hir said grace wold resort to this said towne at any tyme thereafter'.

The famous Stafford knot is to be seen on a building near an iron pump in the High Street and several times on the headings of the windows of the church. The stately, spacious church of St. Mary stands facing a green square which is shaded by a wych elm, so gigantic that it has twisted its bole in its efforts to grow greater. The lofty chancel is Decorated work of about 1340 and includes a very fine east window. The font, with a foliage pattern, is slightly earlier; the rest of the church is Perpendicular of about 1500. The elegant tower, 130 feet high to the top of the pinnacles, has pierced battlements which will probably appear to many visitors to be rather over-decorated in contrast with the simple, lichen-covered lower stage, where the windows have been blocked. The church contains no monuments of any antiquity, but the churchyard wall on the castle side is worth a whole choir full of marble cherubim and a library of complacent verses.

The same road which Mr. Pickwick followed leads us to

Berkeley Heath where, at the 'Old Bell', now 'The Chestnuts', the chaise carrying him and his friends stopped to change horses while the passengers lunched heartily at 11.30 in the morning.

Berkeley itself lies two miles to the west. Few names occur more frequently in Gloucestershire history or few, for that matter, in England's cavalcade of great knights. The name conjures up a picture of valour, murder, remote antiquity. Perhaps that is why the town seems so dull and sleepy and out-of-tune with its past. The animated streets of Thornbury come to mind as we notice the medieval somnolence, the lackadaisical air of the town. Leland aptly describes Berkeley as 'no great Thinge, but standyth well and in very good soyle', so perhaps he too expected a really 'great Thinge'.

Here, where the great Cotswold bastion of Stinchcombe Hill projects to within four miles of the Severn, was the place made by nature to control routes to the north and south. A small plateau some fifty feet above the floodable meadows of the little Avon river, provided a site for the necessary castle, and under its protection the town proceeded to flourish. The castle had the southern extremity of the hillock, the church neighboured it close, and the freetown spread out to the north. Berkeley sent a member to Edward I's parliament, and ranks with Gloucester, Bristol, Dursley and Newnham as the most ancient boroughs in the county. The Avon carried shipping on which the Mayor charged twopence a load, and the Lord in his castle could number scores of retainers, but the clothing trade never grew great here as at Dursley and Wotton, and in 1608 there were only eleven weavers and one fuller. A century later the clothing trade had gone, but the one street of 'mean buildings' was still famous for the best cheese in the kingdom. On August Bank Holiday, when the Berkeley Hunt Agricultural Society holds its annual show, you may still see the great cheeses, the huge Double Gloucesters, which look big enough to feed a baronial army. Rudder says there were over 1,800 people at Berkeley in his day, but these seem to have dwindled away at a remarkable rate, for in 1921 the inhabitants numbered less than 800 and to-day less than 700 —a size which, in Gloucestershire, is usually neither big enough to give a lively appearance nor small enough to induce the rural charm of a village. In winter the folk are rung to supper and to bed by the curfew at eight, and a kindly benefactor with considerable insight has given them a well-endowed and voluminous library.

The pleasant footpath which traverses the damp meadows gives a full view of the great pile of buildings massed above the terraces with their small trees. Leland's words come to mind: 'no great Thinge. Divers Towres be in the Compasse of it. The Warde of the first Gate is mitely strong, and a Bridge over a Dyche to it.' There lies the great castle, a jungle of massive walls, stout buttresses, towers and tall chimneys. Something seems lacking. Defensive strength is there, but no great semblance of majesty. Perhaps however, we become too used to looking at ruinous castles, at the roofless glories of Kenilworth and Chepstow, complete and whole in the imagination, so that we have no mind to look at Berkeley which, although one of the few buildings of its kind intact in England, is like a lion tamed.

The manor of Berkeley was given by the Conqueror to Roger de Berkeley of Dursley. The third Roger de Berkeley espoused Stephen's cause and lost the estates which were subsequently conferred on Robert Fitz-Hardinge, a wealthy citizen of Bristol. This Robert rebuilt the castle about the year 1154, and it remains in his family to-day. The castle was separated from the town by a very deep moat which, since 1587, has been crossed by a permanent bridge. The meadows in which we are sitting formed a morass in medieval times, and could always be flooded, a fact remembered no doubt on the nearby Floodgates Farm.

Of the great lords of Berkeley a library could be written. Their lives are part of English history. Not least among them was Lord Thomas, who died in 1361, to whom Edward II was sent as a prisoner in the spring of 1327. Thomas de Gournay and John Maltravers were the warders, but, in spite of their harsh treatment, the King lived:

'Gurney, I wonder the King dies not,
 Being in a vault up to the knees in water,
 To which the channels of the castle run,
 From whence a damp continually upriseth,
 That were enough to poison any man . . .'

Eventually young Mortimer sent the death warrant:

'This letter, written by a friend of ours,
 Contains his death, yet bids them save his life
 "*Edwardum occidere nolite timere bonum est.*
 Fear not to kill the king, 'tis good he die."
 But read it thus and that's another sense:
 "*Edwardum occidere nolite timere bonus est.*
 Kill not the king, 'tis good to fear the worst." '

Edward was murdered on September 21st in such a way that no exterior marks of violence could be seen. 'His crye', says Holinshed, 'did move many within the castell and town of Berkelie to compassion, plainly hearing him utter a waileful noise, as the tormentors were about to murder him: so that dyvers beings awakened thereby (as they themselves confessed) prayed heartilie to God to receive his soul, when they understood by his crie what the matter ment.'

After several abbeys had refused the body, the Abbot of

Gloucester came in procession to Berkeley, and received his reward when the people of England showed great devotion to the shrine of the murdered King.

The church at Berkeley lies between the castle and town. If the building possessed a tower it would almost have overlooked the castle courtyard, which may explain why the tower has been kept fifty yards away in the corner of the churchyard farthest from the moat. The present tower was built about 1753, but seems to be a faithful copy of a much earlier one. The church, which looks more like a glorious college chapel, is beautiful in spite of the absence of a dignifying tower, and its lichen-covered west front has no equal in this part of Gloucestershire. The noble doorway is surmounted by an Early English window of five graceful lancets with detached marble shafts, and the whole front is flanked by powerful buttresses which rise to a gable once steeply pitched and now, unfortunately, much flattened. The great door shows the holes bored in it to take the muskets of the Cromwellian troopers.

The greater part of the present church was built by Robert Fitz-Hardinge, first Baron of Berkeley, and by his immediate successors. The interior is remarkable for the singularly graceful arcades of the nave, with delicately foliated caps of the late thirteenth century. It will be noticed that some of the clustered pillars have stone seats around them, and that the clerestory has been given windows only on the south side. The north porch, with a fine vaulted roof and the aisles are of a century later, while the timber roof the priest's room above the porch and the Berkeley chapel were added in the fifteenth century. The old stone rood-screen was heavily traceried in the seventeenth century, and the wooden cornice holds nearly two dozen emblazoned shields of the families connected by marriage with the Berkeleys. The considerable traces of medieval mural paintings include a portion of a 'Doom' over the chancel arch, a fine Tudor rose and grotesque patterns in red and black around the windows.

The church contains many fine monuments to its great benefactors. The table tomb in the nave, with fine alabaster effigies of Thomas, eighth Lord Berkeley (ob. 1361), and Katherine, his second wife, has miniature battlements round its edge. This is the Lord Berkeley who was given the custody of the unlucky Edward II. His son, Maurice de Berkeley, was one of the two prisoners said to have been captured by the French at Poictiers. The English took nearly 2,000 knights for ransom, but Maurice de Berkeley, who must have put discretion long after valour, was pierced through both thighs. Froissart says that his ransom was 6,000 nobles, a tremendous sum in those days, and his capturer, Jean de Helennes, was undoubtedly the only Frenchman who became rich at Poictiers *ex spoliis Britannorum.*

The great east window, filled with pictures of Christ healing the sick, commemorates Dr. Jenner, who lies in the chancel. Edward Jenner was born at the vicarage here in 1749, and from his youth upwards trained to become a surgeon. His hut in the vicarage garden is a peculiar structure which, to anyone visiting it for the first time, especially as a patient, would seem black magic enough. A thick thatch roof surmounts a tiny hut composed of gnarled and knotted elm and thick ivy stems with plaster between. It is a witch's hovel with wooden door, groined vaulting and roofing all of contorted wych elm, and even the quaint fire-place bordered with gnarled wooden excrescences. In this curious hut Dr. Jenner conducted his experiments, and here the first person in the country was vaccinated.

North of Berkeley, Frampton is the nearest village to the Severn, and before the canal was cut used to have the tide, so they say, almost up to the churchyard. The charming village consists of two rows of detached houses separated by a broad straight road and a very wide green. Rosamund's Green covers twenty-two acres, and about its shaven lawn horses wander beneath the shade of the chestnut trees, while geese and ducks migrate for spasmodic wettings in one or other of the three large ponds. Outside the 'Bell Inn' a cricket pitch has been carefully prepared, while the children at play find ample space for other pitches at the far end of the green. The houses and cottages are undefiled with signs of buying and selling. Red tiles, Cotswold slates, brick, half-timbers and thatch all find a place here in a picturesque medley. One group of thatched cottages with switch-backed, gabled roofs and gardens merry with fruit-trees and dahlias seems the embodiment of rustic felicity. The old manor, now a farm, is a splendid example of a mid-fifteenth-century house. Stone below and half-timber above, its black and white beauty may be seen from the roadway. The stone roof, tall chimneys and pointed gables, the large timbered barn and the old square dovecot combine to make an attractive picture. On the opposite side of the green, standing on the site of the ancient family mansion of the Cliffords, is the large Court, a beautiful Palladian building erected about 1732 by Richard Clutterbuck from the designs of Vanbrugh. Tradition tells that Rosamund de Clifford, the Fair Rosamund, mistress of Henry II and mother of William Espee, Earl of Salisbury, was born here. The belief is borne out by the fact that the Cliffords held this manor in the eleventh century, and later Walter de Clifford gave a mill at Frampton to the nunnery at Godstow. On her death in 1177 she was buried in the choir of the nunnery at Godstow, and her epitaph tells the passer-by that '*Rosa Mundi*' not '*Rosamunda*' lies below.

At the Court the tall tower-like summer-house, which may be seen above the trees, looks down on a statue of Rosamund, who stands gracefully at the side of a large lily pond. The local people tell of a secret passage from here to the manor-house, but this belief has certainly originated since 1740, when Richard Clutterbuck, a descendant of the Cliffords, drained the morass on Rosamund's Green. Years later the village story-tellers no doubt heard of the finding of an underground drain, and it inevitably became a secret passage for the fair Rosamund. The same Richard Clutterbuck threw up the fine straight road, and 'freed the people from the ague'.

The section of the village near to the church consists mainly of old, thatched, half-timbered cottages and picturesque barns, one of which has its upper story of plaited wattle. The tower of the church is well known to sailors and bargees on the canal, and the field facing it is said anciently to have been a ship-building port. The neat, handsome church of St. Mary was consecrated in 1315 and contains much Decorated and later Perpendicular work. The leaden font, however, is Norman, and its decorations of an arcade, with seated figures alternating with foliated scrolls, show that it was cast in the same mould as half a dozen others in the county. The north aisle holds two effigied tombs as well as memorials to three other Cliffords. The stone effigy of a knight shows a Clifford in mail armour, with surcoat and shield; near by is a woman of about the same date (1310) in a wimple and flowing gown.

CHAPTER XIII: Cheltenham Spa

> 'I'm homesick for my hills again,
> My hills again,
> To see above the Severn plain
> Unscabbarded against the sky
> The blue high blade of Cotswold lie.'
> —F. W. HARVEY, *Flanders*, 1915.

WHERE THE Chelt flows down off the Cotswolds to join the Severn at the swampy Hasfield Ham, it forms with the Coln near Andoversford a gap so conveniently situated midway down the length of the hills that a town to command it was a natural addition. To the north, the higher gap behind Winchcomb was an important route-way at least fifteen hundred years before the one behind Cheltenham was utilized much, and for centuries it was 'Cheltenham near Winchcomb'. To-day the Winchcomb gap is unimportant, and the town had begun to decay two centuries before Cheltenham discovered its mineral waters. But the presence of medicinal springs would have had no more lasting effect on the fortunes of Cheltenham than that of a saint at Winchcomb had not modern route-ways converged upon the town. Now it is 'Winchcomb near Cheltenham', for through the Chelt gap come a main road from London to Gloucester and the only railway across the North Cotswolds.

Cheltenham has a splendid site, sheltered to the north and east by the high protecting wall of the escarpment, and lying open to the warm winds from the Severn Plain on the south and west. To come upon Cheltenham from Cleeve Cloud or the hills above Charlton Kings is a very pleasant way of acquainting oneself with the town which spreads out below one's feet, a beautiful but somehow a defenceless thing. Looking down at the star-like cluster of tall spires and houses you realize something within you of the superiority over the men of the vale which the hill men have always felt.

Cheltenham on closer view has a green, pleasant, open appearance, with cheerful-looking streets, and especially in the High Street and Promenade a dignified beauty equalled by very few towns of its size. There is nothing tawdry or mean in this aristocratic Spa, but on the other hand, neither is there anything old or picturesque, although the town and the parish church of St. Mary belie their ancient foundation. In the reign of Edward the Confessor 'Chintinham' paid the King £9 in rent and 3,000 loaves for his dogs, but at the date of the Domesday Survey 16s. was paid in lieu of bread and £20 together with 20 cows and 20 hogs in taxes.

During the reign of Henry I the church passed into the hands of the abbey at Cirencester, and remained there until the Dissolution when, together with the town, it reverted to the Crown and was reduced to poverty. Leland briefly dismisses the place as 'a long town having a market', and there were very few occurrences of great note in Cheltenham during the sixteenth and seventeenth centuries. The tobacco plantations of 1565 were among the first on English soil and are probably related to the fact that Sir Walter Raleigh's descendants had married into the family at Sandywell Park, near Dowdeswell. In 1576 Mr. Richard Pates founded a Grammar School here, and it is said that Queen Elizabeth visited the school and gave Pates part of the property with which he endowed it. The only building which reflects the early history of the town is the church of St. Mary which was mentioned as early as 773. The oldest parts of the present church, the base of the tower and part of the nave wall, date back to about 1150, while a priest's door and part of the tower are Early English. The fine piscina with statuettes, now unfortunately much mutilated, the north porch with Tudor Roses on the bosses and the remarkable rose window with a circumference of 45 feet are all late Decorated. Around these older fragments the present building, a medley of architectural styles, has grown. The church contains some interesting memorials, among which are fine brass portraits of Sir William Greville (d. 1513) and his wife, their three sons and three daughters in the north porch. A long epitaph to Captain Skillicorne (d. 1763) declares that 'he could do business in seven tongues: he was of great regularity and probity: and so temperate as never to have been once intoxicated'. There is a more amusing elegy in the church-yard which reads:

'Here I lies with my two daughters
 All along of drinking Cheltenham waters
 If only we'd stuck to Epsom salts
 We shouldn't be lying in these here vaults.'

With these memorials St. Mary's Church has brought us to the begining of modern Cheltenham, which owes much to Captain Skillicorne and the health-giving nature of its waters. In 1716 Cheltenham was a collection of small houses grouped on either side of the little street down the centre of which ran the tiny River Chelt, crossed only by stepping-stones. In this year a saline spring was discovered owing to the pigeons which flocked to a certain field to peck up the salt left after evaporation by the sun. Mr. Mason bought the spring and built a shed over it, railed an area round it and laid out a bowling-green. The water was sold as medicine until 1738, when Captain Skillicorne, who had married Mason's daughter, built a small pump-room over the spring. From these humble beginnings Cheltenham became a spa.

Within a few years Captain Skillicorne had built an upper and lower walk so that the springs were reached by a pleasant way through the churchyard, under an avenue of limes and across orchard and gardens, over the Chelt to a beautiful walk of great elms leading to the domed pump-room. There were offices and a library on the right of the entrance, while to the left was the breakfasting room. Before long the water was reputed to be the best purging water in England, 'limpid, a little brackish and nauseously bitter. The dose is from 1 pint to 3 or 4 nor is it ever attended with gripes, but creates a keen appetite. It has been used with success in the gravel, and will cure old scorbutick humours, St. Anthony's fire, and strumous inflammations of the eyes. ' You may, if you wish, find by experiment that 'it will curdle with soap, and lets fall a white glutinous sediment, with the solution of salt of tartar and the spirit of sal-ammoniac. It will ferment with oil of vitriol, spirit of salt and vinegar; beef and mutton boiled therein will become of a pale red, and it turns a deep green with syrup of violets.' Indeed, everything seems to point to the excellency of the water, and Dr. Lucas has seen old men drink Cheltenham water by the quart without any ill-effects '. . . they had drank them on such days and holidays for upwards of thirty year . . . they reckoned it wholesome to clean their bodies, and they had no rule, but to drink till the water passed clean through them.'

The chief drawback to the fame of the Spa was the great difficulty of communication, and visitors from London had to alight from the Gloucester coach at Frogmill and then were accommodated with good post-chaises at a small expense. In 1736 Sir Edward Seymour could find no lodgings in the town and was obliged to send to Gloucester for a coach to fetch him away. Two years later the first coaches ran from Cheltenham to London 'if God permitted' in the short space of three days. Before the end of the century the roads leading to the town had been improved considerably and visitors arrived in growing numbers including Handel, Dr. Samuel Johnson and John Wesley, on several occasions. In 1780 there were nearly four hundred visitors, and Simon Moreau of Bath was appointed M.C. for Cheltenham. As it was said:

> 'Lately an ape in the shape of a beau,
> By the outlandish name of Monsieur M . . . u
> Has officiously come at the balls to preside,
> To preserve etiquette and pay homage to pride.'

The spacious street, however, was 'encumbered' with old 'coarse buildings' on stone pillars called the Corn Market and Butter Cross, and below them was a prison with a motto over the entrance: 'Do well and fear not'. These were ruthlessly demolished in 1786 and foot pavements, then a rarity in England, were built, and 120 lamps erected for lighting the streets in autumn and winter, except when the moon rose. It will be noticed that Cheltenham was fortunate in growing at a time when town-planning was first being followed in England and when the style of domestic architecture was both palatial and dignified.

Cheltenham became fashionable with the visit of George III and the Royal family in 1788, when the Court was removed to Bays Hill Lodge from the 12th of July until August 16th. Their Majesties were greeted with bells and music and general illuminations, and on the day following his arrival the King was at the well soon after six o'clock in the morning. To commemorate the King's recovery M. Moreau had a medal struck showing the King on one side and Cheltenham well on the other. The town now became very popular and the ceremonies assumed the elaborate etiquette and pomp of those at Bath. A ball took place on Monday and Friday and card-playing on the other week-days. The rules at the assembly room left nothing to chance, ladies were 'allowed to change their partner every two dances', while gentlemen were not 'admitted to the balls in boots or half-boots'. In 1802 when the first of many chalybeate springs was discovered there were over 2,000 visitors a year. At that time Dr. Jenner was the only resident physician, whereas forty years later there were twenty physicians, thirty surgeons and nearly forty chemists. Just before the visit of the Duke of Wellington at Cambray House in 1816 it was written: 'Few scenes are more animated and inspiring than the Montpellier promenade, on a fine summer morning. The presence of the lovely, the titled and the fashionable, as they parade up and down the grand walk to the sound of music, and breathing an atmosphere of sunshine and health, present a scene of lively loveliness, unsurpassed by . . . the fairy elysiums of a Spenser; for here indeed it may truly be said that "ladies eyes rain influence".'

Cobbett in his *Rural Rides* thought the place 'a resort of the lame and the lazy, the gormandizing and the guzzling, the bilious and the nervous'. The drinkers of Cheltenham waters would not stomach this, and when Cobbett visited the town a few years later to deliver a political lecture the inhabitants showed their indignation to such purpose that he had to decamp privately and in haste for Stow-on-the-Wold. The populace, disappointed of their opportunity to retaliate, burnt Cobbett's effigy through the streets. Fortunately other visitors were more complimentary, and in the September of 1821 George IV paid the town a flying visit and said he would 'certainly make a point of paying Cheltenham another and an early visit'. Edward VII (1897) praised it even more highly. 'I experience much pleasure in visiting a town so celebrated for its beauty as Cheltenham. Indeed, it is my sincere opinion that it would be difficult to find any part of England surpassing this neighbourhood in loveliness of scenery. . . .'

In the Arms of the Borough is a tree representing the delightful sylvan nature of the spacious streets, two open books symbolical of its educational facilities, and in the crest a globe with waved bands representing the mineral waters which have given the town its world-wide reputation, while surmounting the whole is a pigeon. The motto *Salubritas et Eruditio* can scarcely be more appropriate, for Cheltenham is peopled mainly with educationalists, with retired and leisured people and with those who cater for them. 'When I was in Poona' is no joke in Cheltenham, where the Maharajah of J——r plays polo and one man in twenty has come from the far ends of the earth. As a proof that the town still retains its highly respectable character it is only necessary to state that since 1823 there have been built here over one dozen new churches.

Many of the older houses retain their former 'powdering rooms' and the town keeps much of its dignified Georgian aspect. Its lovely gardens and parks need no mention of mine; the Pittville Pump Room is still popular, but the Rotunda at the summit of Montpellier is often unnoticed although the white statues of buxom matrons warn one of the proximity of something unusual. As a place for retirement Cheltenham, I suppose, has few rivals. You will find its cosmopolitan, mellowed, comfortable spirit in the breakfast-room of your hotel or at the bowling-greens in Suffolk Square or even in the restaurant notices which beseech customers, ladies, I presume, not to seat their dogs on the chairs.

One could almost believe that here

> 'Lord Chancellors were cheap as sprats,
> And Bishops in their shovel hats
> Were plentiful as tabby cats—
> In point of fact too many.

Ambassadors cropped up like hay,
Prime Ministers and such as they
Grew like asparagus in May,
    And Dukes were three a penny.'

We groundlings, however, might comfort ourselves with the thought that

'In short, whoever you may be,
To this conclusion you'll agree,
When every one is somebodie,
Then no one's anybody.'

AROUND CHELTENHAM

'I've tramped a score of miles to-day
And now on Cotswold stand,
Wondering if in any way
 Their owners understand
How all those little gold fields I see
And the great green woods beyond
Have given themselves to me, to me
Who own not an inch of land.'
        —F. W. HARVEY, *On Birdlip*.

Cheltenham has been called a 'city of magnificent distances', for the Cotswolds come very close to its eastern suburbs. It lies in the midst of flat green fields, rich with meadowsweet and dropworts, at the foot of the steep, rocky slopes of the beech-clad hills. Elms are the characteristic trees of the vale; none is more interesting than Maud's elm in Cheltenham, about which the tragic story is told by Humphris and Willoughby in their recent book on the spa. The giants of the hills are beeches, and here the salad burnet, the wild garlic, the lily of the valley and Solomon's seal, Belladonna and the helleborines make their home. Even climatically Cheltenham has access to two spheres, the warm soothing lowland and the cool invigorating upland, where there is always a breeze even under the brazen sky of July and where walking is always a pleasure. Often in late autumn, from the wild hill-tops, the vale may be seen draped in white mists, while the limestones are enjoying the pale sunshine.

The road south out of the town, climbing Leckhampton Hill, gives magnificent views over the vale. Here, in front of a precipitous rock wall which guards the western side of the ancient Leckhampton Camp, you will find the isolated pinnacle of limestone blocks forming the 'Devil's Chimney'. Ruff, in his *History of Cheltenham* (1803), talks of the precipitate and craggy declivity, with its grotesque chimney, built by preternatural hands, and adds in an informative footnote: ' "Built by the Devil" as say the vulgar: it was no doubt built by shepherds in the frolic of an idle hour.' The road continues along the crest of the hill past Shurdington Hill, on whose flanks is the lonely Crippetts, and past Crickley Hill with its woods, of which the Scrubbs, a large, wild and unspoiled portion of the escarpment, was given to the National Trust by Sir Philip Stott. Between the 'Air Balloon' and Birdlip, where Ermin Street climbs the steep slope, the views are wide and majestic, making this one of the most memorable of Cotswold journeys. South of Birdlip lies Cranham with its circle of beechwoods and a wealth of archæological treasures. Here, too, on Whit Monday, you may see the survival of a five hundred years' old ceremony of cheese-rolling on Cooper's Hill. On this day the villagers of Brockworth preserve their grazing rights here by rolling wooden discs (representing the cheeses) from the flagstaff at the top down the hill, and the first to catch the disc wins a real cheese. When the cheese-bowling is finished, the merry company takes part in foot-races on the grassy top of the hill.

Of the villages which lie at the foot of the hills perhaps the most interesting, and certainly the most isolated, is Badgeworth, a large agricultural village two miles from the Cotswold edge and not much farther from Cheltenham. It lies amid elms and poplars and in the midst of well-watered green meadows, and the only approach is from the north. The manor, in the past, belonged to the Clares of Gloucester-shire, the first barons of the realm at a time when earls owned huge estates and were of great personal importance.

Over the west window of the little church of the Holy Trinity at Badgeworth is a sculptured head of Edward II, and below are the supposed effigies of young Gilbert de Clare, owner of the manor, and Maud de Burgh, his wife. The church was under the patronage of the Priory of Usk, a foundation of the Clares, and it was consecrated in 1315, the year after Gilbert was slain. The chancel has been re-built, but the fabric remains almost entirely of the four-teenth century Decorated style. Its windows and doorways are among the finest examples of ball-flower ornament in existence, and there are some extremely skilful mouldings besides. In the lovely little chapel to St. Margaret, the windows are profusely decorated with the delicate ball-flower, both within and without, and there are larger ball-flowers under the eaves. The chapel was probably named after Margaret, Gilbert's sister, who married the King's favourite, Piers Gaveston. There are lines in Marlowe remin-iscent of the occasion, spoken by King Edward III:

> 'Cousin, this day shall be your marriage feast,
> And, Gaveston, think that I love thee well,
> To wed thee to our niece, the only heir
> Unto the Earl of Gloucester late deceased.'

St. Margaret's chapel also contains an interesting com-
mandments' board with the words skilfully inlaid, and
finishing with 'God save the Queen. 1591.' In addition
one of the three old chests in the church is inlaid with
pictures of Adam and Eve and hunting scenes. The cross
in the churchyard has been carefully restored, completing
a pretty scene of fir-trees near a lych gate, charmingly constructed of wood, and a lovely half-timber house with
carved bargeboards facing the tiny village green.

The botanist will be interested in the nearby Cold Pool,
the Badgeworth Nature Reserve, where the very rare
Ranunculus ophioglossifolius or Snake-tongue buttercup is
preserved from extinction. The graceful plant rears its
leaves, which are shaped like a snake's head, high above the
water, and usually in June and early July a large patch of it
may be seen in flower.

Bishop's Cleeve, the largest and most interesting settlement on the north side of Cheltenham, is of very early
foundation, for in 790 Offa of Mercia founded a college of
canons here, and in medieval times the Bishops of Worcester had an important residence at 'Bishops' Cleeve.
At the Dissolution the village came into the hands of Sir
Thomas Seymour of Sudeley, and upon his execution
passed to the Crown. Elizabeth granted it along with
Stoke Orchard to Sir Christopher Hatton, her Lord Chancellor and intimate friend. To Elizabeth he was her 'Mutton' or 'Bell-wether', her *pecora campi* and her 'Lids', and
Sir Christopher used to adorn his letters to the Queen with
a crude device representing a pair of eye-lids. One of his
letters concludes with 'Adieu, most sweet Lady. All and
EveR yours, your most happy bondman, Lids.'

The very large church of St. Michael at Bishop's Cleeve
was already several centuries old when Hatton first knew it.
The present handsome pinnacled tower was built in 1700,
after the spire of its predecessor had fallen down. The

church was carefully restored about forty years ago, and is now well-lighted and very unobtrusively heated. The Transitional building (*c.* 1175) was considerably extended in the fourteenth century, but the west doorway is a magnificent example of Norman work. The west gallery is reached by two winding stairways forming two attractive high turrets with chevron arcading which had to be supported in the fifteenth century by a huge buttress. The graceful porch formed part of the original building and has beautiful vaulting, with chevroned ribs, and wall arcading which has been delicately and most skilfully executed. There is a piscina and a small dug-out chest with iron clamps and three locks, both of Norman date. The lovely ball-flower mouldings, both inside and outside the east window of the chancel and around the lovely priest's doorway at the east end of the church, serve to emphasize the alterations made in the Decorated period. In the north transept an unusual stone stairway is continued to the tower by a remarkable fifteenth-century sloping ladder. Traces of mural paintings remain and the Jacobean west gallery and stairway have fortunately been retained. The large church has many other items of interest for ecclesiologists, but the less expert visitor will probably content himself with three tombs. A handsome recess, again with ball-flower decoration, in the south transept contains a thirteenth-century stone effigy of a knight clad in chain armour and a long flowing surcoat. The unnamed warrior is girt with a sword and bears a large shield on his left arm. He lies with his legs crossed like a knight templar, with spurs at his heels and his feet resting on a dog. Tradition says that this is the tomb of Gilbert the Bold. In the south aisle are the large black and white marble monument designed for Richard Delabere, who died in 1635, and the stone effigy of a lady who is represented wearing over her gown a wimple or mantle of ermine.

CHAPTER XIV: Tewkesbury

'Where Avon's friendly streams with Severn join
Great Tewkesbury's walls renown'd for trophies, shine,
And keep the sad remains with pious care,
Of noble souls, the honour of the war.'
                    —CAMDEN's translation of *Leland*.

THE MYTHE TUTE or Royal Hill, as it has been called since the visit of George III in 1788, is the connoisseur's approach to Tewkesbury. 'The Mythe was a little hill on the outskirts of the town, breezy and fresh. . . . Close below it at the foot of a precipitous slope ran the Severn, there broad and deep enough, gradually growing broader and deeper as it flowed on, through a wide plain of level country, towards the line of hills that bounded the horizon. The Severn looked beautiful here, neither grand nor striking but certainly beautiful. On the left flowed the Avon—Shakespeare's Avon, here a narrow sluggish stream but capable, as we at Norton Bury sometimes knew to our cost, of being roused into fierceness and foam. Now it slipped on quietly enough, contenting itself with turning a flour mill hard by, the lazy whirr of which made a sleepy incessant monotone.' An old branch of the Avon joins the Severn near the mill, but the main stream slips peacefully southwards to meet its parent at Lower Lode, and so encloses 'a wide green level called the Ham—dotted with pasturing cattle of all sorts'. Mrs. Craik omitted to mention in *John Halifax, Gentleman*, the willows which fringe the Carrant brook and the darker green ribbon of the banks of the Swilgate. Indeed a writer might be forgiven on entering Tewkesbury for the first time for not noticing that the noble abbey tower is peninsulated between the Little Swilgate and the Avon, and that the town to the north has its Rubicon in the Carrant. The picture is striking, but whether it be the green flatness or the maze of waterways or the uprightness of the tower which attract, it is hard to tell. These same green meads and somnolent streams which delighted Abbot Gerald in the time of the Conqueror have been associated ever since with his abbey, and in time of flood the tower changes it sombre shadow into a rippling reflection over the swollen waters.

The town is named after Theoc or Theuk, a hermit who lived in a cell near this spot at the close of the seventh century. At Domesday the King held the 'honour of Tewkesbury', and about 1090 Rufus granted it to his kinsman, Robert Fitzhamon. It appears that six years earlier Gerald, Abbot of Cranborne, had visited Tewkesbury and had been so impressed by its lovely riverine situation that he and his monks had commenced to rebuild the abbey. Fitzhamon furthered the project, not only by providing the necessary means, but also by rich endowments of lands. The work progressed so favourably that by 1102 the abbot and fifty-six monks migrated here from Cranborne, which became a cell of Tewkesbury. Five years later Fitzhamon was mortally wounded at the siege of Falaise and was buried in the newly-finished chapter-house. His son-in-law Robert, Earl of Gloucester, continued the building, which was consecrated in 1123 by Theulf, Bishop of Worcester, with the assistance of four other bishops. In 1217 Gilbert de Clare held the manor, and it remained with his family until 1320. The abbey is the last resting-place of the Clares. Gilbert and Richard de Clare, his father, were guardians of the Magna Carta; Gilbert the 'Red Earl' entertained King Edward and his court at Tewkesbury with great splendour in 1262. When the last male of the Clares was slain at Bannockburn the manor descended on the distaff side to the

Despencers, who held it until 1414. Again irrespective of their fate or the scene of their death, the bones of the Despencers were brought for burial home to the great abbey church. Eleanor de Clare married Hugh le Despencer, the favourite of Edward II, the same who was hanged, drawn and quartered at Hereford in 1326. Twelve years later his widow placed seven lovely windows in the choir in memory of him and perhaps to atone, or let us hope to more than atone, for his sins. Under Hugh, fifth Lord Despencer, the architecture of the choir was converted from Norman to Decorated, much of the present stone vaulting was completed and the chevet of seven chapels was built round the apse. The male line of the Despencers ended with Richard, but his sister Isabella married in 1411 Richard Beauchamp, Lord Abergavenny, and later Earl of Worcester. No marriage in the abbey has had more momentous results for Tewkesbury. Isabella was a generous benefactor, and she placed the rich and stately chantry chapel over the grave of her husband while she herself elected to lie before the High Altar in a coffin humbly inscribed 'Mercy, Lord Jhesu'. As a result of the marriage Richard Neville in 1446 inherited the vast possessions of the Despencers at Tewkesbury as well as those of the Warwick family in the Midlands. He was the greatest and 'last of the Barons' of Tewkesbury and of England. Lord Lytton describes him as 'a man who stood colossal amidst the iron images of the Age—the greatest and last of the old Norman chivalry—kinglier in pride, in state, in possessions and in renown, than the king himself. . . . His valour in the field was accompanied with a generosity rare in the captains of the time. . . . His haughtiness to the great was not incompatible with frank affability to the lowly. His wealth was enormous, but it was equalled by his magnificence and rendered popular by his lavish hospitality. No less than thirty thousand persons are said to have feasted daily at the open tables with which he allured to his countless castles the strong hands and grateful hearts of a martial and unsettled population. More haughty than ambitious, he was feared because he avenged all affront, and yet not envied, because he seemed above all favour.'

The fall of the mighty king-maker dragged scores of nobles with him, and three weeks later Tewkesbury, the manor loved by his forebears, was destined to see one of the bloodiest slaughters of a murderous age. Queen Margaret of Anjou, wife of Henry VI, came to support the Earl and landed on the day that he was slain at Barnet Field in 1471. She came with her army to Bristol, augmenting her forces on the way, and tried in vain to gain admittance to royal Gloucester. Thence her army struggled on northwards, and on May 23rd, 'about foure of the clocke in the afternoone, they came to Teukesburie, having travelled that night last past, and that daie, six and thirty long miles, in a foule countrie, all in lanes and stonie waies, betwixt woods, without any good refreshing . . .' The weary army took up a position in a park adjoining the town, part of the battlefield being known to-day as the 'Vineyards' and part as the 'Bloody Meadow'. The quiet meadows to-day have an uneven, cheerless look and their damp surface is broken with many a willow-lined pool.

Edward IV gave Tewkesbury to George, Duke of Clarence, 'false, fleeting, perjured Clarence' who in 1478 was executed in the Tower and was brought to the abbey for burial. He was the last royal personage to find repose in the abbey for the King held the Lordship of the Manor henceforth, and at the Dissolution (January 1540) the monastery went to him also. The list of possessions, the 'Compotus Roll' now kept in the museum at the abbey, occupies both sides of seventy-four skins of parchment and includes the patronage of four dozen livings and silver altar plate weighing nearly a hundredweight. The clear yearly value of all the abbey incomes at the Dissolution was

£1,595 15s. 6d., which is said to be worth more than £60,000 of our money. The subservient attitude of John Wakeman, the last abbot, called 'intriguing' and servile' by a contemporary, may explain why he enjoyed £266 13s. 4d. a year, and a house and park at Forthampton. The priors had £12 6s. 8d. each, and the usual pension for the monks was £6 13s. 4d. Nor, on this occasion, did King Henry forget himself. The Commissioners proceeded to demolish the now superfluous monastic buildings, and the Lady Chapel had already been demolished when the Tewkesbury people came to an agreement with the King. It appears that immemorial usage entitled them to the western parts of the nave, and they purchased the rest of the church, together with some properties, for £453. The indenture of 1543 in the museum tells us that this was mainly for the bells at 2½d. a pound and 5d. a square foot for the lead on the roof. It is a marvel how the corporation has ever since fulfilled the condition of sale that they should 'continually repair, sustain, maintain and uphold' the whole fabric.

To-day the town has all the air and trappings of a city: to visitors it appears populous and rich, yet few realize that it is merely an overgrown village with less people than many a single street in Bristol and with not many more than a thousand families all told.

Yet, especially on a wet day, Tewkesbury is more attractive than any other Gloucestershire town, for the abbey is a constant fund of interest and the streets around it are rich in quaint, half-timbered houses, in pleasant tea-rooms with some old features to offer and enticing alleyways, each a world of its own. The history of the borough has little interest compared with that of the abbey. King John built the bridge over the Avon and the ribbed arches nearest the town are probably part of the original structure, although in the reign of King Charles I the county repaired it to prevent the frequent drowning of would-be travellers.

GARGOYLE ON WINCHCOMBE CHURCH

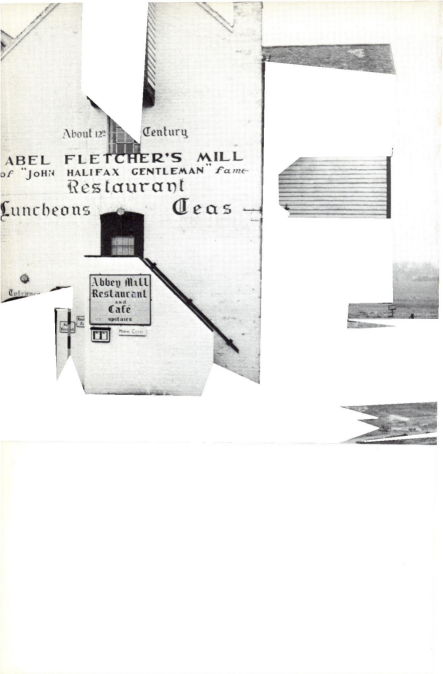

About 12ᵗʰ Century

ABEL FLETCHER'S MILL
of "JOHN HALIFAX GENTLEMAN" fame

Restaurant

Luncheons   Teas

Entrance

Abbey Mill
Restaurant
and
Café
upstairs

Shakespeare gave Tewkesbury a reputation for mustard balls, yet even as early as 1770 no one could remember them ever having been made there. The corporation, however, had grown rich enough to buy the manor for £2,453 from James I on the condition that the King had the right of presentation to the vicarage, which right he keeps to this day.

William III extended the liberties of the borough, and one of his gifts, the right of perambulating the borough, has been revived recently. The coaching traffic proved exceptionally beneficial to the town and explains the large number of hostelries, including, of course, the 'Hop Pole' visited by Mr. Pickwick on his memorable journey from Bristol to Birmingham.

Modern Tewkesbury owes and acknowledges a great debt of gratitude to *John Halifax, Gentleman*, which first drew the attention of readers to the glories of the town. In 1852 Miss Dinah Maria Mulock, later better known as Mrs. Craik, drove over to Tewkesbury and saw for the first time the old abbey above the flat meadows, and the dark intriguing shadows beneath the overhanging stories of the half-timbered houses. She had already determined to make it the background of her fourth novel when a shower of rain drove her into a covered alley where a little ragged boy was also sheltering. Across the street in the window of a grand house a little girl watched the boy sympathetically, and presently came out with a piece of bread in her hand, and beckoned to him. So the story began.

Lunching later at the 'Bell Inn' Miss Mulock was told that a tanner had lived there; this and the smell of the tanyard hard by decided her hero's trade. Abel Fletcher, the mill-owner, a stout-principled Quaker, should apprentice the little ragged boy whose sterling character should make him rise to become owner of all and more than his master

THE MILL AT TEWKESBURY

had. The name John was a favourite of hers, the surname she found on an old stone in the abbey graveyard: the 'Gentleman' was the purpose of the authoress's democratic ideas.

The old mill was then, as now, a beauty of the town, and the shortage of food after the Napoleonic wars led to the touching incident when the old Quaker threw the grain into the mill-race.

Miss Mulock wrote most of the novel in 1856 when staying as a paying guest at Rose Cottage, Amberley, then owned by the Guild family. The last living link with the characters in the book ended eight years ago with the death of Miss E. A. Guild, one of the 'Todd' children. The novel has been printed in nearly thirty foreign languages and its universal appeal, the nobility of man as man, draws thousands of visitors to Tewkesbury to identify the scenery of 'Norton Bury'. Just before her death in 1887, Mrs. Craik lunched again at the 'Bell' and was much touched with 'the feeling of thirty-four years' faithful friendship' with the town.

The picturesque gabled 'Bell Inn' has the initials I.K. and the date 1696 under a bell. Two fragments of medieval wall paintings, once fairly common in the houses of the town, have survived, and the famous bowling-green with its noted yew hedge can yet be seen. 'There was not its like in the whole county. It was about fifteen feet high and as many thick. Century after century of growth, with careful clipping and training, had compacted it into a massive green barrier, as close and impervious as a wall.''

The 'mayor's house . . . porticoed and grand', now the 'Tudor House Hotel' in the High Street, was formerly known as the Old Academy. At this school, founded in 1712 by the Rev. Samuel Jones of Pennsylvania, Archbishop Secker, and Bishop Butler of *Analogy* fame began their education. The noble half-timbered façade with its fourteen windows is dated 1701 and the interior of the house is probably considerably older.

There is no need to search for interesting buildings in Tewkesbury. Any alley way, any street will reward those who look for 'quaint, overhanging, ornamented housefronts—blackened and wonderfully old'.

Mill Street offers the quaint Fire Station with its curious 'look-out' and pretty timbered cottages on a high pavement overlooking the Avon. The mill dates back to about 1300 and was in continuous use until 1920. 'Built on piles, in the centre of the narrow river, it was only a few steps of bridgework to either bank. The little door was on the Norton Bury side and was hid from the opposite shore.' Here Abel Fletcher was made to fling into the river 'the precious wheat, and in the very sight of the famished rioters'. The building is a remarkably fine specimen of mill architecture, and its milling machinery, which is interesting even to the non-mechanically minded, was driven by the great wooden over-shot water-wheel. Now used as a restaurant and information bureau the mill is well preserved and shelters a medley of objects connected with Tewkesbury, including, I notice, some framed woad, a plant which now grows wild only on The Mythe cliffs in England.

Church Street holds many half-timbered houses separated at intervals by the inviting alleyways, some leading to dilapidated cottages and others to picturesque courtyards. The quaint little alms-houses in Gander Street were built, so the inscription says, from an investment of £60. Adjoining the 'Royal Hop Pole' there is Bull Court, entered through a fine archway with carved spandrels and surmounted by a room with traces of Tudor wall-painting. The 'Berkeley Arms' and its fifteenth-century neighbour, the shop with the delicately carved wooden arcading on its front, are perhaps the oldest friends in the town.

The old Baptist Meeting House, tucked away among small cottages, still preserves the gallery, pulpit and table of its seventeenth-century meeting-room. The unhurried will notice, too, the pretty cottages, the profuse greenery and hand-pump of Lilley Alley, the black and white carved front and the sign of a beadle's cocked hat at 'Ye Olde Hatte Shoppe', and the Elizabethan buildings in Tolzey Lane.

High Street continues parallel with the Avon and brings us to King John's Bridge. The commencement of the street is dominated by the four towering, overhanging stories of 'The House of the Golden Key' whose two crazy gables seem to lean proudly away from the electioneering platform over the portico of the 'Swan Hotel Inn and Tavern'. Not far away is the symmetrical black and white front of the 'Ancient Grudge', which, in spite of its name looks like a dignified Elizabethan gentleman well at home, with modern traffic. The interior possesses an old timbered ceiling with a fine central boss and some linenfold panelling dating back to the late fifteenth century, if, as is thought, the intitials R.P. in the spandrels of the great fire-place refer to Abbot Richard (ob. 1509). Clarence House, which lurches rather disconcertingly over the pavement, has a fine plaster ceiling, and the chemist's shop near it, dated 1606, has a charming doorway which shows what the house front would be like if scraped of plaster.

'Ye Olde Fleece', dated 1519, or the 'Wheatsheaf' opposite, cannot but be admired. The mullioned windows and steeply pitched gable of the 'Wheatsheaf' make it the finest seventeenth-century building in the town. The group of houses near the bridge is remarkable, especially for 'ye Old Black Beare', a rambling, picturesque, half-timbered hostelry dating from 1308. The main part of the building is certainly not earlier than Tudor times, but the present lounge, originally the stables, is said to be mentioned in connexion with the Wars of the Roses. No more fitting building could neighbour King John's Bridge, for the 'Bear' in its use and structure typifies the Tewkesbury which grew up as a child of the abbey and a friend to travellers crossing the Avon. Perhaps it is too much to wish all visitors the liberal hospitality enjoyed, or should we say over-enjoyed, by Mr. Pickwick. 'At the Hop Pole at Tewkesbury they stopped to dine; upon which occasion there was more bottled ale with some more Madeira, and some port besides; and here the case bottle was replenished for the fourth time. Under the influence of these combined stimulants, Mr. Pickwick and Mr. Ben Allen fell fast asleep for thirty miles, while Bob and Mr. Weller sang duets in the dickey.'

TEWKESBURY DISTRICT

'It is good to be out on the road, and going one knows not where,
  Going through meadow and village, one knows not whither nor why;
  Through the grey light drift of the dust, in the keen cool rush of the air,
  Under the flying white clouds, and the broad blue lift of the sky.'
                    —JOHN MASEFIELD. *Tewkesbury Road.*

The Mythe Tute looks down upon Telford's Bridge which here, in one sixty-yard span, carries the Ledbury road over the Severn. Two miles of flat and undulating country brings us to the narrow, well-wooded road which leads to Forthampton. The lane forks near an ancient half-timbered barn, and the village is spread out along the way due south, and along the wider route eastwards to

Lower Lode Ferry. Some people will scarcely agree that this straggling dispersion of houses merits the name of village, but the population (160) considerably exceeds that of many well-known hamlets on the North Cotswolds. For those who cherish rural peace and charm Forthampton will become an annual pilgrimage. Almost each house on this small knoll near to the Severn is a gem in itself. Forthampton is a black and white timbered village, with a little brick and much thatch, and ancient barns with cruck timbers, with all the quaintness and charm which half-timbering can give when well preserved and set amid small orchards of apple and pear. The green lane southwards from the barn leads past charming cottages, one with a large chimney almost completely detached, another with a quaint turret gable, to the larger Forthampton House, a picturesque assembly culminating in a black and white dovecot and outbuildings draped in wistaria. The old 'sanctuary house', near to the present school, has an ancient oak-panelled room, and is the house of one's retired dreams. The other way, leading back to the Severn, is equally attractive. The pond near the lovely old barn and the large half-timbered house facing the pump on the opposite side of the road typify the rural charm of the place. The cottage near the pump has been a baker's shop for over a century, and has never yet had a shop front. 'Why should it,' the villagers queried, 'when we all know it's a shop?' Where else in this part of England will you find a village as large and as beautiful with no petrol pumps, no shop fronts, no 'pots of tea', no garish notices? The little church of St. Mary the Virgin, which has been placed on the highest hillock, is mainly fourteenth century, with a few later additions. Beneath the trees the old stocks and whipping-post may be seen close beside the path to the church gate. They are well-preserved, and it will be noticed, with the foresight typical of country folk, that they were built to accommodate three offenders.

The 'Devil-face', like a grinning cat, over the Norman doorway into the church may possibly be Saxon, and welcomes us into an interior attractive both for its arches and its peaceful appearance. The well-preserved thirteenth-century stone altar retains its original stone legs and is one of the very few, three it is said, pre-Reformation stone altars remaining in England in their original position. The woodwork includes fourteen ancient pews with linen fold pattern, and a remarkable pokerwork design of Christ and the two disciples at Emmaus, executed by a curate a century ago.

The road towards Lower Lode Ferry leads past Forthampton Court, a large, rambling old building whose roof-levels vary considerably and whose ivy-covered walls make a fine picture amid the cedars and oaks of the grounds. This house was given to Tewkesbury by Henry II, and was formerly a residence of the abbots, and the yew walks used by the monks are still to be seen. John Wakeman was granted the building and grounds for life at the dissolution of Tewkesbury Abbey, and perhaps that will explain the effigied altar tomb in the garden. When the Lady Chapel at Tewkesbury was destroyed in 1541 this tomb, to William, Lord Zouch (ob. 1335), second husband of Eleanor de Clare, was removed here, and its angels and grotesques take on a new pleasantness amidst the green trees.

Walkers would do well to proceed to the inn at Lower Lode and cross by ferry there to the other bank of the Severn along which an interesting footpath jogs on to Deerhurst, a Severn village standing, as Leland says, *in laeva ripa* three miles below 'Theokesbyri. The site of the town is in the maner of a medow, so that when the Severn much riseth the water cometh almost about the town. It is supposed that it was of old time less subject to waters, and that the bottom of the Severn, then deeper without choaking of sands did at flouds leste hurte. It is now but a poor village . . .' A shallow, reed-grown dyke almost encircles the church and Abbot's Court with a band of willows, and the villagers find therein some compensation from the danger of floods as the withies, made pliable by dipping in boiling water, are woven into baskets for the Evesham fruit-growers.

Deerhurst has a great many claims to fame. A field here called the Naight is said to be the 'Isle of Olney' on which, in 1016, King Edmund 'Ironside' and Cnut the Dane met to make peace. Although possessing a monastery and chapel in pre-Norman times, the village is not mentioned in *Domesday Survey*.

The fine stone farm-house, called the Priory, near the church has incorporated some ancient panelling, very thick walls and a tall, curious, reticulated window, which probably are all that remain of the conventual buildings of the monastery. The cloisters seem to have entirely disappeared, but fortunately the monastic church, one of the largest pre-Norman churches in England, remains for posterity. The simple, dignified church of St. Mary stands in a park-like churchyard beautified by firs, horse-chestnuts and tall, un-clipped yews above which the peculiar oblong tower may be seen. Herring-bone masonry is strikingly plentiful, and it comes as no surprise to learn that the main parts of the church are early tenth-century work. To-day the long, tall nave forms a parallelogram, but once the building was cruciform with a semi-circular eastern apse, traces of which may be seen outside the present church. The western tower, some seventy feet high, has a low gable on its eastern wall, and previous to the gale in 1666 had a spire on the western side. The lower portions, with the bands of herring-bone masonry and a slight but perceptible batter to the wall, are pre-Norman, while the upper half is four hundred years younger. The four super-imposed chambers within it are each divided into two by a wall, and it is the eastern wall of the rooms nearest the nave which is interesting. That on the second stage has a round-headed doorway which once led to a gallery, the supporting stone brackets of which are still visible. Near it a quaint triangular aperture opens into the church. The third stage has the massive, double triangular window which so frequently figures in books on architecture. The two gable-shaped arches of these windows are made of massive stones which rest on three stout pilasters ornamented with a crude form of fluting and ending in stepped capitals. The fourth stage of the tower has a blocked up doorway which used to lead to a chamber between the ceiling and high-pitched roof of the nave, when it was even loftier than now.

The nave retains its pre-Norman walls, and is a very tall, narrow, plain structure beautified by two graceful Early English arcades, the capitals of which are finely and diversely sculptured. The large double clerestory and the roof, which is covered on the outside with lead, were added in the fifteenth century, no doubt after the fire which destroyed the apse.

The south aisle or Petty France, as it was called locally in reference to St. Denis of Paris, was added to the nave in the twelfth century, the walls being extended westwards to enclose the lowest stage of the tower. The sister aisle on the north was constructed about a century later in the same way, but is illumined entirely by Decorated windows. It contains four brasses, of which those to Sir John Cassy and Alice, his wife, are of exceptional interest. Sir John (ob. 1400), shown in his full robes as chief baron of the exchequer, lived at the old manor which preceded the present noble eighteenth-century house at Whitefield Court. Alicia, or Alice, has gained more lasting fame because her pet dog Tirri is the only one with its name on a brass in England. What 'Tirri' stands for I cannot imagine, unless it was one of those endearing nicknames later so much in vogue in Elizabeth's reign. 'Tirri' has only had one rival in England, a mongrel named 'Jakke' which belonged to Sir Bryan de Stapleton (ob. 1438) and Cecilia, his wife, of Ingham. The ravages of time, however, proved too much for 'Jakke'. The rich canopy above the brass at Deerhurst is surmounted by an engraving of St. Anne teaching the Virgin Mary to read.

Nor does this conclude the interesting details of St. Mary's. The seventeeth-century oaken communion seating which once formed a square round the altar and still extends behind the present high altar is almost as rare in England to-day as fonts like the famous one at Deerhurst. This font, an odd tub-shaped, stone structure, richly and skilfully sculptured with peculiar conjoined spirals and scrolls of dog-rose, is tenth-century West Saxon work. It consists of two parts, a bowl and a pedestal; the former was turned out of the church in Tudor or Stuart times and lay derelict in a farmyard. The pedestal was found in a garden at Apperley Court near Deerhurst in 1870 and the two portions were assembled and erected in Deerhurst Church on the grounds that their designs were precisely similar and that their diameters corresponded at the base. Whether the pedestal really belonged to the bowl is open to question.

Not far from the horse-chestnuts in the churchyard stands a quaint hybrid-looking building. A large, attractive, half-timbered house with four stately chimneys has been built on to the end of a small barn-like structure stoutly made of stone and roofed with grey Cotswold slates. The latter is considerably lower than the house and has a retiring appearance, behind a box hedge and overshadowed by a huge red-brick barn which mercifully has mellowed with age. The house is called Abbot's Court and its odd companion, in front of which the chickens peck vigorously, is Odda's Chapel. Sixty years ago the court was, to all intents and purposes, a normal half-timbered residence, but the occu-

pant's curiosity was aroused by certain features in its structure, and investigation showed that the sixteenth-century
house had been constructed round a chapel. The original
doors and windows of the church had been plastered over
and new lights cut to illumine the building. It happened
that in 1675 an inscribed stone, now preserved in the Ash-
molean, had been dug up in the orchard here which said
that the chapel was built by Odda, Lord of the manor, for
masses for the repose of the soul of his brother Elfric who
had died here; Bishop Ealdred dedicated it in the April of
1056. There is a copy of the stone in the restored building
which forms an almost perfect example of a Saxon chapel.
The nave, some 25 feet by 16 feet, is only connected to the
much smaller chancel by a small archway like a doorway,
the jambs of which consist of long and short ashlar work.

CHAPTER XV: The Vale of Leadon

FROM TEWKESBURY to Gloucester the ageing Severn is scarcely fifteen miles from the meanders of the Wye above Ross, and the country between them really belongs to the River Leadon, which comes down from near Ledbury to mingle with the Severn at Alney Island. This land, where Herefordshire merges imperceptibly into Gloucestershire, has attracted less attention than any other part of our country largely because it is off the beaten track, and has not captured the public imagination as much as the Cotswolds or the Forest of Dean. Indeed it is difficult to receive an impression of this borderland as few districts change so completely with the seasons; a rich red soil when the plough has turned it, a blaze of yellow in daffodil time, a mass of fruit blossom in the spring, a reek of cider in the fall, and pigs and poultry all the year.

The flattish aspect gained from a map turns upon acquaintance into a startling jumble of ceaseless undulations; a rapid descent, a wriggle over a stream, and up and over the next hillock and so the narrow road jogs crazily on between high hedges and flourishing orchards until, just when you are beginning to enjoy the scamper, a sudden twist flings you crazily into the midst of a village. Then perhaps expecting a perfection of black and white houses you may be disappointed, but even rural Herefordshire cannot offer finer churches than these nor more genuine hospitality.

The most rural approaches to the Vale of Leadon are over Haw Bridge near Tirley and across the ferry from Sandhurst to Ashleworth, either of which leads straight into the orchard country. Ashleworth has much of a rural nature to attract us. The ferry leads to a tiny dilapidated quay, which is sufficient reason apparently for a public-house, but it is no low water-side haunt for the scene is dominated by a church and a group of monastic buildings formerly belonging to St. Augustine's, Bristol. The huge tithe barn, some 125 feet long by 25 feet broad, makes an impressive picture with its fine old roof, mainly of oak, slated with Cotswold tiles, and its two large projecting porches. The stout buttresses look all the sturdier for their ivy covering while the tiny windows seem ridiculously small for the massive gables. The barn was erected in the year 1500 by Abbot Newland and has been converted by Messrs. Cadbury into an up-to-date cowshed and consequently is in an excellent state of preservation. Near by may be seen the Court House, a graceful building with a handsome door-way and traceried windows, which is quite as old as the barn and is thought to have belonged to the Black Friars of Gloucester. The church completes the little group and, of its type, is the quaintest and smallest of the three. Somehow both SS. Andrew and Bartholomew have become its patrons and the same degree of doubt invades its architecture, much of which shows rebuilding in various old styles. The church-yard contains an old stone well-head and the remains of a fourteenth-century cross, some 10 feet high, with its original lantern head whose four niches hold reliefs of a Crucifixion, two women kneeling to the Virgin Mary, and of other figures, the laity perhaps, kneeling to two saints. The Tudor porch, complete with a stone bench and a stoup, shelters a fine timber door of the same antiquity which still retains its original iron work and its great wooden lock. The herring-bone masonry and the tall, somewhat crude round-headed doorway in the north wall of the nave may be part of the late Norman church, while the plain chancel arch and the lancet archway of the tower belong to the thirteenth century. A mighty coat of arms of Edward VI, blazoned on wood, covers the wall from the top of the door right to the roof ridge, and although much worn, is interesting as being among the earliest of its kind in England.

Newent, six miles to the west as the crow flies and nine by the pretty by-roads, is the ganglion of routes in the Vale of Leadon and consequently also the chief market town. According to Leland a new inn was built on the northern fringe of the Forest of Dean for the benefit of travellers between England and Wales, and a village grew up round the inn. To-day the town is, in a modest rural way, a busy shopping centre and consists mainly of inns and mellowed brick houses spread out along several streets converging upon the gabled Tudor market hall, which with its black and white upper story supported on sixteen oaken pillars, forms quite the most attractive building in Newent. The hall was restored about eighty years ago at a time when the town, even then of over 2,000 inhabitants, was enjoying a coaching traffic, relics of which may be seen in the large cobbled stabling yards, notably that of the 'George Inn'.

The spacious church of St. Mary was mainly rebuilt about 1680, and its tall spire, some 153 feet high, lacks the smoothness of the tapering Cotswold spires. Yet the church contains a good many items of interest, for its oldest portions, the tower base and the chancel arcade, were built in the Early English period. The chancel with its beautiful east window and the Lady Chapel, since adorned with a fine Tudor roof, are fourteenth-century additions. Near the altar a brass to Roger Porter (ob. 1523) shows him sword in hand and clad in armour of the reign of Henry VIII. Two old sculptures discovered in the churchyard are treasured in the south porch. The one is the shaft of a pre-Norman cross probably of the ninth century, which although much defaced bears interesting carvings of Isaac, David and Goliath and an especially fantastic Fall of Man, where the serpent entwines itself around a palm-like Tree of Knowledge with a beady-eyed bony Adam on one side and a tall sylph-like Eve on the other. The second carving is a sandstone tablet remarkably like a brick which on one face has the Crucifixion surrounded by a dozen topsy-turvy figures, whilst on the opposing face is carved an abbot standing amidst a framework of figures, some ape-like and others upside down, which on the whole forms a skilful piece of composition. The tablet is possibly Norman as the name Edred in one corner no doubt refers to one of the twelfth-century founders of Little Malvern Priory.

Those who delight in a health-giving walk could not do better than climb through the fine woods to the thousand foot eminence of May Hill which surveys the dark wooded ridge of the Forest of Dean and the whole rich red Vale of Leadon; from its heather-clad height you may see the 'daffodil crescent' of Gloucestershire, and from that crowning clump of firs, the same which John Masefield mentions in *The Everlasting Mercy*, you may bless once more the National Trust for preserving it unspoiled for ever. Perhaps the walk from Newent should be made in July when the circumspect visitor will be fortified for the climb by a feast of roast duck and perhaps green peas. Avening keeps a Pig's Face Sunday, but Newent smells of roast duck almost every midday for a month, and Gloucestershire folk, unacquainted with the flavour of duckling fattened in the Vale of Leadon, are still not completely aware of the bounty of their gracious county.

The most interesting villages in this district are all within five miles of Newent and are easily accessible by car or on foot along pleasant country lanes. The three miles to Pauntley consist of 'swells and slopes and little vallies' given over to rich meadowland and cider orchards. A gated lane, marked by a signpost labelled 'The Wayfarers' Home', leads to Pauntley Court, which lies a few hundred yards from the road on a hillock overlooking the dark green meadows of the sluggish Leadon. It is hard to imagine a prettier group of buildings; the old church, the substantial court, an ancient dovecot, a brick and timber barn and a long low wooden shed set in a lovely view for a background make up Pauntley village.

The small church of St. John dates mainly from late Norman times, and the grand doorway, with a zigzagged arch and fish scales on its tympanum, makes an entrance worthy of the large chancel arch, which has triple rows of moulding and grotesque monsters on the capitals. The side chapel of St. George, and the square, brown-weathered tower, which gives so splendid a view, were built in the fifteenth century at a time when the Whittingtons were living at the court. In the sanctuary may be seen two handsome old chairs and a quaint fringe of woodwork high up on the walls which may have carried the rood veil.

The triptych reredos showing the Wise Men is probably Flemish work of the early sixteenth century, and a more homely touch is given by the plaited straw hassocks which seem a crude but an ingenious and inexpensive way of providing a necessary comfort, though probably the present-day silk stockinged members of the congregation may find them a prickly penance. The fragments of old glass in the windows include an angel, three swans on a shield and the arms of the Whittingtons impaling those of the Fitzwarrens.

From the high wall of the churchyard knoll you can obtain a splendid view of the great rambling farm. In Rudder's day old Pauntley Court had been taken down and the present manor, a neat, cheerful-looking and spacious house, has been built since amid the ancient farm buildings. The Whittingtons came into the manor about 1300 and the famous Richard was born about 1358. His father, Sir William Whittington, who had married the widow of Sir Thomas de Berkeley, was outlawed, perhaps on account of the presumptuous marriage, and died when the lad was but fourteen years old. Robert de Whittington, later high sheriff of Gloucestershire, succeeded to the Lordship of Pauntley, and 'Dick' went as 'prentice to a merchant in London. Recently the manor has been converted into a 'Home for Wayfarers' largely due to the generosity and support of Mr. John Masefield, who has raised money by public readings of his poems.

From Pauntley it is scarcely four miles to the village of Dymock, which stands on the banks of the Leadon not far from the borders of Herefordshire.

This is the centre of Gloucestershire's daffodil crescent which begins near Bromsberrow and takes its golden course through Ryton, Ketford, Dymock and Newent, and so continues to the flanks of May Hill, fading away through Soudley and Bream and finally it drops its 'golden tide' into the muddy Severn at Awre. The daffodils sometimes gild a whole field or emblazon the orchards with clumps and edges of gold. Perhaps the greatest joy comes from seeing them dance unbelievably wild in the meadows or taking advantage of the secrecy of a churchyard. In April you may pick as many as you want for a few coppers, and the Dymock daffodil fields attract hundreds of pickers who work for the farmers.

John Masefield in *The Daffodil Fields* describes the scene on the Leadon banks:

'Then, on its left, some short-grassed fields begin,
 Red-clayed and pleasant, which the young spring fills
 With the never-quiet joy of dancing daffodils.

. . . .

And there the pickers come, picking for town
 Those dancing daffodils; all day they pick;
 Hard featured women, weather-beaten brown,
 Or swarthy red, the colour of old brick.'

The myriads of blossoms sent to market and the countless bunches carried away by motorists and cyclists seem only to increase the golden harvest which returns each year when the fruit blossoms have spangled the earth with snow.

Here the 'Dymock Poets' wrote themselves into fame during the years 1911 to 1914. In 1911 Lascelles Abercrombie came to Dymock from the north country, and, in the words of John Haines, 'took a cottage . . . standing high above the lane, shrouded in elm-trees flanked by a pretty cherry orchard, and close against the beautiful Redmarley Hills which at that time were densely covered with larchwoods and edged, as they still are, with daffodils. It is a fascinating spot, and the cottage itself, heavily thatched and with a garden yellow with evening primrose and with mullein, was one of the most beautiful I ever saw.' The cottage was at Ryton in the daffodil country of which he wrote:

> 'From Marcle Way
> From Dymock, Kempley, Newent,
> Bromsberrow, Redmarley, all the
> Meadowland daffodils seem
> Running in golden tides to Ryton Firs

> .   .   .   .

> Light has killed the winter and all dark dreams.
> Now winds live all in light
> Light has come down to earth and blossoms here
> And we have golden minds.'

From Ryton, Lascelles Abercrombie, who died recently, published *Emblems of Love* and *The Sale of St. Thomas*, while many of his plays are written round the Leadon country.

In 1913, along with Wilfrid Gibson, who was then living at the Old Nail Shop at Bromsgreen, John Drinkwater and Rupert Brooke, he brought out a quarterly, *New Numbers*, which was printed at Gloucester and dispatched from Dymock itself. This venture was unfortunately brought to an end by the war in the following year. In that year, however, Robert Frost, a young American, came with his family to England, and soon after his arrival, acting on Wilfred Gibson's suggestion, took a small cottage at Little Iddles near Leadington and about two miles from Greenway, but still in Gloucestershire.

> 'Two roads diverged in a wood, and I—
> I took the one less travelled by,
> And that has made all the difference.'

Frost lived at Little Iddles from 1914 to 1915 in close touch with both Abercrombie and Gibson, who sketched the country characters, and here he published *North of Boston*, the book which first brought him a reputation. Here, too, he wrote much of the exquisite poetry that he published afterwards in America, of which the lines about Ryton trees are of especial interest to us:

> 'I wonder about the trees
> Why do we wish to bear
> For ever the noise of these
> More than another noise—
> So close to our dwelling-place?'

The poets no longer live here but the flowers still do. Heath yet flourishes at Bromsberrow, the Star of Bethlehem grows wild and the river-banks are sought by the spikes of small teazel, by the delicate Ladies' Tresses and the spreading Bell-flower.

The village of Dymock is built mainly of brick with a little half-timbering, while one lovely cottage has stout cruck-timbers in its gables. The whole place seems cheerful and prosperous, its gardens are bright with flowers and its population to-day is steadily increasing. Built of warm, reddish stone in a long aisle-less style, the church of St. Mary is made more attractive by a quaint shingled steeple and by niches in the tower buttresses. Some of the herring-bone masonry of the interior may be Saxon in date, while much of the work is early Norman. A string-course and flat buttresses, as well as a small window and two simple doorways in the nave, remain of this date. The shafts and carved capitals of the chancel arch, parts of the chancel arcade and traces of a vaulted roof are also Norman, but the finest remnant of the original church is the main doorway with its double rows of zigzag moulding and a tympanum representing, it is said, the Tree of Life.

On the opposite side of the green to St. Mary's stands the ivy-mantled White House where John Kyrle, the 'Man of Ross', was born in 1637. Kyrle spent most of his eighty-seven years at Ross improving the country-side, building houses and performing alone the functions of an almost complete benevolent institution on an income of a few hundred pounds a year. Pope in his *Moral Essays* describes John Kyrle's boundless charity:

'Behold the market place with poor o'erspread!
The Man of Ross divides the weekly bread;
He feeds yon alms-house, neat, but void of state,
Where Age and Want sit smiling at the gate;

Him portioned maids, apprenticed orphans, blessed
The young who labour, and the old who rest.
Is any sick? The Man of Ross relieves,
Prescribes, attends, the medicine makes and gives.
Is there a variance? enter but his door,
Balked are the courts, and contest is no more.'

His passion for planting trees and beautifying gardens has not been in vain, as some one hundred and fifty years after his death a Kyrle Society was formed to carry on his traditions, especially for the improvement of waste plots of grounds. Octavia Hill was one of its originators, and she later became more famous as one of the founders of the National Trust which continues to do so much for the beauties of Gloucestershire.

Travelling south-westwards towards Ross two miles of pleasant lanes will lead us to Kempley where the fine new church of St. Edward is nearly a mile from the ancient church of St. Mary the Virgin. The old church stands amid a vast cemetery covering nearly an acre of ground; except for the squat, strong tower and the porch, the building is fine Norman work. The stout, heavily-buttressed tower was built about 1280, at the time when the Welsh were revolting against Edward I, and consequently being built partly as a refuge it has no exterior entrances and no windows, for that matter, save the slits in the walls.

The black and white timbered porch, a late fourteenth-century addition, almost hides a grand Norman doorway whose stout shafts and decorated capitals are surmounted by a chevron arch and a tympanum deeply carved with a Tree of Life not unlike an archaic sculpture of a giant moth. The old door, which still works grudgingly on its strap hinges, admits us to a view of a Norman window seen through a magnificent chancel arch enriched with zig-zag and carved foliated capitals. Most of the windows throughout the church are Norman, but the curious visitor will notice no doubt such details as the crude door to the rood loft, the old carved seat in the chancel, the many box-like pews, the quaint wooden supports of the roof, the old scooped-out oaken chest under the tower and perhaps even the three hedgehogs in the arms of the wife of a seventeenth-century vicar. The main interest of Kempley, however, lies in its mural paintings, some of which are faded to-day and have become rather indistinct, but the portions remaining are so considerable that for interest they have no equal in Gloucestershire. The paintings in the nave range in date from the thirteenth to the fifteenth century: on the splay of one Norman window St. Anthony is shown walking upon a red background with his staff and pig. The opposite splay depicts St. Michael weighing damned souls in a balance while the Virgin intercedes on their behalf, and, no doubt, if we could see it more clearly a devil tries to trick the scales. Near by is a large Wheel of Life, with ten spokes ending in discs alternately black and red and now empty of pictures.

The low, barrel vault of the chancel, in itself almost unique in English parish churches, is covered with early twelfth-century mural decorations, some of which are still brightly coloured and for enthusiasts comprise, I am told, the most important group in England. A large 'Glorification of the Redeemer', who is shown on a rainbow in the act of benediction, occupies the whole centre of the vault. The world is His footstool and at His head may be seen the Sun and the Moon and the seven candlesticks of Revelation. Grouped round the figure of Christ are four great attenuated cherubim with six wings each carrying either a book or a pennon, and on either hand are the four Evangelists, the ox and the eagle to the south and the lion and the angel to the north. The western portion of the Glorification ends with figures of St. Peter and the Virgin. Both the north and south chancel walls are richly decorated with a painted arcade showing six apostles, each seated under a canopy. These twelve quaint persons turn their heads inquiringly towards the east and hold up their hands in rapt adoration. Each arcade is separated from a solitary figure by a highly ornamental design painted on the splays and on the immediate surround of a Norman window. The solitary figures, one on each wall, stand under a more elaborately

THE DEVIL'S CHIMNEY

painted canopy and each carries a drawn sword over his shoulder and holds a pilgrim's staff in his right hand. Each faces westward and wears a low dark cap, not unlike a shallow billycock; the figure on the south side, wearing a purple mantle edged with white over a yellow tunic, may represent Hugh de Lacy (ob. 1121), whose fair, long hair and ample beard and even his features can be distinguished. Next to him is a nearly perfect painting of a bishop in Mass vestments raising his right hand in benediction. The faceless figure on the north has faded into a somewhat ghostly state but probably represents Walter de Lacy (ob. 1084) as these two knights owned Kempley Manor after the Conquest and founded the church we see to-day.

CHAPTER XVI: *The Forest of Dean*

'I WAS surprised to find that the road mended at every step, and before I had gone four miles became very good. The country about Gloucester is well enclosed, and near Huntley begins to grow very woody. The road through Long-Hope, and all the way to Mitcheldean, is by most pleasing lanes surrounded by orchards, hills of wood, and several tall plantations of fir-trees. The houses are white, strongly ribbed and seam'd with oak timber, a proof how plentiful this country was of wood and indeed still is, notwithstanding the frequency of iron furnaces, whose smoke, impregnating the air felt to me very wholesome and agreeable. Mitcheldean, twelve miles from Gloucester, is a small market town and here the Forest of Dean begins, which I was very anxious to see (as a place of fame). It fully answered my hopes, being as enchanting as a profusion of noble trees, hawthorns, hollies, on bold scenery can make it. The irregularities of ground are charming, and the noble waving woods, hill above hill, aided by a gloomy still evening, made me feel its awful grandeur:' so wrote the Hon. John Byng, Viscount Torrington, in 1781, and I suppose every one before or since, on visiting the Forest of Dean for the first time, has felt something of his elation. No other woods in Gloucestershire compare with these in solitude and mystery, nor yet in size and compactness, for the Cotswold beechwoods are more like cathedral aisles, and only the Box Wood of the Ozleworth valley can shut out the world and all the noises with a seemingly impenetrable wall of greenness.

The 'eye between the Severn and the Wye' contains 25,000 acres of woodland, coppice and shrub or nearly half the total woodland of Gloucestershire. This primeval forest will tell the whole history of British woodlands for it has withstood the ravages of man ever since pre-Roman times. Man has always been the attacker and despoiler, and the great sea of green would have gone on retreating had not the Crown at the eleventh hour repeatedly saved the woodlands from complete destruction.

Camp-building tribes lurked on the edge of the forest to take advantage of its game, but the Romans came for the iron-ore which they dug in great surface excavations and carried along their roads to the port of Lydney. In Norman times the Vale of Leadon was largely disafforested, as may be judged from the antiquity of the churches there, so that by the reign of Henry II the woods had dwindled to the peninsula between the Severn and Wye south of a line joining Gloucester, Newent and Ross. In the time of Edward I the extent of the forest was further greatly reduced and the iron forges were consuming 4,000 oaks a year. By 1638 the requirements of shipbuilding and of local coal mines had reduced the number of trees fit for navy purposes to about 100,000. Cabins of beggarly people with goats, sheep and swine continued to invade the forest as formerly, but more unfortunate still was the virtual sale of the forest to Sir John Winter. Pepys tells of it June 20th, 1662: 'Up by four or five o'clock and to the office and there drew up the agreement between the King and Sir John Winter about the Forest of Dean. That done, I turned to the Forest of Dean in Speade's Mapps and there he showed me how it lies and the Lea bayly with the great charge of carrying it (the timber) to Lydney.' Winter employed 500 wood-cutters and eventually spared only a few hundred mature trees, whereupon the Crown stepped in to save what was left and in 1668 was empowered to enclose up to 11,000 acres of commonable waste of the forest at any one time. The limit is still in force, and although there is no right of way through the enclosures the foresters will not interfere with trespassers who keep to the paths and drives. The whole of the lawful acreage was quickly enclosed, and in 1675 the bailiwicks were replaced by six 'walks' each with a lodge and a keeper called King's or Speech House Walk, York, Danby, Gloucester, Latimer and Herbert Walks. To-day these lodges form suitable objectives for any one wishing to know all quarters of the forest, and each walk possesses some special sylvan attraction.

The eighteenth century proved a period of intermittent neglect, and the enclosures shrank to nearly 3,000 acres. Consequently, in 1808 the Crown again stepped in at the eleventh hour and ordered the Royal lands to be extended to 18,500 acres, of which the statutory 11,000 acres were to be enclosed and planted as soon as possible. The forest then began to assume its modern aspect. The deciduous trees planted at this time are the giants we see to-day, and in spite of its sage and hoary appearance the forest contains very few ancient trees. Pepys says that a 'great fall' in Edward III's reign left only those which in his time were called 'forbid trees', and five or six of these may have survived to-day, but the grand oaks in Holly Wood near the Speech House or in Churchill Enclosure or near Parkend are probably just about to celebrate their third centenary. In 1924 the woods were transferred to the control of the Forestry Commissioners, who have been planting in recent years an average of nearly 2,000 trees a day. The forest has been turned into a patchwork of green and copper in summer, and in winter the frequent conifers and evergreens give it a verdant aspect even when the silvery greys and browns of the bare deciduous trees merge into a brown carpet of decaying bracken.

The north-eastern edge of the forest forms the best approach to both its woodlands and settlements. From Westbury Halt a narrow road winds up the red-sided 'Vale of Castiard' to Flaxley, where the church, like so many in the region, is not yet one hundred years old. Adjoining it may be seen a large battlemented house standing amid fine grounds, partly ivy-clad and partially moated. Known as Flaxley Abbey, the building incorporates fragments of a Cistercian abbey, which was founded about 1146 by Roger, second son of the Earl of Hereford in memory of his father who was killed hunting on this very spot on Christmas Eve. Fate was kind to the monks as long deliberations could not have chosen a more delectable site for habitation in a vale which was 'fertile, good for fruit, suitable for grain, buried in woods, abounding in springs, a horn of plenty, a place apart from the haunts of men'.

Henry II granted the abbey the tithe of sweet chestnuts and the right of two forges, one to be itinerant, together with two leafless oaks each week to feed them. This proved so destructive of timber trees that Henry III gave them Abbot's Wood instead of the fuel, but the monks still enjoyed the chestnuts which even to-day are more plentiful here than anywhere else in the forest. There remains of the original abbey one range of conventual buildings, which includes a grand hall, severely plain, according to Cistercian needs, and vaulted in five bays with ribs springing form corbels. In addition, two narrow vaulted rooms, one great archway, a smaller doorway and various walls, either in the house or in the private grounds, have been preserved.

The abbey also treasures two portraits of Catherine Bovey, a charming young lady to whom a long inscription may be seen in the church and who also earned by her munificence a monument in Westminster Abbey. Married at fifteen and widowed at twenty-two the rich young widow lived in her manor at Flaxley for another thirty-five years and died here in 1726. Her generosity was remarkable and, remembering that charity begins at home, she left the money for rebuilding Flaxley church and the endowment of the living.

The poor children in the parish were educated at her

expense, and a month before her death she gave some thirty of them a Christmas dinner at the abbey. She was well known to Richard Steele, who thought her knowledge not inferior to that of 'the more learned of the male sex'. In the *Coverley Papers* most of the articles in which the 'Perverse Widow' figures prominently are from Steele's pen. And so it happens that although the perverse widow was probably not intended as a recognizable portrait of Catherine Bovey, there is little doubt that Steel was much influenced 'by the recollection of the stately hostess who had entertained the authors in Flaxley Abbey'.

From Flaxley we may skirt the wooded, camp-crowned Welshbury Hill and proceed past a few pretty cottages until we meet the Roman route, called the 'Dean Road', near Gun's Mill. The substantial dwelling-house with its large mill pool bright with water crowfoot was formerly an iron furnace and later a paper-mill. The pool is fed by a rapid stream which in the eighteenth century drove several mills and three iron forges.

A rough sunken track in front of Gun's Mill leads along the outskirts of Edgehill's Plantation through bracken-lined banks which overlook on the one side the deep gash of the brawling stream. After a few hundred yards a derelict forge-mill may be seen on the right, and just beyond, near to a humble cottage, the tiny stream crosses the trackway. A few yards beyond this narrow ford it is best to plunge fearlessly into the bracken, for after a little floundering you will strike one of the paths which leads to St. Anthony's Well. The well lies beneath fine beech-trees at the foot of the slope scarcely a hundred yards from the trackway just where the bracken ceased for a while and where the bald earth shapes itself into a basin. One of the largest and most picturesque pilgrimage wells in England, St. Anthony's Well probably came into being with the foundation of Flaxley Abbey. The springs collect into a small chamber, and then issue into a large, stone-lined bathing-pool, seven feet square and formerly five feet deep with steps leading into it on the south side. The present large basin was made about the beginning of the nineteenth century and was obviously an immersion well. Rudder says it was good for skin diseases and especially for mangy dogs, but all cutaneous disorders seem to have found relief in its famous waters, especially after nine dippings at sunrise or in May. To-day Gloucestershire folk will be shocked to know that the well is quite dry and that the basin needs clearing of at least two feet of accumulated debris. It seems that forestry operations higher up the hill slope have cut off the well's head-springs and the Flaxley brook now rises several yards below the basin. The Forestry Commission will, no doubt, soon put matters right and thereby earn the gratitude of hundreds of present-day pilgrims who come here each year to find as much pleasure in the charming walk and cooling reflections as the lepers and mangy dogs felt for the efficacious water.

Walkers may continue up 'Jacob's Ladder' to Cinderford, or follow the trackway which strikes the Roman road going northward over 'a land full of dingles and bottoms' to Mitcheldean, where the church, dedicated to St. Michael, is a large building situated in the midst of the long straggling village. The main entrance to the creeper-clad building consists of an ancient porch under the fifteenth-century tower, and on entering the building one is immediately impressed with the lofty barrel roof of the nave and the adjoining aisle. Constructed of oak and enriched with no less than 133 well-carved floral bosses, this beautiful fifteenth century roof has no rival among the forest churches. Other evidence of skill in wood-carving may be seen in the traceried wooden arch between the chancel and nave which extends to the roof by wooden panels decorated with early Tudor paintings showing a Doom surmounting eight scenes from the Life of Christ. The Baynham chapel contains some old glass and fine brasses to Sir Thomas Baynham (ob. 1444) and his two wives who are dressed in strait-laced style with 'butterfly and kennel' head-dresses.

The main road leads westward to Coleford, a cheerful, prosperous-looking market town of 3,000 inhabitants which occupies an important place in the minds of forest folk. In June its two days' pleasure fair makes talk for the whole neighbourhood right from those who strip bark from the trees of the high hills to those who work the coal of the primeval forests 1,000 feet underground. This is the time to see foresters really enjoying themselves, and to watch the carefree gipsies earning a pleasurable penny. If you have never seen a forester ferociously hurtling balls at a coconut you would never credit the skill of their ancestors on moonlit nights in the woodlands. The deer, however, were removed from the forest in 1850 and pheasants comprise the only temptation to-day. The Deputy Gaveller of the forest, a crown official in charge of mining matters, lives at Coleford, but the days are gone by when he called on the Free Miners' workings every Tuesday to collect the Royal Dues. The market hall, the most imposing building in the tiny town, was built in 1662 with the help of a grant of £40 from Charles II. and has recently been enlarged. David Musket (ob. 1847), the famous iron-founder who first advocated the use of blackband iron ore, lived here, and here his son Robert, an equally famous iron-master, was born.

From Coleford a tarmac road leads straight across the heart of the forest on the track of a Roman road to the wide clearing near the Speech House. This is the heart of the forest and here the Verderers and Free Miners still meet. The large, square, substantial house, now an hotel, was built as the lodge for the King's Walk and was probably finished a few years before the year 1682, the date inscribed on the Crown over the west entrance, for another stone removed from the stable bears the date 1676. The old Court Room now forms the dining-hall, and its dais or so-called musicians' gallery and its original panelling have not been disturbed. From the Speech House the beauty and variety of the woods may be sampled at leisure. Perhaps you will be charmed with the rather pathetic avenue of black spruce or with the healthy gloss of the hollies and copper colourings of the beech; the big oaks near Edge End may attract you or the large ponds along the cloudy Cannop stream. Only the occasional bleat of a sheep or the grunt of a pig and the chance meeting with a forester will remind you that the woods are inhabited. The dells and high hills have a carpet of short turf often tinted with harebells, the ground flora is far from dull, and the birds of the forest are more than usually numerous. A favourite walk is that through the Holly Wood south of the Speech House where the noble oaks are interspersed with thousands of stout hollies as old as the Speech House itself. At the New Fancy Colliery the clamber to the top of the great tip reveals the whole vast forest clothing the encircling hills, and rising gradually in great green waves to the high rim of the amphitheatre. Beyond the lower southern edge of the woodlands the Severn estuary may be seen with its twin islands, Flat Holm and Steep Holm, while the horizon fades into the blue edge of the Cotswolds. Only an occasional puff of white smoke tells of the presence of other collieries, for the mining activities cause but insignificant breaks in the phalanx of trees, and the kindly bracken and ubiquitous birch soon clothe the old tips. Here the basin-shaped nature of the forest may be appreciated, and we can realize why the miners everlastingly pump out brown waters which have drained underground into the coal measures occupying the centre of the basin. The forest produces on an average nearly two tons of coal each minute, and the workings vary in size from the large collieries to the small surface diggings or 'scratchings' worked by the Free Miners. Even to-day a few miners work for themselves and pay royalties direct to the Crown rather than sell their 'gales' to the companies; a 'Free Miner' must be born of a 'free' father, and after working a year and a day in a local mine he may then apply for the grant of a 'gale', which entitles him to work on his own.

Across the road opposite the tall chimney of the New Fancy Colliery, cinder tracks lead into the chestnuts and oaks of Russells Enclosure, and the main pathway brings us after a few dozen yards to the famous 'Three Brothers', giant sessile oaks, relics of the medieval forest. These woods are bright with bluebells in May and speckled with foxgloves in June when the bracken begins to thrust its snaky green shoots above its decayed leaves and to dwarf the yellow flares of gorse.

From the colliery the way east leads past the tall beeches of Danby Lodge and along the valley of a small stream to Blackpool Bridge where the 'Dean Road', the best-preserved Roman road in the forest, may be seen to perfection. The trackway and kerb-stones of the route have been traced from near Lydney straight away for ten miles to the present site of Mitcheldean, and at Blackpool Bridge the well-constructed pavement has been revealed by the spade for over fifty yards. The roadway is paved with largish stones to a width of eight feet and enclosed with kerb-stones from ten to twenty inches in length, and I suppose nowhere in an English woodland may be seen a more complete section of a Roman trackway than that ascending from the ford north of this stream. The Roman way continues northwards as a green path to the pretty Soudley villages, whence a charming forest road leads to Little Dean. Here the fabric of the church of St. Ethelbert dates mainly from the early fourteenth century, but the massive pillars are

Norman, and various additions, including the tower and broached spire, were made in the Perpendicular period.

The ancient earthwork on Camp Hill may be sought out, but above all I advise a walk to Littledean Hill just to the west, or to Pleasant Stile a short way to the south of Little Dean village. Here the view can scarcely be surpassed in Gloucestershire; the whole great loop of the Severn lies before us, a mighty river swinging among orchard lands, while beyond it the eye roves southwards from Bredon Hill to the spires of Cheltenham and the glistening tower of Gloucester Cathedral until looking for favourite landmarks we pick out Cleeve Cloud, Painswick Beacon and the Tynedale Monument on Stinchcombe Hill. These scenes were beloved also by our recently deceased Gloucester poet Ivor Gurney, who in his poem 'Near Midsummer' describes the view:

> 'Severn's most fair to-day!
> See what a tide of blue
> She pours, and flecked alway
> With gold, and what a crew
> Of sea-gulls snowy white
> Float round her to delight
> Villagers, Travellers.'

THE CORRIDOR OF THE WYE

'Once again
Do I behold these steep and lofty cliffs,
That on a wild secluded scene impress
Thoughts of more deep seclusion; and connect
The landscape with the quiet of the sky.

Once again I see
These hedgerows, hardly hedgerows, little lines
Of sportive wood run wild; these pastoral farms
Green to the very door; and wreaths of smoke
Sent up in silence from among the trees.'
—WORDSWORTH; from the
Gloucestershire bank overlooking Tintern.

'THE EYE between the Severn and the Wye' does not consist wholly of secretive woodlands. The high lands overlooking the Wye are usually only wooded upon the steep river-side cliffs as the limestone soils were easily cleared of timber in spite of the heaviest rainfall in Gloucestershire, while the flat lands sloping to the Severn and floored with fertile sandstones formed such rich agricultural tilths that they were soon brought under the plough. The Wye woodlands are quite distinct from those of Dean; their hangars are more luminous, and more friendly; we no longer meet miners on bicycles, or start at the sudden appearance of a sheep; even the ground flora is different in that it is richer in species. Bracken and foxgloves still abound, but the yew and whitebeam flourish in the woods; columbines, a rare tall spurge, and several uncommon evergreen shrubs may be found, while the amazing wealth of delicate ferns and mosses more than atones for their marked sparsity in Cotswold Gloucestershire.

The magnificent view from the lip of the crag at Symond's Yat, over the ribbon-like river below to the hills and forests beyond, is too well known to need description. The chequerwork of green meadows in the great loop of the Wye looks marvellously flat, and the river assumes a placid mirror-like surface as if enjoying a leisurely stretch before the hills close in upon it and cause the weirs and pools all the way to Lancaut. Symond's Yat has other attractions to offer; from the beeches upon the high sheer face of the Coldwell Rocks we may peer down to the shimmering river and to the railway clinging to a tiny shelf, on which a train looks so toy-like as it disappears into the twisting tunnel beneath the rock face on which we stand that it is a pleasure to hear the 'Elver Express', as the Chepstow folk call it, shunt away from Symond's Yat station.

A short journey through the Highmeadow Woods brings us to Staunton, which has arisen amid a small patch of farming land in a clearing almost completely surrounded by the great woodlands of the Highmeadow estate. For a forest village, it possesses both charm and tidiness and makes, too, a convenient walking centre. The church of All Saints, which stands in a lovely churchyard on a hillock above the road-side, seems to have been a remarkably long time a-building. Founded originally about 1100 it was still being altered and enlarged in the fifteenth century. The western end of the north arcade consists of two plain Norman arches merging into three Transitional piers with pointed arches, while the south arcade is of a later date still and its mouldings show increasingly Early English tendencies towards the east. The fourteenth-century font has been restored, but the other, somewhat crudely decorated with a diamond design and band of carving, is early Norman work, and some think that it was even hewn from a Roman stone.

Staunton possesses one other treasure, the famous Buck Stone which is to be found on the flanks of Staunton Meend just where the sandstone edge drops precipitously to the valley. From its huge mass, situated at nearly 900 feet above sea-level, we can survey the high wooded hills of Gloucestershire and the Welsh mountains away to the north. The stone balances its thick table-top upon a narrow pedestal, and the whole mass used to rock at a touch until a party of irresponsible tourists pushed the stone off its perch and sent it hurtling down through the bracken and firs clothing the precipice. It cost several hundred pounds to cement the stone back into position, but alas! it rocked no longer, yet the money was well spent for the view is as superb as ever, and the stony climb through a profusion of bracken and elegant brightly-spotted foxgloves is a constant delight.

About four miles to the south-west, just at the entrance to the village of Newland, is the huge stump of an oak, with an excessively gnarled hollow trunk that reaches twelve feet in height and gives forth each year a sprouting of young branches. The girth is enormous, and although measurements vary according to the number of arboreal warts included, we can safely say that the 'trunk measurement' attains 45 feet. The oak, which was probably 400 years old at the foundation of Newland church, is by far the oldest living thing in the county or even in England.

The pretty, clean-looking village of Newland has grown up in the shape of an irregular square around its spacious churchyard. The clearing, which originated probably during the reign of King John, lies in the winding valley of a tributary of the Wye, from which it is hidden by the high ridge crossed by the lane to Redbrook. The houses on the east side of the square are unusually large and substantial for a forest village and several of them are clad prettily in ever-green shrubs and creeping plants. Spout Farm would do credit to a Cotswold town, and adjoining it, some way back from the road, is the Dower House, built in the late eighteenth century by Squire Probyn, whose crest, an os-trich's head with a key in its mouth, explains the name of the nearby inn. All Saint's Church was erected by Robert of Wakering in the early thirteenth century, but the belfry is a century later and some of the windows are, or were before restoration, Perpendicular. From its foundation All Saints' became the mother church of the forest, which has many an older but no nobler or more spacious building. Coleford, Bream and Clearwell were until recently mere hamlets of Newland, whose vast churchyard has been the last resting-place of forest folk for over 600 years, and which still on Palm Sunday becomes the mecca of forest pilgrims with bunches of flowers. The thick stone-slated roofs partly moss-covered, and the great western tower, with its elaborate pinnacles and open-work parapet, complete an impressive picture of strength and simplicity. In some ways All Saints' is almost a replica of the church at Northleach conceived in the dour steadfast mind of a forester, who lacked the artistic polish of a travelled merchant, and built in the local reddish stone which appears dull compared with the lumin-ous Cotswold oolite.

The church contains several interesting brasses; in the south chapel a brass shows Sir Robert Greyndour (ob. 1444) in armour, and his wife in a flowing gown and horned head-dress. A small brass of the same age depicts a miner with a pickaxe in his hand and a naked candle in his mouth, an ancient reminder of the freedom from gas of the local mines. Worth noticing, too, are the effigies of priests in mass vestments and the handsome table-tomb bearing the recut figures of Sir John Joce (ob. 1349) of Clearwell and his wife. For those interested in needlework I must add that the curtains in the side of the south chapel formed part of the hangings in Westminster Abbey at the coronation of George V. In the churchyard may be found the fine panelled tomb of Jenkin Wyrall (ob. 1457), an hereditary forester or Forester of Fee, who is depicted in full proportion wearing his hunting costume: a loose frock with full sleeves and a short kilt split at the sides, trunk hose and low buckskin boots, and with a curious cap on his head. The right hand holds a hunting horn and the left a falchion, whilst the faithful hound at his feet completes a contemporary picture almost unique among English monuments. Near by, just south-west of the restored market cross, another relic of forest life may be found in the form of a stone slab incised with the figure of a bowman with bow and arrows, a portrait no doubt of a royal forester in the reign of James I. The eight pleasant alms-houses and gardens adjoining the tower end of the churchyard were founded together with a grammar school by Edward Bell in 1623, while a long row of symmetrical houses with small windows facing the south side of the churchyard, contains sixteen tenements and a house for a lecturer, founded in 1615 by William Jones and placed in the care of the Haberdashers' Company. The old folk had two shillings each week and a gown yearly, and great is the excitement in the parish to-day when a vacancy occurs or when the 'daber 'ashers' come to visit their wards.

From Newland a hilly upland route skirts Clearwell and brings us right in front of St. Briavel's church and the main gateway to the castle. Both church and castle stand on the northern lip of a platform 800 feet high which commands extensive views ranging in a circle from Trelleck Beacon and the Welsh Sugar Loaf round to the Buck Stone and May Hill and so right over the forest to the Stroudwater Hills. The castle stands on a circular artificial mound which is completely encircled with a deep moat 500 yards round,

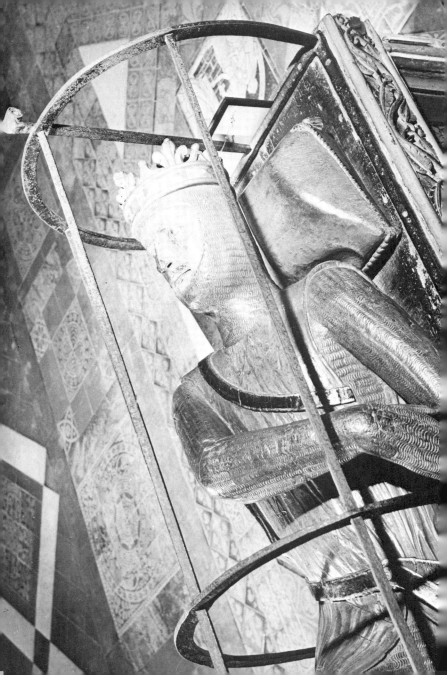

and to-day planted with lovely bushes of blue hydrangeas and quite dry save for the little pool near the entrance towers. Walking around the tall, ruinous, buttressed walls we get some idea of the strength of the tiny stronghold and of the wise choice of the site by Milo Fitzwalter who erected the massive structure about 1131 as a protection against Welsh raids. The two gaunt towers on either side of the present gate-house formed the original north-west front and date from about 1276. By tolling the bell and paying a modest fee we are allowed to see round the three storied towers which contain several hexagonal rooms, including a great kitchen with a ten foot wide hearth and a turnspit wheel and fireplace of Stuart times. The room above built into the nine foot walls of sandstone and used as a prison and bridewell in the eighteenth century was said by John Howard to resemble a common alehouse. This and the adjoining rooms retain their thirteenth-century fire-places and no doubt a 'common ale-house' would gladly resemble these fine rooms to-day. Another archway gives access to Chapel Court, where an arched doorway leads into the chapel which in Elizabeth's time was converted into a Court Room. A room to the south with an original fire-place and rudely sculptured built-up chimney-piece formed the jury room. The shell of the castle walls encloses lawns and gardens as the great keep and nearby portions collapsed two hundred years ago. St. Briavel's, being a private residence, contains many other interesting items, and such details as the portcullis groves, the molten lead-pourer, the horn carved on a chimney and the prisoners' scratchings on the window splays make its grim history more real.

The church of St. Briavel, a pleasantly weathered and splendidly situated little building, has a good deal to commend it. The south arcade and three small, deeply-splayed clerestory windows belong to the church which was consecrated in 1166. The four central arches, once supporting

TOMB OF ROBERT, DUKE OF NORMANDY

a tower, are slightly younger, while the north arcade is Decorated work of the thirteenth century and two curiously carved transept arches are apparently Early English. The chancel tower, and the doorway, in spite of its rounded archway, are modern, but the plain font is genuine Norman. Every Whit Sunday, after evening service, the vicar throws cubes of bread and cheese from the church to the people and so perpetuates a custom started in 1206 to mark the people's rights of cutting firewood and grazing in Hudnall's Wood, and of cutting wood but not timber in other parts of the forest. It is said that these rights were obtained from the Earl of Hereford at the instance of his good lady upon the same hard terms that Lady Godiva wrung the privileges for the citizens of Coventry, but if this is so, the rights stimulated the dour foresters' minds much more than the noble deed.

Narrow, low-hedged country lanes lead southwards to Tidenham Chase, which also makes a delightful walking country. as the plantations are usually threaded by pleasant public footways. Within a mile the road approaches close to the precipitous banks of the Wye, and at one point a platform has been cut to show the lovely view over the great loop of the Wye at Lancaut. Deep below lies Long Hope Reach bordered with the wooded spur of Piercefield Park, and beyond, the winding river hugs the foot of the great amphitheatre which rises up to the mighty Wyndcliff. A lane near this viewpoint leads off to Lancaut, but far more pleasant and vigorous is the footpath along the bank of the Wye, with the high cliffs above you and the deep stream below.

Just where the stone quarry and woods end, the little church of St. James is perched on a low cliff above the river. Its roofless, ruinous walls no longer protect the tombstones within from the wind and rain, but it is lovely as a ruin, and the remarkable two-light window at the peak of the western gable and the early Norman east window are worthy of preservation. In summer an annual service is held in the churchyard in the most pleasant setting imaginable. The old folk take the high road between the hazel bushes of the cliff top, and the young the low path along the Wye whose cliffs again echo on this Sunday to the sound of hymns.

'SABRINA FAIR'. THE TIDAL ESTUARY OF THE SEVERN

'When Noe went sailing with his crew
And waters covered over the earth,
Trees that in Eden-orchard grew
Got washed away to Minsterworth.'
—F. W. HARVEY

The banks and sands and shallow creeks of the Severn, north of Lydney, are the scene of great activity in March and April when the elvers migrate up the river. The young eels, tiny transparent worms like three-inch lengths of thin grey string with a black bead at the end, have taken three years to come from near the Bahamas to their parent river. They wriggle up the Severn, filling its creeks and riddling its water until in good years the river is dense with them. Keeping as close to the shore as possible and moving always against the tide, the elvers are best caught just before or just after the bore. The fishers go out with scoops, which are fashioned of a cheese cloth over a pear-shaped wooden frame securely fixed to a long handle. For the fishing, a position is usually taken up on the shore, and working by means of these scoops and of shallow nets placed just below the surface the water is strained, as it were, of its wriggling elvers, which are tossed into barrels, where, to show their displeasure, they squirm incessantly and fill each cask with foam until it froths over like fermenting home-made wine. In the evening when the fishers take lanterns with them to entice the elvers to the nets, some stretches of the Severn sparkle almost like the quay of a distant harbour. What now of the elvers? Following a cleaning in sieves with saline water, they are tossed into a cauldron of boiling water, during which process they lose their grey shininess and become almost white before being sold to the waiting customer. The billions of elvers in boxes at Gloucester market are dealt with in various ways; the fry-with-milk school may have many followers, but nothing, to my mind, or stomach rather, will ever surpass elvers, scores of them, fried in best dairy butter with a capping of beaten eggs. Thousands more are sent alive in large tanks from the elver depot at Epney to European countries either to stock the rivers or to be cooked in some foreign way. All eaters of elvers, which is the same as saying all dwellers in the Vale of Severn, will welcome F. W. Harvey's saga on the virtues of this jellified boneless worm, the asparagus of the fish epicurean:

> 'Up the Severn river from Lent to Eastertide
> Millions and millions of slithy elvers glide,
> Millions, billions of glassy bright
> > Little wormy fish,
> > Chewed string fish,
> > Slithery, dithery fish,
> > In the dead of night.
>
> Up the gleaming river miles and miles along
> Lanterns burn yellow: old joke and song
> Echo as fishermen dip down a slight
> > Wide frail net,
> > Gauzy white net,
> > Strong long net
> > In the water bright.

From the Severn river at daybreak come
Hundreds of happy fishermen home
With bags full of elvers: perhaps that's why
> We all love Lent,
> Lean mean Lent,
> Fishy old Lent
> When the elvers fry.

When elvers fry for breakfast with egg chopped small
And bacon from the side that's hung upon the wall
When the dish is on the table how the children shout
> "Oh, what funny fish,
> Wormy squirmy fish,
> Weeny white fish,
> Our mother's dishing out!"

But any way, good people, you may search the river over
Before a breakfast tastier or cheaper you discover
Than elvers, and if all the year the elver season lasted

> I wouldn't mind a bit,
> I wouldn't care a bit,
> Not a little tiny bit,
> *How* long I fasted!'

Newnham is by far the prettiest and most pleasurable
town on the banks of the Lower Severn. It perches itself
upon a cliff overlooking a fine stretch of sand, and whether
approaching from north or south we climb sharply from
the flat river-bank to the lime avenue of the churchyard.
The wide, sloping, tree-lined street of substantial houses
possesses an air of pleasant tidiness rather than of antiquity,
for Newnham, although one of the five ancient boroughs
of Gloucestershire, has little of architectural interest. From
here, in 1171, Henry II with the great Strongbow, Earl of

Pembroke, set sail for his expedition to Ireland. Yet the shipping does not seem to have brought much profit, as in the thirteenth century the citizens begged successfully to be excused representation on the grounds of expense.

In the fifteenth century vessels of 500 tons were still being built and owned by Newnham merchants, and the Pyrke family had built a quay for small boats. Newnham is now mainly a local 'riverside resort', although forest coal is still shipped from Bullo Pill Wharf and ferries run across to Arlingham. The church of St. Mary, twice re-built completely in the nineteenth century, contains little of interest save a sculptured tympanum and a fine Norman font, carved with an arcade of the Apostles, which was removed from an ancient chapel at Nab's End before the Severn swallowed up the site. The manor-house of Stuart times is now probably the large hotel with a great porch surmounted by a stone eagle which faces the church. Its interior contains panelled rooms and a grand oak staircase in which a small window is filled with early seventeenth-century glass illustrating the fable of the grasshopper and the ants.

Along the stretch of Severn from Newnham to Epney, or from 'Stonebench Inn', or Lower Parting near Gloucester, the bore may be seen and heard to perfection at times of high spring tides. The wave begins to appear near the Guscar Rocks at Woolaston and grows gradually in height as the river narrows and becomes shallower past Sharpness and The Noose beyond Frampton. Opposite Awre the vast sandy estuary of the Severn suddenly contracts to only one-quarter of its previous width, and here the rushing tide hurls itself into the river's current and thrusts it upstream as a wall of foaming, gurgling, resisting water. The wave travels up-river at the rate of a dozen miles an hour and reaches a height of over three feet in mid-stream and of five feet near the sides. John Speed, writing in 1607, tells us that the Severn has no rival in England 'for Channell broader, for Streame swifter, or for Fish better stored. There is in it a rage and fury of waters, . . . raising up the sands from the bottom, winding and driving them upon heapes; sometimes overflowing the bankes, roveth a great way upon the face of the bordering grounds, and again retyreth as a Conqueror into the usuall Channell. Unhappy is the Vessel which it taketh full upon the side . . .' The phenomenon, except for the persistency and marked punctuality, thoroughly belies its name and a long acquaintance will not dim the wonder of a great bore. The distant murmuring like low rumbling thunder which is heard coming up the river quickly changes to a sibilant roaring just as if the 'Elver Express' were ploughing a swift furrow in the very midst of the mighty stream. Then a white wall of tumbling water races round the bend, and behind it great undulations form which fill the sandy bed and lap noisily over the banks before retreating into the murky, seething channel.

We cross three miles of flattish orchard country to reach Westbury, a village less attractive but considerably more interesting architecturally than Newnham. The tower stands some fifty feet from the church and is crowned by a magnificent octagonal spire rising to a height of 160 feet. The tower itself, erected in the Early English style, has a turret with slot openings for arrows, and a priest's chamber floored with stout elm planks. The spire, which was added about 1270, forms a remarkable example of skill in carpentry, especially for the intricate network of oaken beams and for the perfection of the shingling, done, so they say, with staves from old cider casks in the reign of Charles II. The oldest parts of the church, including the north arcade, with its aisle and porch, date back to about 1300, but considerable enlargements were made during the next 150 years, and to recent times we owe the clerestory and a thorough 'restoration'. Ecclesiologists will notice the Tudor font, while the less expert but equally curious visitor will find an Elizabethan chalice, an old alms-box with triple locks attached to an ancient iron chest, and on a window-sill, the remains of a medieval piscina carved into a rose with eight holes for drainage. The chained copy of Foxe's *Book of Martyrs*, which may be seen in a glass case, was presented, it is said, by the printer, perhaps because of its intimate account of the persecution of James Baynham, the son of the lord of Westbury manor. After much torture the unlucky Baynham was burnt over a barrel of pitch on May Day, 1532, but with a fortitude so typical of the martyrs described by Foxe he is supposed to have cried out during the burning that the fire and stake felt to him like a 'bed of roses'.

CHAPTER XVIII: *Gloucester, the County Capital*

Caer Glow, 'the splendid city', so they called it,
Those funny beggars brilliant in woad;
And then the tramping Roman came and walled it
And called it Glevum, throwing many a road
Through and around it. Dane and Saxon strode
Awhile its streets; then they whose quills did blot
That Domesday Book which every city showed.
Old Gloucester reigns the King of all the lot.
                                              —F. W. HARVEY.

AT GLOUCESTER, amid meadows beloved of dropworts and meadowsweet, the Severn parts its waters to enclose Alney Island and to form two shallower streams fordable by primitive man. Iron Age man favoured the gravelly site, which the Romans renamed Glevum and fortified to resist the inroads of the Silures. Ermin Street came here from Corinium and later route-ways led southward to Abone near Bristol and northward to Worcester. In 97 A.D. Emperor Nerva raised the settlement to the status of a colonia and Glevum became a 'Cheltenham' of Roman Britain. Little may be actually seen of the Roman town save the relics in the museum and a few patches of tessellated pavement, such as that preserved at the National Provincial Bank in Eastgate Street, on the site of the Prætorium. The walled city of medieval days seems to have corresponded with the Roman town and the four main streets which to-day meet at the Cross are modelled on the rectilinear plan of the Romans.

Although the Battle of Deorham (577) led to the sack of Gloucester, it soon recovered and was the residence of

Alfred in 595 and the deathbed, in 940, of Athelstan, Emperor of all Britain.   The town has been rightly called Royal Gloucester.   William the Conqueror spent many a winter here and in 1085–86 Domesday Survey was started in the Chapter House.   It was at Gloucester that Rufus was prostrated in 1093 by a serious illness which terrified him so much that he swore to reign more justly in future.   Henry I made his son Robert its earl and Henry II built two bridges with a strong castellated west gate on the longer one, which was demolished only a century ago.   At Gloucester in 1216 the boy king Henry III was crowned by Cardinal Guala, the Papal Legate, with a sinple ring of gold as the crown jewels were in the Wash.

Most of the pre-Tudor kings held Parliaments at Gloucester and here Richard III is said to have found it in his heart to issue the order for the murder of his two nephews in the Tower.   Henry VIII favoured the citizens with the sight of the two prettiest of his six wives, Anne Boleyn and Jane Seymour, while Elizabeth slept at St. Nicholas House and gave the city the privileges of a seaport much to the chagrin of the merchants of Bristol.   The walls were still strong and the four gates still in use, when Royal Gloucester betrayed its name in the Civil War and, owing partly to dislike of Laud, then Dean of the Cathedral, took up the Parliamentary cause and withstood a month's seige in 1643. Charles II remembered this at his Restoration and the walls were razed to the ground.   Only one of the wooden gates survived and that is in the museum.   To-day, Gloucester has grown into a bustling city, with the Severn its main asset, a son of the King its namesake, and the Cathedral tower still the pride and glory of the countryside.

The original Benedictine monastery of St. Peter was founded by Osric, a viceroy of King Ethelred, in 681, for both sexes under the control of Kyneburga, his sister.   Upon the death of the third Abbess in 767 the building lay desolate until 823 when Beornulf, King of Mercia, rebuilt it and granted it to the secular canons. Two centuries later, according to Leland, King Cnut expelled the secular clerks for ill-living and on the advice of Wulfstan, Bishop of Worcester, immediately re-established it on a slightly different site, actually athwart the Roman wall. The fortunes of the house were low until Abbot Serbo began to erect the new church which was consecrated in 1100. Within a few years the number of monks had increased from ten to one hundred. An earthquake and many serious fires which damaged the church, and the incessant alterations of the fabric are too numerous and technical to concern us. In the August of 1534 Abbot Parker and his thirty-five monks acknowledged the royal supremacy and in the day following New Year's Eve six years later the abbey was dissolved. The clear annual value of its revenues, including the four cells, was £1,846 5s. 9d., for the abbey owned lands and churches throughout the length and breadth of the Cotswolds, from Buckland in the north to Beverstone and Winterbourne in the south. The prior and monks were given particular lands and rents or profits for their several offices, the prior having £20 a year, the chamberer £10, and Richard Anselm the kitchener £8 a year. The list of offices of the abbey was astonishingly long and included a master of the choristers, of the organ and of the grammar school, a principal shepherd, a valet of horse, and of the brewhouse, a tailor and a keeper of the felling-axe for the trees.

In 1541 by a charter of the King, the see of Gloucester was founded and the abbot's lodging became the bishop's palace. The Abbey Church of St. Peter was in future to be known as the Cathedral of the Holy and Undivided Trinity of Gloucester. The moveable properties of the church had been inventoried and handed over to the King's commissioners in Bishop Hooper's time but in 1553 a chalice and the nine great bells had been graciously returned for use 'until the King's Majesty's pleasure shall be therein further knowen.' Three months later King Henry died and his pleasure was never 'further knowen', so Gloucester kept its ancient bells.

No tower is more familiar to Gloucestershire folk than the one at Gloucester. It dominates the whole city and the vale around and is a pharos for all the neighbouring hills. It is at once majestic, massive and lovely and from a distance becomes a fairy growth of delicate tracery and crocketed pinnacles.

> Now, on the tower top, where crockets ceased
> Like lace against the sky, they set at pause
> The golden wind-vane, that from west to east
> Would turn his beak to tempests or to flaws.
> It poised, it swung, it breasted the wind's stream,
> The work was done, the hands had wrought the dream.

The interior of the church is interesting as the evolution of various architectural styles can plainly be seen and much liberty has been taken with the Norman framework, the prevailing idea being apparently that Norman walls and foundations, like donkeys, serve best when heavily laden. The ground plan still remains much the same as it was in the twelfth century but most of the interior has been transformed from plain dignity to flippant airs and graces, frills and furbelows, that are strangely out of place neighbouring the great gaunt pillars.

The south porch was built by Abbot Morwent (c. 1430), who also reconstructed the western bays of the nave and had designs on the rest of the building. Ever since, the remaining seven Norman bays with their massive piers and plain capitals have been menacingly viewed by would-be restorers. The dwarf triforium above the chevron mouldings of the high arcades was restored and practically spoilt by

Abbot Foliot's masons in the thirteenth century but the schemings hatched against the great pillars culminated five centuries later when Bishop Benson actually wanted to flute them. Byng, in the *Torrington Diaries*, describes them as seemingly 'gouty and immoderately swelled'.

The Early English vaulting of the nave is less successful than at Tewkesbury. The corbels with quaint grotesque heads for their bases are pleasant enough, but the vaulting which springs from marble shafts seems too meanly conceived to suit the lofty, unadorned and giant piers.

The north aisle is the work of Abbot Serbo and his immediate successors and here the capitals and ribs of the Norman vault are Decorated and the original windows filled in with Perpendicular tracery. The south aisle, with its ball flowers and pointed windows, does much credit to Abbot Thokey (*c.* 1318) and is more pleasing than its fellow.

At the west end of the north aisle are two markedly contrasting memorials, both ill at ease in the Norman church. The one, a vast tablet to an insignificant local doctor of medicine, is called by Edward Foord, 'a Sahara of aridity and bad taste, with an epitaph of fearful and wonderful length and pomposity'; the other, a relief in marble by John Flaxman, has the imaginative beauty and appeal of the work of a great artist.

There are two ancient monuments at the east end of the south aisle also. The rather plain chantry tomb, bearing traces of its original colour, holds the alabaster effigy of Abbot Thomas Seabroke (ob. 1457) who built the tower. In a recess almost opposite lie the effigies of an armoured knight, probably Sir Thomas Brydges (ob. 1407) and his lady, both wearing SS collars.

The south transept has a peculiar interest for lovers of architecture. The original walls have been pared down and lined with Perpendicular tracery, a means adopted by the monks in the choir and north transept also, to hide the grimness of the Norman work. The casing consists of a scaffolding of open panels filled with foliated headings and elaborate tracery which is vaulted with a 'cob-web' roof, having no bosses at the joints. If, and the weight of opinion inclines to the view, this is the work of Abbot Wygmore (ob. 1337) then this south transept is the birthplace of the lovely Perpendicular Gothic style.

The transept has two doors; one, now built up, is surmounted by an apish monster with a double body, while the other, usually called the Pilgrim's Door, is guarded by angels with faces of great beauty. Near the chapel of St. Andrew may be seen the Prentice's Bracket, consisting of the figure of an apprentice supported by a mason's square and a master mason, which commemorates either the workmen or an apprentice who lost his life when working on the tower. Richard Pates (ob. 1588), the founder of Cheltenham Grammar School, lies here, and Alderman Blackleech who is shown in full Jacobean dress and the widest of wide bows on his shoes.

The ambulatory is of much architectural interest since it stands on another of similar plan in the crypt and is surmounted by a wide triforium which corresponds to it even in the subsidiary chapels. This imposition of three galleries in the form of three stories is unique in England. The ambulatory itself, a curious mixture of plain massive Norman work and delicate Perpendicular screens, leads us to the north transept, which is richer and more ornate than that on the south.

The choir, which is the great glory of the cathedral, always comes as a surprise as it is almost completely screened off from the nave. It is indeed like a magic cave. The Perpendicular Gothic casing of the walls has a splendour and an elegance which belittle description. The strong light pilasters spring upwards for seventy feet as clean as the bole of a beech tree and then branch into a gorgeous lofty canopy of intertwining branches. The details are well illumined for the whole eastern end of the choir consists of tracery and glass, thus forming a window 72 feet high and 38 feet wide, the largest in England. In plan it is slightly elliptical and so exceeds the width of the choir and that of its only rival, the great East window at York Minster, by just five feet. The mid-fourteenth century glass contains a rich variety of blues and reds and a very silvery white, but the figures themselves do not show the same artistic skill. The coronation of the Virgin with a company of saints and angels occupies most of the window, and the remainder is filled with kings and heraldic devices of the warriors who fought at Crecy.

The stalls of the choir with their fine pinnacled canopies retain much of their ancient woodwork and the misericords are beautifully carved with objects of everyday interest to the medieval woodworkers. Here a fox is seen carrying off a goose; there an owl is being attacked by small birds, but we must carry our thoughts further afield to meet the elephant and the grotesque dragons, the mis-shapen monsters so beloved by that romancer, Geoffrey de Mandeville. The sports of the day have their places too, such as wrestling and backswords, hawking and hunting, while the pageantry loved by the people is represented by a coronation scene and a tournament. The sins of the daughters of Eve were never far from the mind in medieval times; Eve is shown tempting Adam, and Samson shorn of his hair by Delilah.

Another fine piece of carved woodwork is the painted panelled chest, decorated with armorial shields, which stands in the midst of the choir and supports the effigy carved in bog oak, of Robert of Normandy, the eldest son of the Conqueror. The Duke is finely depicted as a Crusader accoutred in chain mail and wearing a coronet decorated with fleur-de-lis and strawberry leaves. Old folk say that formerly the Duke used to raise himself up if you pressed hard upon his uplifted foot.

The stonework of the tombs shows less inspiration and happiness. The Perpendicular canopy covers an effigy of Osric, the founder of St. Peter's; adjoining, and cramped by the lowness of the arch in which it was erected, is the gorgeous Decorated tabernacle of Edward II. Abbot Thokey fetched the body of the murdered king here from Berkeley in 1327 and the glorious choir was built out of offerings laid at his shrine.

The choir and parts of the nave look magnificent when viewed from the triforium which is well-known for its 'Whispering Gallery', a narrow passage passing right behind the great window and having acoustic properties which considerably augment the faintest whisper. The visitor for the first time to Gloucester Cathedral has, however, a greater joy in store, for hidden behind the great window of the choir is the large Lady Chapel built by Abbots Hanley and Farley during the later half of the fifteenth century. The last of the great additions made to the building by the monks, it is, perhaps, the finest of all, being a product of imagination, ingenuity and superb craftsmanship. The great choir window remains unspoiled by the addition and the original Norman apse was replaced by a beautifully vaulted vestibule upon which a screen of open tracery rises to the roof of the Lady Chapel. The interior of this chapel forms the climax of the loveliest inspiration of English architecture for the Perpendicular style has hardly been better understood than at its birthplace here in Gloucester. The Chapel is as light and cheerful as an open forest under a cloudless sky in May and here at last is a roof which must have satisfied even its builders. The graceful shafts of the vaulting and the cunning simplicity of the cobweb roof combine with the coloured foliage bosses to form a natural conclusion to the lovely design.

Before visiting the cloisters at Gloucester it is perhaps advisable to see the crouching sullen piers of the crypt which has the same plan as the east end of the church above it, excluding the Lady Chapel. A greater contrast between crypt and cloisters can hardly be imagined. Abbot Horton commenced building the latter about 1360 but Abbot Froucester (1381–1412) duly completed a structure unrivalled in England. The columned archways and exquisite fan vaulting give a sense of serenity and repose, which seems to embody the monastic ideal of the daily contemplation of the beauty of God.

The cloisters were devised as a quadrangle with ten bays on each face, each bay illumined by a Perpendicular window looking out upon the cloister garth. Two of the galleries were used as promenades, while that on the south was used for reading and meditations, and that on the north for ablution and maybe occasionally for recreation. Each side is nearly fifty yards long and when viewed from one end becomes a vista of shafts of sunlight coming through columned arches which rise to delicate fan-vaulting, the earliest of its kind in England. It is indeed as Leland says 'a right goodly and sumptuous piece of work'. The most satisfying gallery is possibly that with the twenty arched recesses, two to each window; the most interesting is that with the monastic lavatory, a narrow corridor-like apartment which projects from the main cloister into the garth. Here, opposite the long and somewhat primitive stone water trough once lead-lined, may be seen the groined recess in which the monks kept their towels.

The main cloisters communicate with the small Abbot's Cloister and with the Chapter House, both Norman in style except for the east end which has been transformed to Perpendicular. The Norman part of the Chapter House includes a fine doorway with zig-zag moulding and a blind arcade along the lower wall beneath which may be traced the line of the original stone benches, the meeting place of many a Norman parliament. The names on the wall of the barons buried here have recently been restored and they mainly consist of contemporaries of the Conqueror, Walter de Lacy, Bernard de Neufmarche, Roger Fitz-Osbern, Earl of Hereford, and Richard 'Strongbow', son of the Earl of Pembroke.

A few other portions of the conventual buildings of St. Peter's are still standing.   Of the remains of all four gateways, that leading to St. Mary's Square is the most perfect and retains an upper room decorated with a typical Early English arcade. An irregular quadrangle of archways, called the Little Cloisters, may be seen and these probably enclosed the monks' herbarium. Near to them are six graceful arches, formerly part of the infirmary which was pulled down at the Reformation as being superfluous.   The present deanery, formerly the Prior's Lodgings, contains much Norman and Early English work as well as the timber-framed roofs visible from College Square where Richard II is said to have held his Parliament.

It would be ungrateful to expect the city of Gloucester to prove as interesting as the Cathedral. A modern city of 60,000 inhabitants, teeming with transit traffic, cannot hope to retain as much of its old-world buildings as the inhabitants would wish. The Cross itself had to go and the old castle has long been replaced by the County gaol. Yet enough remains of the old town to give interest to each of the four thoroughfares. Previous to the Dissolution there were two monasteries here in addition to St. Peter's. The site of the priory of St. Oswald has been largely covered by St. Catherine's church, but a few fragments of its walls and several late Norman arches are still to be seen in Priory Road. Ethelfleda, Lady of the Mercians, and her husband Ethelred, founded this house in 909 and hither brought the body of St. Oswald, martyr-king of Northumbria.   Llanthony Priory, the other minor monastic foundation, was used by King Charles' forces during the seige of the city, and the buildings not battered by gun-fire were later greatly reduced when a canal was driven straight through the church. To-day the priory is still worth a visit for the sake of the ruined gateway adorned with the arms of de Bohun, descendant of Milo, and of Henry Dean, prior here in the late fifteenth century, and later Archbishop of Canterbury (1501). Portions of the walls of the great barn remain, while the farmhouse, so prettily placed between the canal and the Severn, consists of half-timber work upon a lower story of stone which, as its Gothic windows indicate, was part of the domestic buildings of the priory.

The existing old churches of Gloucester are situated near to the Cross and the Cathedral. The Church of St. Nicholas contains much Norman work and a fine ancient bronze closing ring. The little church of St. Mary de Lode, named after a passage of the Severn, stands on the site of a Roman building. Here, too, good Norman work is visible and, rarer still in Gloucestershire, a fine pre-Reformation carved oak pulpit. In the churchyard Bishop Hooper was burnt in 1555 within the shadow of the Cathedral of which he was the second bishop. The glory of St. Mary de Crypt lies in the three beautiful Perpendicular stone screens dividing the chancel from the aisles. Robert Raikes was buried here in 1811 and the desk and bell used by him at his first Sunday School are preserved in the south aisle.

The old houses of Gloucester also stand mostly close to the Cross. Robert Raikes' House, a fine half-timbered building with rather elaborate woodwork and carved bargeboards, has its rivals in the 'Old Blue Shop', St. Nicholas House, Bishop Hooper's Lodging, the Old Judge's House and several others.

Southgate Street leads to the Spa Pump Rooms, to the Park with its fragments of Roman pillars and above all to the docks, which have a flavour of the sea, although distinct from the tidal Severn. Truly, Gloucester is, as Charles

Dickens said, 'a wonderful and misleading city: a city which you dispose of, in your mind, as a combination of an ordinary capital, and a cathedral town, till you happen to see a man in complete maritime costume turning down an obscure lane which, apparently, ends in the County Gaol. You follow this mariner, saying to yourself: 'And why a sou'-wester hat, why a blue flannel jersey, why these canvas trousers in Gloucester? Why? Follow the seaman but a little bit farther and you will see!'

You may, of course, follow the sailor in the reverse direction and perhaps come across one of the many old inns of Gloucester. The Fleece in Westgate Street retains some pre-Tudor half-timbering, and the 'Monks' Retreat', a stone-vaulted underground chamber of the thirteenth century, formerly part of a medieval monastic foundation. The New Inn in Northgate Street is among the dozen oldest hostels in England, having been built about 1455 by John Twining, a monk of the Abbey, in Thomas Seabroke's day. Originally intended to house pilgrims to the shrine of Edward II, it has kept the ancient balconies around its courtyard. In addition, nearby, on the corner of New Inn Lane, is a medieval carving of an angel beneath a Gothic canopy.

The Bell Hotel has neither the charm nor the antiquity of these inns but is noteworthy as the home of George Whitefield who was born here a few days before Christmas, 1714. His father died two years later but his mother kept on the inn and brought up seven children of whom George was the youngest. He was educated at the Crypt School, Gloucester, and after serving for two years as a pot-boy at the 'Bell', went to Oxford in 1732, where he met Charles Wesley who was largely instrumental in attracting him into the Methodist movement. Four years later Whitefield was ordained and preached his first sermon at St. Mary de Crypt, the same which Southey says caused complaints to the Bishop of it having driven fifteen people mad. Within a few years

Whitefield began his open air sermons and showed that as a public orator the church in England had never known his equal. The carrying power of his voice when he was 'constrained to lift it up like a trumpet' was tremendous, and Benjamin Franklin ascertained that it would carry to a congregation of thirty thousand people. At times Whitefield's voice would choke with tears, at others it would sink to the merest but clearest whisper, only to rise again to an oratorical thunder. The skilful modulations of his musical voice and the beautiful gestures of the speaker affected the feelings of educated people as well as those of the ignorant Kingswood colliers. What mattered it if Whitefield's logic was scant, his imagery coarse and his experience limited, if, as Garrick affirmed, he could pronounce 'Mesopotamia' in such a way as to move his audience to tears? Poor folk in their thousands, courtiers, authors, critics and actors flocked to his open-air meetings. His audiences reached extraordinary numbers for, as Hume thought, it was worth going twenty miles to hear him. Lord Chesterfield unconsciously paid a great tribute to the orator's skill; the preacher was comparing the sinner's way of life with the progress of a blind man, groping along a narrow ledge above a precipice. The helpless, wretched sinner drew ever nearer to the ever-deepening chasm and the awful catastrophe was at hand when, above the silence of the spell-bound audience, Lord Chesterfield was heard to gasp, 'Good God! he is gone!'

THE INTEREST of Bristol lies in the history of British sea-borne traffic; the city links Gloucestershire with the age of Elizabethan sea-dogs, with slave trading and privateering, with the literature of the sea and, above all, with America. The great Norman castle in the peninsula between the tidal Avon and the tiny Frome played an unhappy part in the growth of the town, for its lords were usually at logger-heads with the citizens. The stronghold disappeared after the Civil War and in spite of Robert Fitzhamon's great fortifications little is left of the building save traces of the moat and portions of the foundations of the massive walls.

Bristol first creeps into history as a seaport; in 1062. Harold sailed from here on an expedition against the rebellious Griffith of Wales. At this time, too, slaves were lined up and sold in Bristol market place before being despatched to Ireland. Wulfstan, Bishop of Worcester, induced the Conqueror to stop the trade which, however, was found to be flourishing again in the reign of Stephen at which time also a deep harbour was constructed to hold a thousand ships. The traders were soon to learn that the sea brings ill as well as good fortune, for in 1349 the Black Death crept in through the maritime ports. Bristol, whose narrow twisting streets were honeycombed with storage cellars, suffered so badly that grass grew on the roadways and the living were scarcely able to bury the dead. Yet within a few years the Gascony wine trade was lining the traders' pockets with silver and the first group of a succession of merchant princes arose in the city.

The Canynges family is best remembered by William the junior, who was born in 1399 and owed much of his vast fortune to the cloth trade, and a good deal no doubt to legacies from his father John, twice mayor, and to his grandfather William, six times mayor of Bristol. About 1460 the great William possessed at least nine vessels afloat and a total of 2,000 tons of shipping which employed 800 seamen as well as a host of carpenters and other artisans. Five times mayor of the city and twice its representative in Parliament, the rich trader practically rebuilt the church of St. Mary Redcliffe and the fine college at Westbury-on-Trym. Of his palatial house in Redclyff Street, with its four bay windows and tall towers, to-day only the fine timber-roofed hall behind No. 97 remains.

In 1480, a few years after Canynges had retired from business to become Dean of Westbury College, Thomas Jay sailed west from Bristol to look for the mythical 'Island of Brasylle and the seven lost cities'. Jay, who died on the fruitless voyage, is remembered by a brass set in the floor of the Lady Chapel in St. Mary Redcliffe. The westward voyages were continued by John Cabot with the permission of Henry VII provided that the King had one-fifth of the profits. In the spring of 1497 the little *Matthew* with a crew of 18, mostly Bristol men, sailed down the Avon and in June landed in the New World in the vicinity of Cape Breton Island. On St. Augustine's Bridge, Bristol, used to be a tablet inscribed:

From this port John Cabot and his son Sebastian (who was born in Bristol) sailed in the ship Matthew A.D. 1497 and discovered the Continent of America.[1]. .

Historians do not gainsay that Cabot set foot on the American continent before Columbus, but Bristol writers even claim a further honour for the town. The chancel in St. Mary Redcliffe contains a fine brass of John Brook, one of Henry the Eighth's judges, with his wife Joan, daughter

---

[1] The tablet was removed recently during road alterations and is awaiting re-erection on another site.

of Richard Amerycke. It is generally held that America
was named after Amerigo Vespucci, a friend of Columbus,
and, if his travel accounts are valid, the discoverer of parts
of the shores of the continent named after him. Arguments
by no means altogether refutable can be brought forward
to show that the name might have originated from the
Amerycke family of Bristol for Richard was a friend of
Cabot and as sheriff of the city presented the King's gift of
£12 'to hym that found the new Isle'. The whale's rib
hanging in St. Mary Redcliffe was brought home probably
by the Cabots, as a record tells us, '1497. Item. Paid for
settyng upp ye bone of ye bigge fishe . . . vid.'

Four hundred years later the high Cabot tower was built
on Brandon Hill overlooking the quayside from which
Cabot sailed. Although the great city sprawls out on both
banks of the Avon almost as far as eye can see, the harbour
near the bridge where the masts of ships show up among the
old house-tops is still the focus and heart of Bristol.

In the sixteenth and seventeenth centuries Bristol was next
to London in the trade and maritime affairs of the country.
The Merchant Venturer's Society was incorporated by
Edward VI in 1551 and still exists to-day as a philanthropic
body although its noble Merchant's Hall was totally
destroyed by bombing a few years ago. Queen Elizabeth
duly respected the town's position and importance when she
allowed Bristol to amuse her for a week in the August of
1574. She was met at Lawford's Gate by the Corporation
and trade companies each marching under its proper ensign,
while four boys representing Salutation, Fame, Gratulation
and Obedient Goodwill made speeches at strategic spots in
the luscious flowery strain of

'All hayl, O plant of grace and speshall sprout of fame . . .'
As the Queen entered her lodgings in John Young's great
house, 300 soldiers fired their muskets and the cannons of the
castle and city fired an answering salvo. The next day, a

Sunday, the Queen heard a 'sarmond' in the Cathedral and an 'imme' specially composed for the occasion. Two days of pageantry followed which the citizens found 'verie costlie and chargeable, especially in gonnepowder. . . .' The Great House where the Queen stayed was built on the site of the Carmelite Friary by Sir John Young, and is now covered by Colston Hall, but Sir John also built about 1590 a mansion in the Friary gardens and this, the Red Lodge, with a fine carved staircase, and one gorgeously decorated room, still remains.

About the time of Queen Elizabeth's visit the growing hatred between Spanish Catholics and English Protestants was showing itself in ever increasing acts of plunder and revenge. In 1576, Andrew Barker, presumably a law-abiding Bristol merchant, had his cloth and wine seized at Teneriffe and his factor imprisoned by the Inquisition. Whereupon, the good Andrew with the help of friends fitted out the *Bear* and the *Ragged Staff* and, by way of reprisal, plundered the Carribbean coast and harassed any Spanish ships he could. Twenty years later when John Hopkins, a local fishmonger, took his own ship with the English expedition against Cadiz, his glory so inflamed his fellow-citizens that on his return they marched to Durdham Downs to lead him home in triumph and (in true Protestant fashion!) 'lighted all their tallow candells, and a great bonfire at the High Crosse, very beautiful to behold'.

During the years 1586–90, Richard Hakluyt, the compiler of the *Principal Navigations* of Elizabethan seamen, was a prebendary of Bristol Cathedral and it was largely owing to his incitement that several Bristol merchants fitted out an expedition after the failure of Sir Humphrey Gilbert's last voyage. Under the leadership of Martin Pring and Edmund Jones, the Bristol venturers sailed in 1603 into Whitsun Bay where they encountered unfriendly Indians. Fortunately the natives were frightened off by two great mastiffs which the sailors had brought from Bristol and these famous sea-dogs are remembered in a curious old print entitled 'Bristol Mastiff charging the Indians'. Seventeen years later the Pilgrim Fathers, financed by Thomas Weston, a Merchant Adventurer of Bristol, went ashore at Pring's landfall and re-named it Plymouth Bay. Martin Pring lies under an imposing monument in the church of St. Stephen.

Not the least among the great Adventurers was Captain Thomas James who was sent out by the Bristol Merchants in the *Henrietta Maria* to seek a passage to the Indies round the North-West of 'Asia'. James was not accustomed to ice and as his ship of seventy tons burthen was badly battered in Hudson's Bay, he wintered there in 1631, and he and his crew are justly famous as the first English party to brave an Arctic winter. Scurvy emaciated the crew and the cold became so severe that a sick man with clothes piled upon him and a pan of hot coals in his bed, had the wine frozen in the bottle under his pillow. Yet the following spring saw James returning safely to Bristol, and, ever since, James Bay in Canada has preserved his memory.

Cromwell came to Bristol in July 1649, driving his six favourite Flanders mares, and spent a fortnight in the town preparing for his notorious Irish expeditions. His joyous reception was probably largely due to his many influential friends here, notably Sir William Penn, the joint commander of the fleet that seized Jamaica and the same Admiral who fixed a whip to his masthead in reply to Van Tromp's broom. Sir William now lies beneath his armour and pennons which hang on the wall of St. Mary Redcliffe.

It was the port of Bristol that brought Samuel Pepys, clerk of the Acts of the Navy, hither in 1668, with his wife and her pretty maid Deb. Willet. They stayed the night of June 11th at a little inn on Salisbury Plain where they found the 'beds good, but lousy, which made us merry'. The following night was spent at Bath, and early next morning

Pepys took a bath, although 'methinks it cannot be clean to go so many bodies in the same water'. The party reached Bristol about two o'clock, 'the way bad but country good, where set down at the Horseshoe, and there being trimmed by a very handsome fellow, 2s., walked with my wife and people through the city, which is in every respect another London. . . . No carts, it standing generally on vaults, only dog-carts, and so went to the Sun; and there Debs. going to see her uncle Butts . . . and I to see the quay which is a large and noble place, and the new ship building. . . . It will be a fine ship. Walked back to the Sun, where I find Deb. come back, and with her, her uncle, a sober merchant, very good company, and so like one of our sober, wealthy, London merchants, as pleased me mightily. Then walked round the quay, and to the ship; and he showed me the Custom-house and led us through March Street, where our girl [pretty Deb] was born. And so brought us a back way by surprise to his house, a substantially good house, and well furnished; and did give us good entertainment of strawberries, a whole venison pasty, cold, and plenty of brave wine, and above all Bristol Milk: Servant maid, 2s. So thence took leave, and he with us through the city. . . . He shewed us the place where the merchants meet here, and a fine cross yet standing, like Cheapside." A copy of the cross may be seen to-day on College Green and 'the place where the merchants meet' was the Tolzey in Corn Street, which in the eighteenth century was replaced by the present exchange, a building in the classical style erected by the Woods of Bath. The 'nails', or curious brass pillars, now standing outside the Corn Exchange belonged to the old Tolzey where the bills used to be settled; hence the expression 'to pay on the nail'.

Long before the close of the seventeenth century, the selling of slaves in Bristol market place had been largely replaced by negro-catching expeditions, but the kidnapping of children continued and seems to have been leniently dealt with by the British magistrates. This leniency was violently denounced by Chief Justice Jeffreys during the Bloody Assizes of 1685. Jeffreys forced the mayor, clad in all his civic pride, to step from the bench to the criminals' bar where, to the amazement of the citizens, he called him a kidnapping knave and having thoroughly terrified him, fined him £1,000. Even this vehemence did not stop the slave trade, and a few years later some sixty local ships were employed in carrying negroes either captured, or exchanged for brass goods manufactured in the city.

The eighteenth century brought a marked increase of privateering, and Bristol became the headquarters of the British pirates. The most famous of early privateering voyages was that of Captain Woodes Rogers and William Dampier in 1708. Sixteen Bristol merchants fitted out the *Duke* and the *Duchess* with 56 guns and a crew of 333. The robbers set sail in the August and passing by chance round Cape Horn more to the south than usual, they rescued Alexander Selkirk, a Scotsman marooned on Juan Fernandez Island. The ships continued their plundering raids all round the world and three years later brought home, it is said £170,000 worth of booty. Woodes Rogers wrote an account of the voyage which gave Daniel Defoe the idea for *Robinson Crusoe*. Bristol historians like to fancy that Defoe met Selkirk here and heard the sailor's own story but the supposed meeting is based only on conjecture.

The finest picture of Bristol during these buccaneering times may be caught from the pages of Robert Louis Stevenson's *Treasure Island* for the Spyglass Inn was situated on the quayside and from this harbour the *Hispaniola* sailed. The old half-timbered house near the waterside overhanging the cobbles of King Street and partially occupied as the quaint Llandoger Trow Inn, might easily be the original 'Spyglass'.

The most notable of the honest traders of this age was Edward Colston, a Merchant Adventurer who amassed a huge fortune in the West Indian trade. Born in 1636 at a house in Small Street, the site of which is now occupied by the Assize Courts, Colston was educated at Christ's Hospital, London, and although in later life he gave liberally to London, his chief pleasure was to do good in his native town. He founded the almshouses on St. Michael's Hill and a home for aged sailors, as well as a charity school and the Colston Hospital. Before his death in 1721 he had given tremendous sums to various deserving charities and every year since his death his birthday has been celebrated in a most fitting way; at midnight the church bells ring a muffled peal and on that day, November 13th, a public collection is made for the poor by the four chief Bristol Societies. Colston is buried in All Saints' Church, a small building almost embedded in a crush of houses in the very heart of Bristol. His effigy, the most notable monument in the church, is decked each Sunday with flowers and nearby a painted window and a fine statue by Rysbraek also commemorate his good deeds.

Bristol had indeed need of many such benefactors as its streets were cramped and insanitary. Alexander Pope (1735) describes how 'you come first to old walls and over a bridge, built on both sides, like London Bridge, and as much crowded with a mixture of seamen, women, children, loaded horses, asses and sledges, with goods dragging along together. . . From thence you come to a quay along the old wall with houses on both sides, and in the middle of the street, as far as you can see, hundreds of ships, their masts as thick as they can stand by one another, which is the oddest and most surprising sight imaginable. . . .' The only part of Bristol the poet liked was Queen Square which had originated with Queen Anne's visit in 1702, and which, with the adjacent streets, occupied the tip of the peninsula between the Frome and Avon rivers. To-day it is difficult to imagine this close-packed city of 80,000 with its sledge-drawn traffic and its cobbled streets, lighted by candles in lanterns, hung, according to an order of 1660, by the wealthier citizens outside their houses from 6 till 9 p.m. Many of the old storage cellars survive to-day, including those under the General Post Office in Small Street, which are double-storied and supported by church-like pillars and vaulted roofs.

For some decades after the Declaration of Independence the distress in Bristol, owing to the loss of the American trade, was terrible, but affairs gradually mended after 1792 when the first American consulate in England was established at 37, Queen Square. Bristol maintained its connection with the colonists in many ways. Here Benjamin West, the American painter and friend of George III, identified a manuscript left by an old sailor who died in the seamen's almshouses. This, the *Journal of Llewellyn Penrose* was the sailor's own story and it gave Poe the idea expressed in the *Gold Bug*, one of the earliest stories of buried treasure. Furthermore, the Bristol Art Gallery possesses pastel drawings by the Sharples of the first four American presidents and of Mrs. Martha Washington, a kindly determined-looking lady in a cotton cap.

When the *Great Western* in 1838 steamed down the Avon to New York the event would have marked the rejuvenation of the port had not the dock-owners partly ruined this early lead by neglecting to improve the harbour sufficiently. Liverpool outrivalled Bristol but the Gloucestershire port was not long in awakening; prosperity returned with the building of new docks at Avonmouth, and the city is still famous for bananas, tobacco, cocoa and sugar. The floating harbour among the old houses and the docks at Avonmouth afford endless delight and if you care to tread King Street at the first flush of dawn or at the time of the full moon, you can yet recapture something of the atmosphere and spirit of Bristol, the merchant adventurer.

BRISTOL: THE CHURCH-GOER AND POET

To-day, the vast sprawling city engulfs many old buildings, the chief of which from an architectural point of view are the Abbey Church, or Cathedral, with its lovely chapter house and Lady Chapel; the stately church of St. Mary Redcliffe, and St. Mark's or the Lord Mayor's Chapel. Of the numerous new religious influences embraced by the people of Bristol, Methodism was the chief, having its cradle here in the 'room' between Broadmead and Horsefair, where Wesley seldom held a meeting without someone falling in agony on the floor. So strong was nonconformism that when Powell opened a theatre in 1766 he tactfully billed the first performance as a 'Concert of Music and a specimen of rhetoric'.

In literature Bristol has nurtured a few notables, and a room in the City Museum is devoted to relics of poets and authors who were either natives of the city or regular visitors to it.

The first Bristol poet to acquire more than local fame was Thomas Chatterton who was born in Pile Street a few yards from St. Mary Redcliffe. His father, a peculiar man, fond of inns and antiques, died in 1752 three months before the birth of his son. The boy was duly christened at St. Mary's but he proved of little solace to his family who looked upon him 'as an absolute fool'. Eventually when nearly seven years old Thomas learnt his letters with the help of illuminated capitals and then quickly learnt to read out of a huge Bible for he always objected to read in a small book.

The next seven years of his life were spent at the Blue Coat
School attached to the Colston Hospital where he showed a
fondness for reading about medieval life, antiquities and
heraldry. He was well acquainted, too, with the muniment
room over the porch of St. Mary Redcliffe containing
chests of parchments and parochial documents, one of
which was called Master Canynges' coffer. A few years
before Chatterton's birth these chests had been opened and,
after the removal of the church documents, the rest were
left for anyone to pilfer. His father had helped himself
liberally to the parchments to use them for covering books
and other kindred purposes, and the boy had collected these
parchments and stored them in his attic-study.

When scarcely twelve years old Chatterton took an
'antique' poem to the usher of the school who immediately
proclaimed it genuine. The boy proceeded to test his
ability to write in an ancient style on anyone he could, and
he happened to find three men particularly gullible: Burgum,
a pewterer craving for a noble ancestry; Catcott, his assistant,
vain and foolish; and Barrett, a surgeon interested in the
history of the city. When fifteen years old, Chatterton
called on Henry Burgum and showed him an emblazon-
ment of the coat of arms of the de Bergham family whose
descent he had traced from Simon de Seyncte Lyze alias
Senliz, Earl of Nottingham, down to Sir Alan de Bergham,
Kt., of the thirteenth century. Burgum was too elated to
suspect a forgery or hoax, and saw nothing amiss in the
prominence of the name Radcliffe de Chatterton of Chatterton, as the whole genealogical tree was verified by numerous
marginal references to the *Roll of Battle Abbey*, Ashmole's
Order of the Garter and other historic documents. The reward of a five shilling piece no doubt assisted in the discovery a few days later of *The Romaunte of the Cnyghte*,
composed in 1320 by John de Bergham, one of the greatest
ornaments of his age. It was some years before Burgum

submitted the document for verification to the College of Heralds and become once more a disillusioned common citizen.

William Barrett proved equally credulous. Chatterton supplied him with materials for his *Antiquities of Bristol* in the form of ancient manuscripts supposed to be written by a priest, Thomas Rowley, the friend and confessor of the William Canynges who had built St. Mary Redcliffe. The manuscripts were included in Barrett's volume, and George Catcott, Burgum's assistant, began to collect with zeal these 'Rowley Poems'. In 1768 a new bridge was built over the Avon and Chatterton produced an 'ancient account' of the ceremonies connected with the opening of the old bridge during the reign of Henry II. Upon inquiry the youth admitted that the documents came from the muniment room and so it happened that as a boy of sixteen he found he could hoax his fellow-citizens given only the aid of a glossary of old words and a little candle-black to age the parchments. Hitherto he had been paid such meagre sums for his discoveries that he resolved to extend the scope of his work, and forged a *Rise of Peyncteyne yn Englande* which temporarily deceived Horace Walpole just as completely as the genealogy had duped Bergum.

Chatterton took up political writing, mainly of a satirical nature, and his articles were regularly published. In 1770 he departed for London, where he found little difficulty in selling his writings, until, probably haunted by the burden of an insidious disease, he poisoned himself with arsenic at his lodgings in Holborn.

A statue standing in the corner of the St. Mary Redcliffe churchyard depicts Chatterton as a schoolboy and so he should be remembered. He is grouped among the great literary forgers of England but he takes a more honourable place among the boy-poets of the world. The Rowley Poems, written in ordinary language and then transliterated with the help of a glossary, are unskilful forgeries, some of the stanzas being comically 'antique':

> 'Ynne Whilomme daies, as Storie saies,
>   Ynne famous Brystowe towne
>   Dere lyved Knyghtes, doughtie in fyghtes,
>   Of marvellous renouwne.'
>   (*A Chronycalle of Brystowe*).

Yet some of the poems show a lively imagination, as for instance in the following lines from the *Ballad of Charity*:

> 'The gathered storm is ripe, the big drops fall;
> The sunburnt meadows smoke—and drink the rain;
> The coming ghastness doth the cattle appal,
> And the full flocks are driving o'er the plain;

and in the Minstrel's Roundelay in *Aella*:

> Hark! the raven flaps his wing
> In the briar'd dell below;
> Hark! the death-owl loud doth sing
> To the nightmares as they go
>   My love is dead,
>   Gone to his death-bed
>   All under the willow-tree.
>
> See! the white moon shines on high;
> Whiter is my true love's shroud,
> Whiter than the morning sky,
> Whiter than the evening cloud.
>   My love is dead,
>   Gone to his death-bed
>   All under the willow tree.

Bristol owes a debt of gratitude to Chatterton as he aroused a great deal of interest in its vast wealth of historical records, and, what is more, he indirectly gave the city a small niche in the intellectual life of the nation. He seems to have influenced some of the works of Coleridge who in 1794 wrote a monody on his death, and of Keats who dedicated *Endymion* to him. It was characteristic that Coleridge

> Dare, no longer on the sad theme muse,
> Lest kindred woes persuade a kindred doom

but that Robert Southey was moved by the penniless condition of Chatterton's sister to edit the youth's works so that the proceeds might go to the family. This act is typical of Southey who of all the notable poets intimately associated with Bristol was probably the most balanced, most kindly and most practical. Born in the autumn of 1774 at his father's linen shop in Wine Street, he was adopted by a well-to-do aunt who sent him for a while to a school at Corston, near Bath, and later brought him with her to Bedminster, then a pleasant country walk from Bristol. Southey passed nearly five years at a school on St. Michael's Hill where his industry and obvious literary taste was envied by his fellows who once, so he says, waylaid him with the demand that he should at once say what *i.e.* meant, which he unhesitatingly interpreted as 'John the Evangelist'. The boy had already scribbled a few highly unsuccessful verses when, at the age of fourteen, he went to Westminster. Four years later the *Flagellant*, a school serial started by himself and three others, accepted his article denouncing flogging, and this, his first public appearance in print, was rewarded by private expulsion.

Southey proceeded to Balliol where, after two years of exemplary industry and self-control, he published a collection of poems by himself and Robert Lovell, the Quaker poet. In this year, 1794, Coleridge came down from Cambridge to Bristol to explain to the two poets his scheme of pantisocracy: on the Susquehanna they would lead a life of common unselfishness and common helpfulness, each to contribute to the general elevation of the mind and each to be blest with the society of a young, beautiful and helpful wife. The last condition, although seemingly impossible, proved the least obstacle as Lovell was already married to one of a family of three sisters, Southey was engaged to the second, and Coleridge shortly afterwards married the third. The pantisocratic idea failed because of the shortage of money and, to make matters worse, Southey's aunt heard of the hare-brained scheme and, enraged beyond measure at his engagement to Miss Fricker who had recently been left penniless, turned her adopted son out on the spot never to return. Early in 1795 Southey fetched Coleridge away from the Angel in Butcher Hall, London, to share his rooms in 48 College Street, where they obtained a living by writing articles and by giving historical lectures in the city. This year Mr. Cottle, the generous Bristol publisher, gave Southey one hundred guineas for his *Joan of Arc*, and it was Cottle also who later published the earliest poems of Coleridge and Wordsworth. Southey at this time was obliged to go to Lisbon for six months with the uncle who had paid his college fees, but on the day of departure he frustrated the main purpose of the voyage by privately marrying Miss Fricker at St. Mary Redcliffe. In the meantime Coleridge was offered a post as co-editor of a London paper which he was forced by poverty to accept although, to use his own words: "My heart is very heavy for I love Bristol, and I do not love London."

Southey, upon his return to Bristol, took seriously to the study of law, yet two years later we find him in a pleasant country residence at Westbury-on-Trym, his wife's former home. Here, in twelve months, he produced the laborious

Madoc and at least a dozen of his most popular minor poems, including *Blenheim*, the *Inchcape Rock*, *Bishop Hatto*, and the *Well of St. Keyne*. At the same time the industrious poet lectured with Coleridge at Bristol, wrote for magazines, periodicals, and reviews to make a living, and could still find time occasionally to walk over the Downs for a talk with Humphrey Davy, who was head of the Pneumatic Institute.

The year 1798 also marked the publication by Joseph Cottle of *Lyrical Ballads* by Coleridge and Wordsworth, a most notable volume as it contained *Kubla Khan* and the *Rime of the Ancient Mariner*, the last named of which is probably influenced by Chatterton's ballad and perhaps, as regards choice of subject, by Coleridge's residence at Bristol. Wordsworth's *Tintern* was included and this, the first poem to show his future greatness, was actually composed, after an excursion along the Wye, in Cottle's bookshop.

In 1803, Southey left his native Bristol for Greta Hall, Keswick, where he stayed till his death in 1843. Coleridge had urged him to come—'Behind us the mossy Skiddaw, smooth, green, high, with two chasms and a tent-like ridge in the larger. A fairer scene you have not seen in all your wanderings.' Southey found it even more beautiful than he had hoped and here the kind-hearted, hard-working poet supported Mrs. Lovell, and Mrs. Coleridge and her family as well as his own.

Coleridge preferred to shirk his marriage responsibilities and his wanderings brought him frequently to Bristol where he could borrow from Joseph Cottle. On one occasion, in 1813, when on his way to lecture at the Great Room, Coleridge discovered that a fellow passenger was a sister of a particular friend, so he gallantly escorted her to North Wales and arrived at Bristol a few days late. At the rearranged meeting he was collected and delivered on the platform just one hour late but apparently the six lectures gave complete satisfaction, the last being gratuitous to recompense for the diffuseness of the introductory talk.

BIBLIOGRAPHY

General

> *The Bibliographer's Manual of Gloucestershire Literature.*
> Hyett and Bazeley. 1895–1916. 3 vols. Two supplements by Hyett and Austin.
>
> *Catalogue of Local Collection of Gloucester Public Library.*
> Roland Austin. 1928.

Periodicals

> *Transactions of Bristol and Gloucestershire Archæological
> Society.* 1876 *et seq.* Contain history of almost every
> parish in county.
>
> *Proceedings of Cotteswold Naturalists' Field Club.* 1846 *et seq.*
>
> *The Gloucestershire Countryside.* 1931 *et seq.*

Works on the County

> *The Ancient and Present State of Gloucestershire.* Sir Robert
> Atkyns. 1712. 2nd edition. 1786.
>
> *A New History of Gloucestershire.* Samuel Rudder. 1779.
>
> *The Rural Economy of Gloucestershire.* Marshall. 2 vols.
> 1789.
>
> *A Collection of Gloucestershire Antiquities.* S. Lysons. 110
> plates. 1804.
>
> *Agricultural Survey of Gloucestershire.* Rudge. 1807.
>
> *Records and Manuscripts Respecting the County of Gloucester.*
> T. D. Fosbrooke. 2 vols. 1807.
>
> *Parliamentary History of the County of Gloucester: 1213–1898.*
> W. R. Williams. 1899.
>
> *Victoria County History of Gloucestershire,* Edited by W. Page.
> Vol. 11. 1907.
>
> *Descriptive Catalogue of the Printed Maps of Gloucestershire,
> 1577–1911.* T. C. Chubb. 1913.

The Ancient Wells, Springs and Holy Wells of Gloucestershire.
    R. C. Skyring Walters. 1928.
Gloucestershire, A Survey. Gordon E. Payne. 1945.

Archæology

Archæological Handbook of County of Gloucester. C. B. Witts.
    1883.
The Ancient Entrenchments and Camps of Gloucestershire.
    E. J. Burrow. 1924.
The Long Barrows of the Cotswolds. O. G. S. Crawford.
    1925.

Church Details

The Old Crosses of Gloucestershire. Charles Pooley. 1868.
The Church Bells of Gloucestershire. Rev. H. T. Ellacombe.
    1881.
Monumental Brasses of Gloucestershire. C. T. Davis. 1894.
The Church Plate of Gloucestershire. Rev. J. T. Evans. 1906.
The Ancient Mural Paintings in the Churches of Gloucestershire.
    W. Hobart Bird. 1927.
Old Gloucestershire Churches. W. Hobart Bird. 1928.
The Monumental Effigies of Gloucestershire and Bristol. Ida M.
    Roper. 1931.
Gloucestershire. J. Charles Cox. 1914. 7th edition. Revised
    1937.

Flora

Flora of the Bristol Coalfield. J. C. White. 1912.
Flora of the Chepstow Neighbourhood. Schoolbred. 1920.
Flora of Gloucestershire. Edited by Rev. H. J. Riddelsdell.
    To be published shortly by Cotteswold Field Club.
    Also contains full account of Climate, Vegetation, etc.,
    of the county.

Geology

Memoirs of Geological Survey: especially those by L.
    Richardson.
The Country around Moreton-in-Marsh. 1929.

Wells and Springs of Gloucestershire. 1930.
The Country around Cirencester. 1933.
Bristol and Gloucester District. F. B. Welch and R. Crookall.
    1935.

Modern Poetry by Gloucestershire Poets or touching on the County
    A Gloucestershire Lad. 1916.
    Ducks and Other Verses. 1919.
    Farewell. 1921. F. W. Harvey.
    Severn and Somme. 1917.
    War's Embers. 1919. Ivor Gurney.
    Selected Poems. 1922. John Drinkwater.
    Collected Poems of John Masefield. 1928.

A Few Volumes dealing with Parts of the County
    Cotswolds
        *Old Cottages: Farm Houses and Other Stone Buildings in the
            Cotswold District.* W. G. Davie and E. G. Dawber.
            1905.
        A Cotswold Village. J. Arthur Gibbs. 1898. Travellers'
            Library, 1929.
        A Cotswold Shrine (Hailes). W. St. Clair Baddeley. 1908.
        Ancient Cotswold Churches. Ulric Daubeny. 1921.
        The History of Painswick. Sir. F. A. Hyett. 1928.
        A Cotteswold Manor (Painswick). W. St. Clair Baddeley.
            1929.
        A Cotswold Year. C. Henry Warren. 1936.
        Wild Visitors to a Cotswold Garden. Ernest C. Harris. 1936.
        Winchcombe Cavalcade. Eleanor Adlard. 1939.

Vale of Severn
        History of Cheltenham. S. Griffith. 2 vols. 1826. Wealth of
            illustrations.
        At Cheltenham Spa. Humphris and Willoughby. 1928.
        Gloucester in National History. Sir F. A. Hyett. 1907.
        Roman Gloucester. C. Fulbrook Leggatt. 1947.
        Bristol: Birthplace of America—and other brochures. Bristol
            Development Board.

Bristol Privateers and Ships of War. J. W. Damer Powell. 1930.
A Gateway of Empire. C. M. MacInnes. 1939.
English City. H. G. Brown. 1945.
A Life of Thomas Chatterton. E. H. W. Meyerstein. 1930.

Forest of Dean
    The Forest of Dean. H. G. Nicholls. 1858.
    The Forest of Dean. A. O. Cooke. 1913.
    The Dean Road. A. W. Trotter. 1936.

A Note on Maps
    The following small scale Ordnance Survey maps deal with the county:
    $\frac{1}{4}$ inch. Sheet 8A.
    $\frac{1}{2}$ inch. The Cotswolds. An Ordnance Survey District Map.
    1 inch to 1 mile. New Popular Edition.
      Sheet 143. Gloucester and Malvern.
      Sheet 144. Cheltenham and Evesham.
      Sheet 156. Bristol and Stroud.
      Sheet 157. Swindon and Cirencester.

Youth Hostels
    Full information may be obtained from
      Regional Secretary of the Y.H.A.,
        Folk House,
          College Green,
           Bristol 1.

For list of Gloucestershire gardens open in aid of the Queen's Institute of District Nursing, apply to the County Organizer,
    Miss Ratcliff, O.B.E., J.P.,
      Southam Delabere,
        Cheltenham.

INDEX